MY DARLING
HERIOTT

MY DARLING HERIOTT

*Henrietta Luxborough, Poetic Gardener
and Irrepressible Exile*

JANE BROWN

Harper*Press*
An Imprint of HarperCollins*Publishers*

Harper Press
An imprint of HarperCollins*Publishers*
77–85 Fulham Palace Road,
Hammersmith, London w6 8jb

www.harpercollins.co.uk

Published by Harper Press 2006

1

A catalogue record for this book
is available from the British Library

ISBN-13 978-0-00-712994-2
ISBN-10 0-00-712994-7
ANZ ISBN 0-00-723570-4

Garden plans redrawn by Rex Nicholls
Family trees by Leslie Robinson

Set in PostScript Linotype Minion with Spectrum display by
Rowland Phototypesetting Ltd, Bury St Edmunds, Suffolk

Printed and bound in Great Britain by
Clays Ltd, St Ives plc

CONTENTS

ILLUSTRATION CREDITS

Henrietta St John [Knight] (1699–1756). English School though variously attributed to Michael Dahl (c.1659–1743) or Charles Jervas (c.1675–1739); possibly her wedding portrait painted c.1727. (*Lydiard House, Lydiard Tregoze, Swindon. Photograph © The De Morgan Centre, London/Bridgeman Art Library*)

Sir Oliver St John of Thorpe Hall (1598–1673) by Pieter Nason (1612–1690), painted in 1651. (*National Portrait Gallery, London*)

Johanna St John (1631–1705). By [John] Michael Wright (1617–1694), possibly her wedding portrait c.1651. (*Reproduced by kind permission of Lydiard House, Swindon*)

Angelica Magdalena, Viscountess St John (1667–1736) by an unknown artist. (*Reproduced by kind permission of Lydiard House, Swindon*)

Henry, 1st Viscount St John (1652–1742) by an unknown artist. (*Reproduced by kind permission of Lydiard House, Swindon*)

Lydiard Tregoze c.1700, the south–west front in elevation and part with the family wing, the newly–planted avenues and formal flower and fruit gardens. (*Warwickshire County Record Office: MA1793/1/1–5*)

Battersea as it was during Henrietta's lifetime.

Henrietta St John (1699–1756) c. 1703, possibly by Maria Verelst (1680–1744). (*Reproduced by kind permission of Lydiard House, Swindon*)

Sir Thomas Coke (1674–1727) of Melbourne, Vice-Chamberlain to Queen Anne, by Michael Dahl (c.1659–1743). (*Reproduced by kind permission of Ralph Kerr, Melbourne Hall*)

Frances Winchcombe (d.1718) 1st wife of Harry St John, 1st Viscount Bolingbroke by Michael Dahl (c.1659–1743). (*Lydiard House, Swindon. Photo: The Paul Mellon Centre for Studies in British Art*)

Henry [Harry] St John, 1st Viscount Bolingbroke (1678–1751). Attributed to Alexis Simon Belle, painted c.1712. (*National Portrait Gallery, London*)

Henrietta St John (1699–1756), c.1719, possibly her debut portrait which remained in the St John family until modern times, English School. (*Reproduced by kind permission of Lydiard House, Swindon*)

Robert Knight (1702–1772), later Baron Luxborough, Earl of Catherlough by an unknown artist. (*Photograph of portrait reproduced by kind permission of Arthur Carden*)

Elizabeth Rowe [née Singer] (1674–1737). Etching by an unknown engraver after Richard Baldwin. (*National Portrait Gallery, London*)

Illustration by William Kent (1684–1748) for 'Spring' in James Thomson's *The Seasons*, 1730, showing in fanciful pastorale the mount and grotto at Marlborough Castle, with Silbury Hill in the background.

Frances [Thynne] (1700–1754), Countess of Hertford, later Duchess of Somerset, by Thomas Hudson (1701–1779). (*Collection of the Duke of Northumberland*)

Marlborough Castle and its gardens, a bird's eye view dated 29th June 1723: illustration from William Stukeley's *Itinerarium Curiosum*, 1776.

Alexander Pope's Thames-side villa and garden at Twickenham, Heckell & Mason engraving, 1749.

The Shell grotto in Pope's upper garden, by William Kent (1684–1748). (*British Museum Prints and Drawings – ref. 1872–11-9–878)*)

The Weekly Journal or British Gazetteer May 1721, 'Lucipher's new Row-barge for First-Rate Passengers'. (*British Museum Prints and Drawings*)

Paris, Les Promenades du Palais des Tuileries, *c*.1730, engraving by Jacques Rigaud (1681–1754). (*Hulton Archive/Getty Images*)

Luxborough, Chigwell, Essex: extract from Chapman & Andre's 1777 map showing the location of Luxborough mansion and gardens. (*British Library*)

Robert Knight (1702–1772), in his robes as Baron Luxborough by Thomas Hudson (1701–1779). (*Photograph reproduced by kind permission of Canon Walter King*)

Maddalena Henrietta (1729–63), pastel portrait attributed to Rosalba Carriere (1675–1757). (*Reproduced by kind permission of Lydiard House, Swindon*)

Henry [Harry] Knight (1728–62), attributed to Joseph Highmore (1692–1780) and painted *c*.1745. (*Reproduced by kind permission of Mrs D.P. Johnson*)

Henry [Harry] St John, 1st Viscount Bolingbroke (1678–1751). (*Reproduced by kind permission of Lydiard House, Swindon*)

Marie Claire, Marquise de Villette, Viscountess Bolingbroke (1675–1750). (*Reproduced by kind permission of Lydiard House, Swindon*)

Holles 'Holly' St John (1710–38). Reproduced by kind permission of Mrs P. Pulzer)

William Shenstone (1714–63) and his greyhound with The Leasowes as the backdrop, 1760 by Edward Alcock (d.1782). (*National Portrait Gallery, London*)

Vignette with the last two stanzas of 'The partially retir'd Venus' from *The Works in Verse & Prose of William Shenstone Esq.,Vol II* 1768.

William Somerville (1675–1742) of Edstone. (*National Portrait Gallery, London*)

Garden at Woodside, Old Windsor, *c*.1750, by Thomas Robins the Elder (1716–70). (*Private Collection/Bridgeman Art Library*)

The Orangery at Woodside, *c*.1750, by Thomas Robins the Elder (1716–70). (*Reproduced by kind permission of John Harris from his book Gardens of Delight*)

Somerville's Urn beneath the oak tree in Henrietta's garden by Thomas Smith of Derby (*c.*1720–1767). (*Reproduced by kind permission of Lydiard House, Swindon*

Barrells House, designed by Joseph Bonomi the Elder (1739–1808) and exhibited at the Royal Academy 1796. (*RIBA Library Drawings and Archives Collection*)

FAMILY TREES

The St John Family Tree

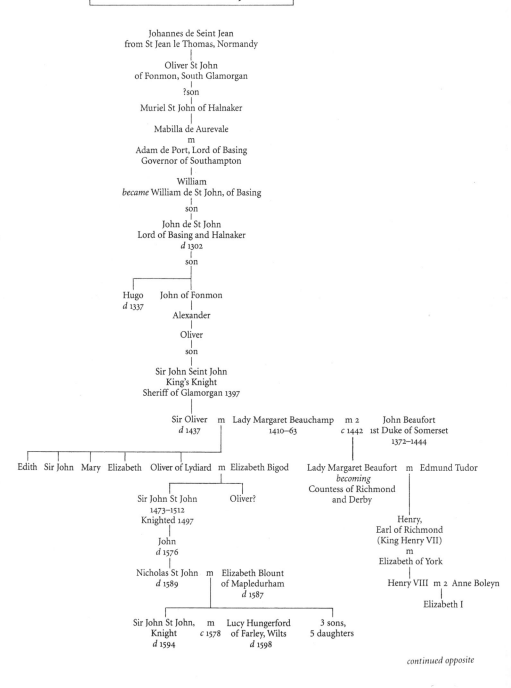

Johannes de Seint Jean
from St Jean le Thomas, Normandy
|
Oliver St John
of Fonmon, South Glamorgan
|
?son
|
Muriel St John of Halnaker
|
Mabilla de Aurevale
m
Adam de Port, Lord of Basing
Governor of Southampton
|
William
became William de St John, of Basing
|
son
|
John de St John
Lord of Basing and Halnaker
d 1302
|
son

Hugo   John of Fonmon
d 1337 |
       Alexander
       |
       Oliver
       |
       son
|
Sir John Seint John
King's Knight
Sheriff of Glamorgan 1397

Sir Oliver   m   Lady Margaret Beauchamp   m 2   John Beaufort
d 1437   1410–63   *c* 1442   1st Duke of Somerset
                                               1372–1444

Edith   Sir John   Mary   Elizabeth   Oliver of Lydiard   m   Elizabeth Bigod   Lady Margaret Beaufort   m   Edmund Tudor
                                                       becoming
Sir John St John   Oliver?   Countess of Richmond
1473–1512   and Derby
Knighted 1497
|
John   Henry,
d 1576   Earl of Richmond
| (King Henry VII)
Nicholas St John   m   Elizabeth Blount   m
d 1589   of Mapledurham   Elizabeth of York
                  d 1587 |
                                     Henry VIII   m 2   Anne Boleyn

Sir John St John,   m   Lucy Hungerford   3 sons,   Elizabeth I
Knight   *c* 1578   of Farley, Wilts   5 daughters
d 1594   *d* 1598

continued opposite

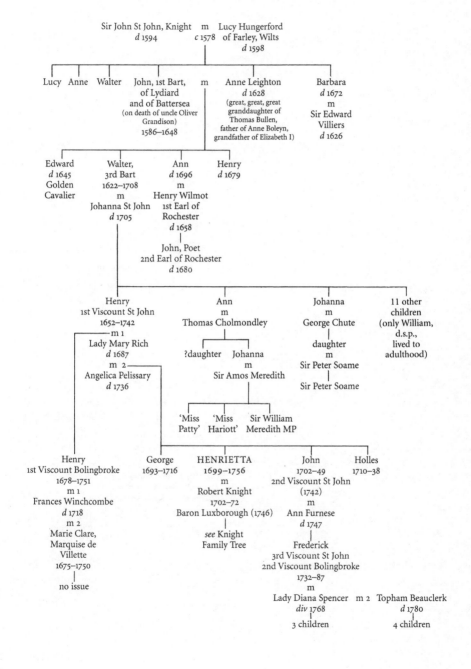

Sir John St John, Knight m Lucy Hungerford
d 1594   *c* 1578   of Farley, Wilts
                                        d 1598

Lucy   Anne   Walter   John, 1st Bart,   m   Anne Leighton   Barbara
                       of Lydiard   *d* 1628   *d* 1672
                       and of Battersea   (great, great, great   m
                       (on death of uncle Oliver   granddaughter of   Sir Edward
                       Grandison)   Thomas Bullen,   Villiers
                       1586–1648   father of Anne Boleyn,   *d* 1626
                                             grandfather of Elizabeth I)

Edward   Walter,   Ann   Henry
d 1645   3rd Bart   *d* 1696   *d* 1679
Golden   1622–1708   m
Cavalier   m   Henry Wilmot
              Johanna St John 1st Earl of
              d 1705   Rochester
                               d 1658

                               John, Poet
                               2nd Earl of Rochester
                               d 1680

Henry   Ann   Johanna   11 other
1st Viscount St John   m   m   children
1652–1742   Thomas Cholmondley   George Chute   (only William,
— m 1   d.s.p.,
Lady Mary Rich   lived to
d 1687   ?daughter   Johanna   daughter   adulthood)
m 2   m   m
Angelica Pelissary   Sir Amos Meredith   Sir Peter Soame
d 1736   Sir Peter Soame

                               'Miss   'Miss   Sir William
                               Patty'   Hariott' Meredith MP

Henry   George   HENRIETTA   John   Holles
1st Viscount Bolingbroke   1693–1716   1699–1756   1702–49   1710–38
1678–1751   m   2nd Viscount St John
m 1   Robert Knight   (1742)
Frances Winchcombe   1702–72   m
d 1718   Baron Luxborough (1746)   Ann Furnese
m 2   *d* 1747
Marie Clare,   *see* Knight
Marquise de   Family Tree   Frederick
Villette   3rd Viscount St John
1675–1750   2nd Viscount Bolingbroke
                                                    1732–87
                                                    m
no issue   Lady Diana Spencer   m 2   Topham Beauclerk
                                                    div 1768   *d* 1780

                                                    3 children   4 children

The Knight Family Tree

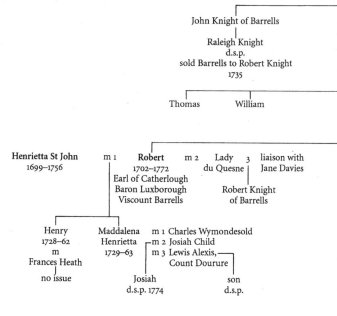

John Knight of Barrells

Raleigh Knight
d.s.p.
sold Barrells to Robert Knight
1735

Thomas   William

Henrietta St John   m 1   **Robert**   m 2   Lady   3   liaison with
1699–1756   1702–1772   du Quesne   Jane Davies
                        Earl of Catherlough
                        Baron Luxborough   Robert Knight
                        Viscount Barrells   of Barrells

Henry   Maddalena   m 1 Charles Wymondesold
1728–62   Henrietta   m 2 Josiah Child
m   1729–63   m 3 Lewis Alexis,
Frances Heath   Count Dourure
no issue   Josiah   son
                   d.s.p. 1774   d.s.p.

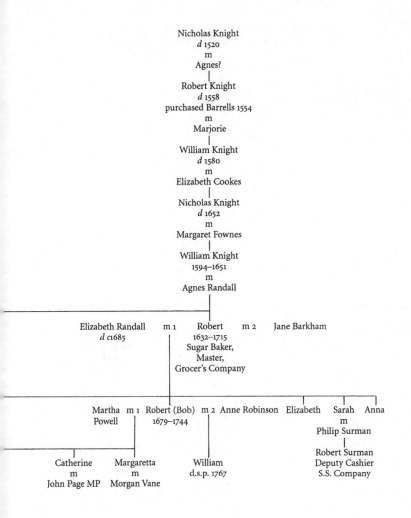

Nicholas Knight
d 1520
m
Agnes?

Robert Knight
d 1558
purchased Barrells 1554
m
Marjorie

William Knight
d 1580
m
Elizabeth Cookes

Nicholas Knight
d 1652
m
Margaret Fownes

William Knight
1594–1651
m
Agnes Randall

Elizabeth Randall   m 1   Robert   m 2   Jane Barkham
d c1685   1632–1715
                 Sugar Baker,
                 Master,
            Grocer's Company

Martha m 1 Robert (Bob) m 2 Anne Robinson Elizabeth Sarah Anna
Powell   1679–1744   m
                                        Philip Surman

Catherine   Margaretta   William   Robert Surman
m   m   d.s.p. 1767   Deputy Cashier
John Page MP Morgan Vane   S.S. Company

The Bull-Finch in Town

Hark to the blackbirds pleasing note
Sweet usher of the vocal throng;
Nature directs his warbling throat,
And all that hear admire the song.
The bull-finch, with unvary'd tone
Of cadence harsh, and accents shrill
Has brighter plumage to atone
For want of harmony and skill.
And, while to please some courtly fair
He one dull tune with labour learns,
A well-gilt cage, remote from air
And faded plumes, is all he earns.
Go, hapless captive, still repeat
The sound which nature never taught;
Go, listening fair! And call them sweet
Because you know them dearly bought.
Unenvy'd both! Go hear and sing
Your study'd music oe'er and oe'er;
Whilst I attend th' inviting spring
In fields where birds unfetter'd soar.

HENRIETTA LUXBOROUGH

FOREWORD

This is the story of a vivacious and resourceful woman who, though she lived through the first half of the eighteenth century, refused to be imprisoned by any of our perceived stereotypes of her time. She was neither a court beauty, nor a courtesan, nor a milkmaid, and yet she was a little of all three. She was not an accepted bluestocking though perfectly qualified to be so. She was a wife, mistress and mother, but above all these, a beloved sister. When all these roles had faded she found her solace in making her picturesque landscape garden, at a time when the concept had hardly been invented.

Like so many other women her history is confused by her changing names. She was born as Henrietta St John, she became Henrietta Knight by marriage, and by virtue of her husband's acquisition of an obscure Irish barony, which matched the name of his inherited home in Essex, she was finally known as Lady Luxborough. Under any or all three names she will be found, lightly indexed, in volumes of memoirs and letters, and in books on politics and manners. The sum of these references, together with a volume of her own letters published in 1775, earned her a column and a half in Sir Leslie Stephen's original *Dictionary of National Biography*, which was an unusual place for a woman. More recently she has crept into garden history, notably into Peter Martin's *Pursuing Innocent Pleasures: The Gardening World of Alexander Pope* (1984) and Mark Laird's *The Flowering of the Landscape Garden: English Pleasure Grounds 1720–1800* (1999). She is sometimes said to have invented the term 'shrubbery', though she would have laughed at that notion.

She lived in the lee of history; indeed, it would be appropriate to say that Henrietta's life was truly Hogarthian. Her family, the St Johns (*not* pronounced 'Sinjun' in her day, but having parity with the Baptist and the Evangelist as will become clear), was one of the most colourful dynasties of British history, from the time of the Norman invasion. Consequently she was born to a certain splendour and security, but neither could protect her from the rogues and tricksters of her early Georgian society. The likely rogue-in-chief was her adored and 'adoring' half-brother, Harry St John, 1st Viscount Bolingbroke – the fallen angel of Tory political history or the most brilliant prime minister that Britain never had, to position him in a popular idiom of today. She grew up in his shadow and they had much in common. She typifies a species that I find especially fascinating: a sister equally as talented as a brilliant brother, but with nowhere to go. And, as if being the sister of an attainted traitor in the age of Jacobite plots and invasion-fevers was not enough, she also became the innocent victim of the greatest financial scandal of her age, or any other: the South Sea Bubble.

In appearance and personality she was an unconventional enchantress; she was no blushing English rose of a peaches-and-cream variety, but perhaps more the velvety dark red rose of Lancaster. As she was neither a celebrated beauty nor a great heiress, she was not grand enough to have been painted by Kneller, and the glittering quartet of Allan Ramsay, Reynolds, Gainsborough and Zoffany were all but infants when she was in her prime. All her surviving portraits have questions over their attributions. The portrait of her as a doll-like child is possibly attributed to Herman Verelst. The two portraits of her as a young woman, one that remained with the St John family at Lydiard until modern times (her debut portrait showing her in an orange and scarlet satin sack dress, *c.* 1719) and one that was treasured by the Knights' descendants (a more mature Henrietta in silver and blue satin, her wedding portrait, *c.* 1727), have been variously dismissed as 'English School'. The second, the 'Knight 1727', has been attributed either to a popular painter to the gentry, Charles d'Agar or, more interestingly, to

Michael Dahl, though Dahl in decline, for he had lost his Court patronage in 1714 and was reduced to country house commissions. Both have such a sameness with so many contemporary women's portraits that they cannot be said to lift Henrietta beyond the charming. Conversely quite by chance I found her personality springing from the page in a word picture of another heroine who was far from her in space and time: 'the young woman was tall, with a figure of perfect elegance, on a large scale. She had dark and abundant hair, so glossy that it threw off the sunshine with a gleam, and a face which, besides being beautiful from regularity of feature and richness of complexion, had the impressiveness belonging to a marked brow and deep black eyes.'[1]

This is Hester (a diminutive of Henrietta?) Prynne, as introduced by Nathaniel Hawthorne at the beginning of *The Scarlet Letter* of 1850. In type, she is, of course, eternal; but it is as though time had stood still (as we know it did in customs, language and fashions) while a woman of Henrietta's time had crossed the ocean to the New World. Henrietta's Puritan pedigree is also an important ingredient in her character.

Other certainties are hedged about her. Her half-brother Harry Bolingbroke was judged a classicist and philosopher of genius by his friends – who included Jonathan Swift, Alexander Pope and Voltaire – and his enemies alike, and it was said that he made at least half a scholar of her. She was mistress of her own mind, she disliked formalities and whited sepulchres, she loved poetry and literature, but was acutely critical of florid style and mannerisms. She was not interested in money, but then it might be said that there was always enough for her not to notice it! However, she was taught to be appreciative and economical, the Puritan streak from her grandmother, while at the same time she loved beautiful things and fine clothes, as she was also the child of post-Restoration prodigality. She was contemptuous of excessive money-love and shied away from grandiloquent show. She was a romantic at heart, but – having a French mother and Frenchness in her blood – she loved

the philosophical light-heartedness of the Gallic temperament, and
yet was fretful of her own fate. Henrietta was openly intolerant of
fools, and therefore conscious that – unlike her mother, her best
friend Frances Hertford, her contemporary Mary Delany and subsequently Fanny Burney (who was only four when Henrietta died)
– she was unacceptable at Court. She had no position on which to
hang her memoirs of the great and the good and I fear she was
rather isolated in her eccentricities; all the more reason, I believe,
for searching out her story.

What was there left for her to be but a gardener? She was a
gardener, hands-on and muddily booted, from her childhood and
though she had no garden of her own until she was in her late
thirties, she served her apprenticeship through peculiarly interesting
times in the history of gardening fashions. Sir Thomas Robinson's
much quoted letter to his father-in-law, the Earl of Carlisle, of 1734
reported what Henrietta had seen with her own eyes, that 'there is
a new taste in gardening just arisen, which has been practised with
so great success at the Prince's garden in Town [Carlton House] that
a general alteration of some of the most considerable gardens in the
kingdom is begun ... to lay them out, and work without either
level or line'. William Kent had worked the Prince of Wales' twelve
acres beside The Mall into 'the appearance of beautiful nature', with
lawns, open groves and walks winding through clumps of trees and
shrubs, in defiance of the prevalent fashion for straight canals, allées
and terraces in the French/Dutch tradition, as in Henry Wise's
St James's Park and the late Duke of Buckingham's famous formal
garden at the end of The Mall. As Sir Thomas added, the celebrated
gardens of Claremont, Chiswick and Stowe were 'full of labourers,
to modernise the expensive works finished in them, even since
everyone's memory'.[2] This was the much-vaunted 'Transition' when
fashions were changing very quickly, and though it has always been
assumed that Chiswick and Claremont were leading the way in the
breaking of avenues and serpentining of waters, by the time their
frantic 'loosening' works were under way some smaller gardens

had stolen the lead. Henrietta's friends the Earl and Countess of Hertford were in the avant-garde of fashions. She saw Charles Bridgeman's stripped-down geometry of her brother's Dawley, the graceful and flowery charms of Lord Bathurst's Richings and Alexander Pope's pioneering of the poetical and picturesque, with optical illusions, in his own gardens at Twickenham and at Marble Hill. Her most treasured and used books included Philip Miller's *Gardener's Dictionary* (1731), her volume of Isaac Ware's edition of drawings by Inigo Jones, and the design manuals of new ideas by Stephen Switzer and Batty Langley. When she came to her own gardening she found herself within reach of the most important smaller gardens where the new taste was being pioneered, the most important of all being William Shenstone's *ferme ornée*, The Leasowes, which she immediately recognised for its worth and beauty. She was there, an acute observer, a spectator, at the birth of the English landscape style; but more than that, gardening was in her genes and the gardens that featured in her life play a prominent role in the pages that follow. Gardening sustained her sanity and brought her friends. For Henrietta, friendship, another virtue of her age, was her lifeblood.

Her high spirits and intelligence led her into trouble, she was hustled into a bad marriage, accused of infidelity by a pompous husband, and sent into the wilds of Warwickshire to moulder and die. In refusing to fulfil these cruel expectations, at least for twenty years, she created for herself and for us an eccentric and enchanting circle of friends from the understorey of mid-eighteenth-century society. Her circle – they liked to set their light wooden Windsor chairs in a group round a favourite 'bustoe' or memorial urn in the garden, sip port and gossip on warm, moonlit nights – was a lively collage of characters living in the heart of England far removed from the Court and the City, and yet occasionally touched by great events. Henrietta's was the reality of Henry Fielding's England, and yet when she eagerly purchased and read *Tom Jones* as soon as it appeared in 1749 her verdict was that more happened in Squire

Allworthy's Somerset in Book One than would happen in 500 years in her corner of Warwickshire. Fanny Burney's *Evelina* was not published until twenty-two years after Henrietta's death, and yet those who tremble with forebodings at the pernicious Madame Duval and her cohorts, at those neat betrayals of a heroine's 'nearest and dearest', may tremble for Henrietta, too. Perhaps, after all, Henrietta's England has the most parallels and fascinations in miniature with those of Jane Austen's, but twenty-five years before the incomparable Jane was even born.

Au fond my reasons for searching for Henrietta St John are that she appears to have been a wholly enchanting and comparatively ordinary mortal who lived in a distant time, and yet reaches out across the years with her sorrows and her laughter. To say that she was born too early is ridiculous, but to say that she died too early is purely regret. She died before the eighteenth century, as we assume its enlightenments, had hardly begun. Bach, Vivaldi and Handel (her admired Mr Handel whom she knew) composed the music of her life. Mozart was only born the year she died, 1756. Her landscape, such as it was painted at all, was portrayed by George Lambert and Richard Wilson, artists for landscape connoisseurs. The great gun Turner (born the same year as Jane Austen, 1775) was far too late, and even Gainsborough was only starting to be successful in faraway Suffolk in the last years of Henrietta's life. William Hogarth was her near contemporary, but those pertinent, and impertinent, fellows, Thomas Rowlandson and James Gillray, were only born within months of her death.

Of most fascination is the way that the dates of garden and landscape history seem to slip: Henrietta appreciated Hogarth's *Analysis of Beauty* and was surprised that he could write so philosophically and well, but she did not live long enough for Edmund Burke's *Essay on the Sublime and the Beautiful* (1757). With William Kent, and her country neighbours of Taste, William Shenstone and Sanderson Miller, she was a practitioner and a philosopher of that elusive moment when the idea of an ornamental farm, a *ferme ornée*

– or *ferme negligée* as she dubbed her own unmanicured groves –
merged pleasure ground into agricultural landscape and evolved
into that visionary achievement for the philistine English (their only
world-class artistic coup), the English Landscape Style, *le jardin
anglais*. Lancelot 'Capability' Brown only began his park-making
career in the last decade of her life, and Humphry Repton was still
a toddler of four when she died. In gardening fashions it is too easy
to dismiss the early eighteenth century with trite repetitions of Pope's
satire on topiary, 'the lavender Pig with sage in his belly', and Kent's
'leaping the fence', and then almost immediately land in the lushly
documented acreages of the 1780s and afterwards. Henrietta's story
occupies the gap, the fragile, interesting years when garden-making
had a political potency and the future appearance of the English
landscape hung in the balance.

And so, to her world. My required reading for this could not
but begin with George Macaulay Trevelyan's thundering fanfare
for Queen Anne's England. Henrietta was just old enough to be
bounced on her half-brother Harry's knee to hear the story of the
little moley gentleman in brown velvet who had done his work,
tripping the king's horse and so dispatching William of Orange,
leaving England to Queen Anne. Trevelyan's 'great issues', 'brilliant
societies' and 'distant landscapes' that formed his themes were the
stuff of the St John household as much as any home in England.
Harry St John was the absurdly young Secretary at War who found
the pay for Marlborough's 'many-coloured columns winding along
the banks of Rhine, Danube and Maas', and Harry argued with his
navy colleagues over the money for 'the English fleets heaving on
Mediterranean and Biscayan waters, or coasting the West Indian
islands and the misty Newfoundland shore'. The news was ever of
the 'envoys posting over land and ocean with Godolphin's gold and
Marlborough's persuasive counsel to half the Courts of Europe from
Lisbon to Moscow'. In London 'the fashionable arena of sedan chairs
and glass coaches between St James's Palace and the Parliament
House, the battle ground of political and literary intrigue', was

Harry St John's home territory, its travails and excitements conveyed to his adored little sister. Sir Christopher Wren's dome of St Paul's was 'rising to its completion above the masts of the river, and beyond it the Tower, the workshop of Newton as Master of the Mint'. Trevelyan's vignettes of London are of Henrietta's England as well as Queen Anne's, and because Henrietta's childhood was spent largely in the St John family home at Battersea, of her river, Father Thames. 'But,' Trevelyan asserts, 'all these fine doings had their roots amid homely scenes.'[3] These 'homely scenes' are the backdrop to Henrietta's story.

Finally, on a personal note I should add that I have always found myself helpless once my subject taps me on the shoulder. Henrietta St John, though she was born over three centuries ago, has haunted me for years, as if her sometimes laughing, sometimes pensive, sad ghost lingers in shrubberies, waiting to remind me of her story. Of course, I am much, much too late, and the rushing modern world has obliterated almost everything of the one she knew. For this reason I have tried to document the fate of all her places and gardens in the pages that follow, with special emphasis on what there is of Henrietta's world that may still be found.

CHAPTER ONE

On Being Henrietta St John

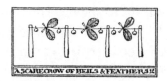

HENRIETTA ST JOHN was born on 15 July, the feast of St Swithun, in the last year of the old century, 1699, at Lydiard Tregoze in north Wiltshire. She was fond of her birthday saint, the ninth-century bishop of Winchester, who wished to be buried where God's good rain fell on his bones and who slept peaceably for more than a hundred years. When Winchester's monks, looking to swell their profits from pilgrims, planned to move his remains inside their cathedral, his saintly curse made it rain for forty days and forty nights – a curse carried down the centuries so that people came to believe that whatever the weather on 15 July so it would remain, interminably wet or dry as dust. St Swithun was a fitting birthday saint for an outdoor girl and Henrietta remembered all her life that they shared their day.

Henrietta's birthplace, Lydiard Tregoze (so named for a medieval baron Tregoz), is on the western outskirts of modern Swindon. A warm and welcoming grey stone mansion and country park, a convenient refuge from the M4, it is now marketed as a 'Swindon Surprise'. In 1943 the almost derelict house and 147 acres of run-down parkland were bought from the St John family for Swindon Corporation by a far-sighted Town Clerk, David Murray John, who anticipated our leisured lives from those dark days of wartime. He paid £4,500 for it, at a time when a 1930s semi-detached house with a 200-foot-long garden cost about £1,500.

This Lydiard House, however, is not overtly the house Henrietta was born in, but a rebuilding, in the 1740s, of the old house by her brother in the manner of Inigo Jones' Wilton House at the other end of Wiltshire. She saw this grand new house only once. Something of her childhood home is buried behind the façade, though invisible to a visitor's eyes, but glimpses of old walls and roof-lines are more likely to be seen from the rear, the side of the house next to the ancient little church of St Mary's. The church she would recognise, for it is little changed from her day. On my first visit to Lydiard it was a busy and fine bank holiday afternoon. I stood beneath the trees (none of them, sadly, old enough to have been seen by Henrietta) and watched a smart wedding party spilling out on to the lawn for photographs. The guests fluttered around the bride and her maids dressed in pink crinolines and carrying roses; the groom and his friends were in vivid brocade waistcoats and elegant trews. It was not hard to imagine the young Henrietta in their midst, but the harsher truth is that there is little remaining of the house, gardens and park of her childhood. Her grandmother's walled and terraced gardens, where she loved to play and where she grew into a gardener, are razed to nothing but shadows in the grass in dry weather.*

It is ironic that Swindon the saviour of Lydiard Tregoze was also its destroyer, for Henrietta's Lydiard is far from us, far beyond Swindon's two great reinventions of itself, as the present high-tech and Honda-hub of the M4 corridor, and as the Great Western Railway's town. By the 1940s, apart from deaths and taxes, the absentee St Johns had had 100 years of the noise, dust and sprawl of the railway town, and only the far greater sprawl of post-war development to anticipate. Their long tenancy of Lydiard – almost exactly 500 years – was ended.

Swindon had become a railway town as a result of a letter in 1840

---

* The post-1740s gardens and landscape are part of the Lydiard Park Restoration Project.

from Daniel Gooch to Isambard Kingdom Brunel, pointing out that it would be necessary to change engines in view of the steep gradients of the new Great Western line to the west of the town. A station at Swindon would divide the journey from Paddington via Reading and so on to Bristol into three more or less equal parts.[1] Before that great railway moment Swindon was a small market town of white stone houses, where nothing in particular happened: 'the great names of England's past did not visit the hill-top town – King Alfred burnt no cakes in a Swindon oven, Queen Elizabeth did not sleep in a Swindon bed, neither Monmouth nor William the Dutchman marched through the High Street . . .'[2]. Swindon was comfortable in its unimportance, and had been so since Roman times and earlier, the home of the Holloways, Herrings and Haggards, of the Goddards who were lords of the manor, of less than a thousand souls, pious pew-holders, dame schoolmistresses, and shop- and innkeepers. It had, though, something of a reputation for smuggling, sheep stealing and bull baiting – 'the absence of any Grammar School may be remarked as being in part both cause and effect of this unsatisfactory state of affairs'.[3]

John Andrews' and Andrew Dury's map of Wiltshire of 1773, the first of the county to be based on an original survey, with prominence given to the great estates and their parks in the hopes of patronage, gives the clearest picture of Henrietta's landscape. Swindon, a one-street town, is dominated by the Goddards' manor house and park; to the west is 'Liddiard' then belonging to Henrietta's nephew (and, I fear, with his new walled garden prominently shown and her grandmother's gardens already apparently destroyed). 'Liddard Tregooze' is shown in the northern part of the old Hundred of Kingsbridge, a well-watered and undulating country extending southwards to a scarp of downland from Broad Hinton to Wroughton.[4] The chief town, and parliamentary borough in the pockets of the St Johns, was Wootton Bassett, just south-west of Lydiard Park.

In the year of Henrietta's birth, 1699, Lydiard was the family's summer home, a comfortable old house caught in a prosperous rural ease, not grand nor particularly fashionable, and in the heart of the fertile estate of rolling pastures and woods that sprawled across some 5,000 acres. The house had been enlarged by Henrietta's great-grandfather, Sir John St John, 1st baronet, who sired many children and built a family annexe. It was a Jacobean-fronted medieval timbered building patched with Swindon stone and local bricks. The entrance door led into a screens' passage, with parlours and solars tucked away and endless kitchens and pantries, stillrooms and sculleries at the rear. It was a lovely house in fine summer weather, with the casements opened, velvet curtains lifting in the breeze, and everything smelling of applewood smoke and lime flowers. Immediately outside the sunny south front the little Henrietta had ducklings to chase across the paved terrace, safe in a railed court. A second court was laid out with four beds, with clipped box or yew pyramids at the corners. These were the formal front courts for greetings and leave-takings. There were more flower gardens to the south-east, and farther still there were the old walled gardens that Henrietta's grandmother, Johanna, and her gardeners had tended since her first arrival at Lydiard, as a bride in the 1650s.

The Lydiard to which Henrietta was born seemed timeless; it was the oldest of English agricultural landscapes, with as yet few false pretensions or divisions. The villagers of Lydiard still lived in the park, which was open to their comings and goings, their cottages and workshops were clustered near the church and along the lane to Hook Street, and the estate provided their work and food and play. The cows at spring pasture were tended by maids, undoubtedly named Marian, Rebecca or Madge, who called their charges named Marigold, Daisy and Winsome into milking. Tom Durfey, the popular balladeer (a Huguenot, as was Henrietta's mother), sang of these earthy maids making festive haymakings with 'Kate o' th' Kitchin, and Kit of the Mill, Dick the Plowman', the young gardeners and the 'Shepherd's boy (he seeks no better name)' from over the hill:

To solace their Lives, and to sweeten their Labour,
All met on a time with a Pipe and Tabor.[5]

Durfey's last song (of 1700) for merrie England merges into Alexander Pope's earliest Augustan pastoral, *Summer*, of 1709:

A Shepherd's Boy (he seeks no better name)
Led forth his flocks along the silver Thame,
Where dancing sun-beams on the waters play'd,
And verdant alders form'd a quiv'ring shade.[6]

In other words, Henrietta was born into a remote corner of England – and her other home beside the Thames at Battersea was equally bucolic – and into a country life that was the very stuff of pastoral.

The St Johns had been at Lydiard ever since they had gained it by a prudent marriage in the early fifteenth century. Before that they had a proud, and strangely obligatory for the British aristocracy, line of descent from the Norman invaders. One Johannes de Seint Jean, from Seint Jean le Thomas in Normandy, which is across the bay from Mont St Michel in Brittany, was one of a dozen knights who subdued south Wales for William Rufus. The Vale of Glamorgan was parcelled out to his fellows by their leader Robert Fitzhamon, and Johannes de Seint Jean netted the Fonmon (pronounced Funmun) estate, a mile from the sea in the beautiful vale.[7] His great-great-granddaughter and heiress, Mabilla de Aurevale, was likely to have been the end of the line, except that her son William, who found himself inheriting the lovely Fonmon as well as the estates of Basing in Hampshire and Halnaker in Sussex, decided to call himself William St John. It was William's grandson who was the Crusader, earning the two golden mullets or stars that can be seen still in the St John armorial window in Battersea church, which were to be pointed out to Henrietta's grandmother by her chaplain, Revd Symon Patrick, and would have been pointed out to Henrietta in due time.

The generations rolled on, to the early fifteenth century and a particularly fortunate marriage between Oliver of Fonmon and

Margaret Beauchamp, who brought with her the estates of Bletsoe in Bedfordshire and Lydiard Tregoze. Oliver and Margaret had two sons and three daughters, and then, after about ten years of marriage, Oliver died in France in 1437. He was only about thirty, which was sad for him but for the St Johns it was the greatest sacrifice that he could have made, and they were to be eternally grateful; so grateful that Oliver – or at least his rebus of an olive tree with his coat of arms – takes centre stage in the great east window of St Mary's Lydiard Tregoze, where he is flanked by two other St Johns, St John the Baptist and St John the Evangelist.

The sainted Oliver left a widow of twenty-seven, and after about five years, around 1442, Margaret St John married John Beaufort, 1st Duke of Somerset, the son of John of Gaunt, Duke of Lancaster. At this moment the family entered upon their most glorious inheritance, which would have been explained to Henrietta as soon as she could understand. It was to be a strange and remarkable story, woven from the history of England, which gave the St Johns their pride and their continuing prosperity.

At first the Beaufort marriage did not seem all that exciting; indeed John Beaufort at not yet forty was sickened and disillusioned by his life. He was one of John of Gaunt's children by the family governess, Katherine Swynford, and though Gaunt eventually marriage Katherine and their children were declared legitimate three times, by the Pope, the King and by Parliament, John Beaufort found all this very difficult. At sixteen he had been sent soldiering in France, where he was almost immediately captured and imprisoned for another whole lifetime, seventeen years, as a pawn whom no one deemed valuable enough for a successful ransom or escape.[8] No one thought much of him, or his marriage to the widow St John, who in 1443 gave birth to a daughter, also named Margaret. Beaufort's daughter, Tacyn, sired during his French imprisonment, came to live with them in England, made a good marriage, and apparently lived happily ever after.

Beaufort, now Duke of Somerset, was given a last chance and

appointed to lead an expensive military expedition to France, which failed entirely. Completely disgraced he retired to Dorset with his duchess and their daughter, where he died (he is likely to have committed suicide) three days before little Margaret's first birthday, 27 May 1444. Beaufort was buried in Wimborne Minster, and after her death in 1463 he was joined by his duchess. Diminutive figures, he in armour, she with a daintily folded marble skirt, they lie there still.

That same little Margaret, a great-great-granddaughter of Edward III, was now seen as something of a political prize. Aged seven she was 'married' to her guardian's son, John de la Pole, but she was allowed to live with her mother, and spent her happiest times with her St John half-brothers Oliver and John and her half-sisters Edith, Mary and Elizabeth at Bletsoe, or at Maxey Castle on the edge of the fens north of Peterborough. After a while the grown-ups grew impatient and the de la Pole 'marriage' was annulled, and Margaret, aged twelve, was married to Edmund Tudor, the Earl of Richmond, who was twice her age. This time consummation was immediate and ensured, but before Margaret gave birth her husband died of the plague. She was so young that the birth was difficult, and left her emotionally and physically scarred.* Her son, Henry, Earl of Richmond, born at Pembroke Castle on 25 January 1457, was destined to be king of England.[9]

But first, the lady Margaret, his mother, had to champion his cause through the squabbles of the Yorkists and Lancastrians, and her role was crucial. In *Richard III* Shakespeare makes Edward IV's queen, Elizabeth, wary that the lady Margaret 'loves me not', and later Richard himself threatens the lady Margaret's husband, Lord Stanley, 'Well, look unto it. Stanley, look to your wife: if she convey Letters to Richmond, you shall answer it.'[10]

The lady Margaret, 'the active political partisan',[11] trod the tightrope lightly between her husband's overt loyalty to Richard III, 'oft

---

* She was to marry twice more, both affectionate and happy relationships, but she had no more children.

in jeopardy of her lyfe',[12] and the secret plotting with her son. As a result Henry Richmond eventually returned from exile to Wales, landing at Milford Haven on a fine August morning in 1485, making his way with his supporters – St Johns of Fonmon amongst them – to the battle of Bosworth Field. After his victory Richard III's coronet was retrieved from a thorn bush and placed on the new king's head.

All this stirring history was very much alive to the St Johns in Henrietta's day, especially to Harry St John with his acute sense of being part of England's destiny. Back in the fifteenth century, with her son Henry VII on the throne, the lady Margaret, Countess of Richmond and Derby, officially titled The King's Mother, became the most powerful woman in the land. Her half-brother, Oliver St John, was a senior member of her household, and for his son, John, she arranged a knighthood. She presented him with an embroidered carpet with golden threadings (the work of herself and her ladies), depicting the St John lineage, upon his marriage in 1498. Lady Margaret also managed the marriage of her niece Alice St John to her protégé Henry Parker. She was apparently a continuing fairy godmother to Alice and Henry's family, and eventually she found Henry a place in her grandson Henry VIII's household.[13] Sir John St John became her last chamberlain in her household and executor of her will. She outlived her son, was present at the marriage of Henry VIII to Catherine of Aragon on 11 June 1509, and at their coronation on 24 June. The lady Margaret died just five days later, aged sixty-six, and she – who on occasion had signed herself ambivalently 'Margaret R' – was buried in regal splendour in the King Henry VII Chapel in Westminster Abbey. On her tomb her beatific, long-nosed face, framed in a nun's wimple, tells us little other than that she was pious and wise, and a survivor. Her gentler spirit more likely walks on the fields and relict gardens – she made the most splendid and beautiful terraced gardens – of her favourite home at Collyweston in the Welland valley just west of Stamford town.[14] Her kindnesses to the Stamford anchoress, Margaret White, are legendary, as are the colourful pageants and the music and the laughter that used to enliven these lost gardens and their now deserted meadows.

The King's Mother had died an enormously rich woman, with properties in twenty-five counties, and revered, as she is still, as the foundress of two Cambridge colleges, Christ's and St John's (named for the Evangelist not the family). She had faithfully provided well for her relatives, both materially and with their lineage of pride, their consanguinity with Henry VIII and Elizabeth I. Later St John generations came to regard her, at least as far as the First Commandment would allow them, as something of a demi-goddess. So enriched, the St John generations continued to roll on at Bletsoe and Lydiard, which had been shared between the Lady Margaret's sons Oliver and John.

At Lydiard the 1st Baronet, Sir John St John, became the great memorialiser, who taught his family of their grand inheritance. He filled the little church of St Mary's with images of St Johns, making it a crowded place even before the living congregations arrived. Here, in the church, we can still see, as Henrietta saw, the wooden panels intricately painted and gilded with the family genealogy and coats of arms. These panels open like cupboard doors, revealing ten pairs of piercingly dark eyes, those of the baronet's parents, the Elizabethan Sir John and his wife Lucy Hungerford, the baronet and his wife Anne Leighton, and six be-ruffed sisters in a pious line, their white hands fluttering like doves on their dark gowns. In the south chapel is the marble funerary bed which Sir John, who died in 1648, arranged for himself, where in armour and ruff he lies with his wives, Anne Leighton, who died in 1628, and Margaret Whitmore, who died in 1637, and thirteen children. These children were all Anne's, she cradles the doll-like thirteenth, and the others gather round like toys in a marble trance. Anne Leighton thus appears twice, in 'life' and in death; she was the great-great-great-granddaughter of Thomas Bullen, the father of Anne Boleyn, mother of Elizabeth I, and so another treasured royal connection. Of the

toy-like marble children, three died fighting for the Royalist cause
in the Civil Wars. Sir John set up a striking monument to Edward,
his favourite son who died from his wounds after the second battle
of Newbury in October 1644, an almost life-like figure of a cavalier
emerging from his canopied tent. In Henrietta's day the figure was
painted in rich colours, but it is now traditionally gilded, and known
as the Golden Cavalier. Like so many families the St Johns were
divided by war. Oliver St John at Bletsoe was a firm Parliamentarian,
and though exiled in France for his money troubles he returned to
lead a troop of horse soldiers at the battle of Edgehill (23 October
1642), where he was captured and died in captivity. At Lydiard, with
the deaths of his brothers, it was Walter, the least Royalist of the
Royalist St Johns, who was left to carry on the line. Sir Walter was
Henrietta's grandfather and head of the household for the first eight
years of her life. With the Golden Cavalier we leave the dead for the
living, at least at the time of Henrietta's birth.

In St Mary's at Lydiard, a crowded little church, cool even on the
hottest day, glistening with gold, scarlet and blue, the baby Henrietta
was presented to her ancestors. There is no record of her baptism
in the Lydiard registers, but her grandmother Johanna was extremely
pious, and would not have allowed her to go unblest.*[15] It seems
likely that the family trooped into church in their habitual way, on
a Sunday in August or September of 1699, and gathered around the
font whilst the baby was sprinkled with holy water. Her grandfather
Sir Walter, or perhaps Henry her father, pronounced it done then
slipped a modest gold coin – enough for one Christian name, which
is all she had, and for a girl at that – to the priest, who hurried off,
forgetting to write anything down.

---

* The records are so haphazard that for her book *Married to Mercury*, 1936, Lady
Hopkinson had horoscopes drawn to establish the birthdays of Henrietta's half-brother
Harry, 16 September 1678, and of her brothers, George, St George's Day, 23 April 1693,
John, 3 May 1702, and Holles, 24 November 1710. She asserts that 'these dates can be
accepted as authentic'. The boys were baptised at St Mary's, Battersea, but no mention is
made, nor any horoscope drawn, for Henrietta; perhaps because her birth on 15 July was
the only one when the family were sure to be at Lydiard for the summer.

Henrietta was in fact doubly a St John, for her paternal grand-parents, Sir Walter and Johanna, came from the Lydiard and Bletsoe branches of the family respectively. Sir Walter was nearing eighty when she was born, a stern and respectable old man devoted to his estates and his charities, and her grandmother Johanna was almost seventy. Henrietta, a vivacious and intelligent child, an only girl surrounded by brothers, seems likely to have amused them so that they gave her special attention. If anything she absorbed more from her grandmother in her first five years than she ever did from her own shy French mother, Angelique. All the evidence is that Henrietta's relationship with her parents was ever merely dutiful – Angelique definitely preferred her sons – whereas Henrietta's passion for growing fruits, flowers and vegetables, her pride in frugal housekeeping but setting a lavish table for friends, her Christian conscience, her appreciation of architecture and poetry, all these, along with a good supply of gritty genes, seemed to stem from her grandmother.

When Johanna was born, in 1630, her father Oliver St John, a brilliant son of Bletsoe, was a prisoner in the Tower of London. He was freed from the charge of inciting anti-royalist revolution by courtesy of a general royal pardon to celebrate the birth of a son to the king. Johanna and her mother had taken refuge in the house-hold of Sir William Masham of Otes at High Laver in Essex, where Johanna was baptised. When released, Johanna's father, a more determined republican than ever and a clever lawyer, made his reputation defending reformist John Hampden in the Court of Star Chamber.[16]* Oliver St John spoke for two days, he lost his case but found himself to have become indispensable to the reformers. Very soon after the case, his wife died and his links to the reformers were further strengthened by his marriage to Oliver Cromwell's cousin

---

* '[L]earned St John, a dark, tough man . . .' was the verdict of Thomas Carlyle, 'of the toughness of leather, who could speak with irrefragable eloquence'. Hampden was fighting the imposition of 20s. ship money, ordered for the defence of coastal towns, on his land-locked Buckinghamshire home, as a test case.

Elizabeth, the young daughter of Henry Cromwell of Upwood in south Cambridgeshire. Seven-year-old Johanna and her young step-mother were to be the best of companions.

Oliver, 'a man reserved and of a dark and clouded countenance, very proud and conversing with few, and those men of his own humour and inclinations',[17] was now Solicitor-General, master-minding Parliament's assertion of its rights and privileges, preparing every dreadful step that would inevitably lead to war.

Johanna grew into a young woman in the turbulent Civil War years, though she was kept clear of sieges and battles in the quiet of Parliamentary Essex or in London. In 1645 her stepmother, Elizabeth, died, and once again St John married quickly, this time to a widow, Elizabeth Cockcroft, the sister of John Oxenbridge, a fiery Nonconformist preacher, fellow at Eton College and friend of the poet Andrew Marvell. Elizabeth Cockcroft seems to have been a formidable and educated woman, and undoubtedly strong in her radical beliefs. St John himself had wholly rejected the Church of England and the Book of Common Prayer and regarded himself as a Presbyterian. It was little wonder that Johanna felt she 'never understood' what religion was about, so much had changed so quickly in her short lifetime. Equally it is easy to imagine that she found a surer and more certain world in her gardening and in herbals. John Gerard's *Herball*, which was first published in 1597, was revised in a popular second edition by Thomas Johnson in 1633. William Lawson's *A New Orchard and Garden* (1618), which included 'the Country Housewife's Garden', was also in popular use into the mid-century. In 1655 *The Queen's Closet Opened*, purporting to be the secret recipes of Queen Henrietta Maria, was published. Perhaps that did not find its way into Johanna's collection (for, as Antonia Fraser has remarked, the 'desire to cash in on a famous name is no modern phenomenon'![18]).

Johanna never seems to have lived anywhere for very long, so even her gardening must have been frustrated. When she was about seventeen or eighteen, though before Charles I's execution in

January 1649, St John moved his family to Thorpe manor at Peterborough, where he began to exhibit a much more sympathetic side to his character, his plans for his own fine house and garden. He had travelled in his undergraduate days studying his admired Dutch republicanism. He had Dutch friends, and his admiration had extended to their architecture and gardens, particularly the work of the Stadholder Frederik Hendrik, who died in 1647.* Frederik Hendrik had laid out Honselaarsdijk on a polder south of The Hague. An assemblage of buildings, gardens, courts, avenues and canals, it was designed with the harmonic proportion of width to length of 3:4, from the inspiration of Vitruvius and Alberti and a revival of Italian classicism. Honselaarsdijk inspired Frederik Hendrik's son William of Orange's Het Loo, and in turn William and Mary's Hampton Court, but St John was there first, with his own plans for Thorpe Hall and his gardens.

At Peterborough Johanna watched – how much she was involved we cannot know – while her father went about his scheming. The great Norman cathedral, the former abbey of Gildenburgh, had been treated comparatively gently at the Dissolution (because, it is said, Henry VIII remembered it fondly from his visits to his grandmother, Lady Margaret, at Collyweston and wished it little harm) but more recently, in 1643, Colonel Richard Cromwell and his soldiers had reduced many of the precinct buildings, including the chapter house and cloister, to rubble. It was also said that Oliver Cromwell had his eye on this 'quarry' of good building stone, Barnack rag from Ketton and Collyweston quarries, for a house for himself, but the wily St John beat him to it. He ingratiated himself with the bewildered townspeople, who were angry at the

---

* The Dutch influence stemmed from his youth. The St Johns of Bletsoe and their cousins at Old Bolingbroke in Lincolnshire had long had interests in the vast salterns of the south Lincolnshire fens, and with competition from rock-salt mining they diverted their influence to fen drainage schemes. Both families were represented in the 1630 Adventurers' Company with Francis Russell, 4th Earl of Bedford, and as a young man Oliver St John would have heard much talk of Vermuyden's plans and probably visited the Low Countries to see his work. The Earl of Bedford paid a large fine to free Oliver St John from prison on his first charge of sedition when he was at university.

cathedral's fate: 'whereas the minster of Peterborough,' wrote St John, 'being an ancient and goodly fabric was compounded to be sold and demolished I begged it to be granted to the citizens, who at this present, and ever since, have accordingly made use of it'.[19] While the citizens kept their minster there was abundant building stone from the cloister and the chapter house and other buildings, which was spirited away to Thorpe to build St John's new house.

The surprise is in the house he built, which now rides high amongst the trees of the Nene valley, just west of Peterborough, carefully sited to avoid having the cathedral anywhere in view. It is a rectangular house of seven bays, its axial plan extending to the garden courts, all on the Honselaarsdijk principle. It is an exceptionally pretty house, with a cap of a roof of Collyweston slates, deep eaves and tall chimneys. It is just such a house as Christopher Wren would have built had he not still been stargazing at Oxford and not ready for architecture for another ten years. Like its dark builder, Thorpe Hall has held many mysteries. Who was the architect St John employed? Long thought to have been John Webb, it is now agreed that it was the artisan-mason Peter Mills.*[20] The names of other St John's craftsmen are now known. He ordered '38 windows of freestone' from the Ketton masons John Ashley and Sampson Frisbey; exquisite interior doors and doorcases were made by John Whiting and Richard Cleere, who later worked on Wren's Great Model for St Paul's. The Thorpe chimneys, four great stacks 'crowned with acanthus-palmette capitals', delight stone-addicts still.[21]

Whether Johanna St John was married from her father's new house is uncertain. Staunchly Royalist John Evelyn passed by the 'newly completed' Thorpe Hall in August 1654, his eyes tinged with bitterness at the 'stately palace' of 'one deep in the blood of our Good King'.[22] By that date Johanna was settled at Lydiard with at

---

* Mills also built Wisbech Castle, Thorpe's twin, for another Cromwellian, John Thurloe, Secretary to the Council of State, of which St John was a member.

least two children, Ann and Henry. Henry, born in 1652, was to be
Henrietta's father. It is possible that St John, now Lord Chief Justice,
presented his daughter in marriage to her Royalist cousin as a
symbol of reconciliation, setting a good example in anticipation of
the Act of Oblivion which was 'to bury all Rancour and Evil' (and
passed in February 1652)[23]. This explanation does not quite fit –
Walter St John was not like his Cavalier brothers, he was thought
to be something 'of a rogue and a rebel, an anabaptist and a
quaker'.[24] Was it simply a matter of money? The Lord Chief Justice
had made his fortune and was on the winning side, the Royalists at
Lydiard had lost and were poor; it was in the family's interest to
balance things out. Of course, it cannot be discounted that the
two young people loved each other – theirs was to be a long and
companionable marriage – and Cromwell himself was a firm
believer in marriage for love.

Johanna must have revelled in her new life at Lydiard; she was
mistress of it all, with no mother-in-law nor maiden aunts to
restrain her, and away from the harshly Puritan regimes which
puzzled her. Her portrait from the time of her wedding, reveals a
proud young woman with a pale face and mocking smile, and eyes
that are curiously watery, almost filling with tears. Her fair hair is
dressed simply in a jewelled band, and she wears a demure silver
satin gown. In successive portraits as she became older so she grew
farther from the Presbyterian ideal of a modest and 'guid' housewife,
her necklines were lowered, her curls tumbled freely and she became
much more the Restoration lady. But, regardless of her costume,
she seemed to inspire love in those round her, she enjoyed the
company of loyal friends and servants, and she bequeathed to
Henrietta some of her goodness of nature. Chief Justice St John
seems to have been concerned for his daughter's spiritual welfare, for
round the time of her marriage he had a hand in the appointment
of her chaplain, the young Symon Patrick from Gainsborough in
Lincolnshire, a graduate of his old college, Queens' at Cambridge,
who had taken Presbyterian orders. Symon Patrick took his new

post seriously, studying the St John lineage and making it his business to visit the ancestral Fonmon in Glamorgan and putting his observations to pious use: 'there is a spring in that country where your name first took root in British soil,' he wrote in a later sermon,

> which is very low and empty of water when the sea flows and swells the neighbouring river Ogmar, and again ascends and rills itself when the sea retires out of the [Bristol] Channel. It will be a most lovely sight, both to God and man, to see you humble and lowly in the highest tides of a swelling fortune; and if your fulness should abate and draw back into the ocean from whence it came, to behold the elevation of your spirit and the greatness of your mind rising above all the reach of these worldly changes. Then would you most truly imitate those stars in your escutcheon which are not seen in the day and shine most brightly in the night.[25]

Whether Johanna's father ever knew that Symon Patrick was privately ordained, in the Bishop of Norwich's parlour, into the Church of England is not clear; perhaps he just turned a blind eye. Sir Walter and Johanna certainly approved; their chaplain was appointed as vicar of St Mary's Battersea, a living in their gift, and became an ever more beloved shepherd of his flock.

Throughout the late 1650s, after Cromwell's death in September 1658, Symon Patrick – 'too wise to betray the opportunity then opening by unduly precipitating a return to forms and practices long dis-used' – carefully led the way 'by familiarising his flock with the nature and the advantage of the Church's system and the beauties of her liturgy'.[26] He read the Book of Common Prayer for the first time at Battersea on 22 July 1660. For Johanna St John, who declared 'she never understood religion till she knew me', it was a relief and a homecoming. The young clergyman was greatly beloved at Battersea for the way he cared for the village in the Plague year, but he was clearly destined for greater things. Of his time with the St Johns he wrote, 'Never was any man, I have often thought, more beloved in any family than I was; specially by the lady of it who was very pious.'[27] Revd Patrick eventually moved to St Paul's in Covent Garden, from where he stayed in touch with the family, and was appointed Dean of Peterborough in 1679.*

And what of the Chief Justice's end? He was painted by a pupil of Van Dyck sitting amongst the folio volumes of his library at Thorpe. Outside his garden courts flowered, though whether the widow Cockcroft was a gardener I do not know. Thorpe had a river gate to the Nene, and was probably intended to be completely moated, as at Honselaarsdijk. This fortress element came to take on a more sinister meaning, together with all the railings, gates and walls. The Lord Chief Justice knew that he did not have long to enjoy his lovely house. From that Friday evening, 3 September 1658, when the messenger came riding up the Great North Road with the news that the Lord Protector was dead, he was a prey to fears and vacillation. With others he swore to hold up the 'Good Old Cause', but soon sided with General Monck so as to be seen as supportive of the return of the king.

Charles II offered Oliver St John an amnesty if he would betray his fellow regicides, but he would not. Instead he worked up his complex legal defence on the basis that his was not amongst the signatures on Charles I's death warrant, which he had taken good care to see that it was not. Thorpe's walls were well guarded, horses were ever ready in the stables, St John was haunted by dread. In the end, on a gloomy November evening in 1662 he rode away, to a hiding place in the Bavarian mountains, where he died at the good

---

* He further distinguished himself by publishing Simon Gunton's history based on the medieval chronicles, adding his own supplement which included Francis Standish's eye-witness account of Colonel Cromwell's soldiers' attacks 'with Axes, Poleaxes and Hammers' on the monuments, including the tomb of Catherine of Aragon, and all the other furnishings of the cathedral's interior. Dean Patrick had asked for this rare and harrowing account to be written, and it includes the following: 'for Mr Oliver St John Chief Justice then of the Common Pleas, being sent on an Embassy into Holland by the Powers that govern'd then, requested this Boon of them at his Return, that they would give him the ruin'd Church or Minster at Peterburgh; this they did accordingly, and he gave it to the Town of Peterbrugh for their use'.[28]

age of seventy-five. Johanna, happily at Lydiard, had plenty to fill her prayers.

These turbulent years in the lives of her ancestors were to have a profound influence on Henrietta St John. She, it might be supposed, inherited her dark colouring, darker than any of her brothers, from some stray genes of her great-grandfather. His lovely Thorpe Hall, quite the loveliest of all the St John houses, remained in the family, with his son and grandson, throughout her lifetime. Surely, her natural curiosity drew her there? She certainly visited Cambridge (perhaps to see her ancestress Lady Margaret's colleges, Christ's and St John's), which was not far away. And was it a remnant of the Chief Justice's radicalism that made her so impatient of royalty and Court life, when all around her pandered and did their duty? She definitely had an anti-royalist streak, finding all the panoply of rituals and parades merely fit for ridicule. Her outspokenness and her low threshold of tolerance for pomposity and affectation were more than likely an echo caught from her grandmother Johanna's republican upbringing.

Sir Walter and his wife Johanna were to impart a great sense of security to Henrietta's childhood, which is more than can be said for her own father. Henry St John, their heir, was second-born. He was extraordinary as a young man, a paragon: tall and proud, handsome and well built, good-natured and apparently viceless as well as being brilliantly clever. After six years at Eton College, he gained bachelor's and master's degrees at Cambridge and entered the House of Commons in the family's seat at Wootton Bassett as soon as he came of age. Soon he made a brilliant marriage, to Lady Mary Rich, a daughter of the 3rd Earl of Warwick. Her father was dead so Lady Mary lived with an aunt, also Lady Mary Rich, at Leez Priory in Essex. The aunt was surprised, and pleased, at how Henry St John seemed so 'free from the reigning vices of these loose and profane times'.[29]

Poor Lady Mary St John went through a succession of miscarriages and still births for five years, until she finally managed a healthy son, on 16 September 1678. She died within a few days, and as the baby was born at Battersea, Henry had the melancholy task of taking his young wife's body to Lydiard for burial on 2 October, before returning for his son's baptism at Battersea on 10 October. The baby was called Henry, though was always to be known in the family as Harry.

We have become inured to the swift litany of childbed deaths when riffling through the generations, as any history dictates. The inevitability of procreation, the availability of an easy succession of young wives, seem to be 'normal' for past centuries. Did they not, the survivors, shed a swift tear and carry on? At least this time, the signs are that it was not so. Those five years of loving hopes and disappointments, and their tragic ending, seemed to have changed Henry St John from a vital young man with the world at his feet into a listless and idle and absentee father, who became a prey to bad company. His little son had no power to save him, and their relationship was ever to be marked by bitterness. Did he blame the baby for living, while Mary died? Was there something that we cannot know of that changed Henry St John, or was it that he understandably felt bereft, emasculated even, that his existence was pointless? Little Harry did not need him, for he was brought up in the more than capable hands of his grandmother, Johanna. Yet the boy missed his father, and he was always to be looking for a hero to worship. Sir Walter seemed rejuvenated in his hopes for his grandson, to whom he transferred the mantle of St John pride. Harry was to feel that he was 'thrown early into the world', and was strictly educated to make him ambitious before he could even understand the meaning of the word. Henry must have looked askance at Sir Walter, who carried his sixty-plus years so lightly, despairing of ever coming into his own inheritance (Sir Walter was to live to be eighty-six).

When Harry was six, disaster struck. The household was thrown into a frenzy of concern. Henry and a drinking companion were accused of the murder of a gentleman, variously named Escott,

Estcourt or Hescot, in a brawl at the Globe Tavern in Fleet Street. They were put on trial and found guilty at the Old Bailey. Indeed, according to Bishop Burnet's *History of His Own Time*, Henry St John was subjected to plea bargaining; he was 'prevailed on to confess the indictment, and to let sentence pass on him for murder; a pardon being promised him if he should do so, and he was threatened with the utmost rigour of the law if he stood upon his defence'. That 'utmost rigour' was, of course, a death sentence, which was passed, swiftly followed by an offer of a royal pardon.[30]

Sir Walter was shocked, but he thought the king's friendship would soften the blow. Had he not 'put on his rich red riding coat' and joined the company of nobles on that joyful day, 29 May 1660, with 'the bells ringing, the streets hung with tapestry, fountains running with wine' as Charles II had returned to his own City of London?[31] Had he not confirmed his loyalty with presents of venison from Lydiard, and Muscovy ducklings for the royal aviary in St James's Park, both regularly offered? Had not the king, quick to recognise the sources of good things, not taken to halting his royal barge at Battersea stairs for a game of cards with Sir Walter and one of Johanna's sumptuous suppers? Put not your trust in princes, for Sir Walter's efforts were to no avail and the shade of Chief Justice St John leaned down. Bishop Burnet noted that the prisoner's 'was a rich family, and not well affected to the Court, so he was told he must pay well'. Henry's pardon apparently cost £10,000, some said £16,000, a year's salary for a minister of state, and it was paid by his mother Johanna out of the Chief Justice's legacy. Bishop Burnet added, with feeling, that 'old Sir Walter would not meddle with it'.[32]

Freed from the gallows and probably under duress, Henry St John resorted to a good woman. His new bride, Angelique Madelaine de Pellissari, was a French Huguenot just twenty years old and already widowed. They were married on 1 January 1687 at St Anne's church in Soho Square. Angelique came from a well-connected and distinguished family of French Protestants; her father was treasurer-general of the French navy, and her mother was a daughter of a senior member of the French East India Company. Angelique had a brother and a half-sister and they had all fled to the safety of Geneva after the Revocation of the Edict of Nantes, that scourge of French Protestants of 1685. Angelique came to England to marry a son of the Wharton family, who promptly died.[33] Henry St John must have been just as much a port in a storm to her as she to him. At least he could converse with her in French, for she had very little English. She was unfamiliar with English ways, rather quiet though very beautiful. She was certainly no match for the formidable Johanna, who ruled at Battersea and Lydiard, and at first she was treated much as a guest in her own homes. This meant that she had time for her stepson Harry, to whom she taught French conversation and a love of all things French, and who grew to love her in return.

Harry was just over eight when his stepmother arrived. He was desperately ill later that year, a crisis that consumed everyone's efforts, from which he was almost certainly saved by his grandmother Johanna's knowledge of medicines and herbal remedies, aided by Angelique's gentle nursing. Harry's first half-brother, named George, which was for Angelique's father and to mark his birthday, was born on 23 April 1693. The following year Harry was again seriously ill, his 15-year-old constitution overstrained by his ruthless educational regime of Latin, Greek, rhetoric, logic, history and politics overlaid by the ogreish Dr Manton's 'daily task book'. Dr Manton was Symon Patrick's predecessor at St Paul's, Covent Garden, who famously composed 119 sermons upon Psalm 119. These sermons Harry later recalled 'taught my youth to yarn'.[34] After this second illness, in 1694, Sir Walter put up a medallion portrait of his grandson in the church at Battersea.[35] Was it in thanks for his recovery, or an appeal to his forebears, the lady Margaret, Henry VII and Elizabeth I, who are all pictured in the St John east window of the church, to watch over him?

A little ancestor-worship seemed quite usual to the St Johns, and this time it worked. Their precious Harry, with some irregular and unrecorded attendances at Eton and rumours of an Oxford college and a little European travel, but mostly by dint of the home efforts of the family, grew up into a dazzling young man, whom Jonathan Swift was soon to dub 'the greatest young man I ever knew'.[36] The Wootton Bassett seat, which seems to have reverted to Sir Walter after Henry's misdemeanour, was his when he came of age. Soon he was being called 'the most brilliant of the younger Tories'[37], the faction he affected to join, even though Sir Walter's (and his father Henry's) were Whig preferences. In 1702 at the age of twenty-four he was Secretary at War, 'at an age,' wrote Lord Chesterfield, 'at which others are hardly thought fit for the smallest employment'.[38] Harry's quick perception, his prodigious memory and hard work were his virtues, though Swift suspected too much work, 'for he would plod whole Days and Nights like the lowest Clerk in an office'[39], which meant too little delegation. In the House of Commons his appearances attracted a crowd, for his tall and graceful figure, long expressive hands and good voice 'and, above all, the purest and most florid diction, with the justest metaphors and happiest images'[40] made Harry St John what we would call a star. His father Henry, who was by now Henrietta's father too, was more jealous and disaffected than ever.

Harry, ever in search of a hero to worship, claimed to have modelled himself on his cousin, John Wilmot, 2nd Earl of Rochester, the Restoration poet of sex and satire, of whom Dr Johnson observed that 'he blazed out his youth and health in lavish voluptuousness'.[41] Rochester died at thirty-three, Harry was to make three score years and thirteen, so his 'blazing' was more equivocal – but then, he was a politician. Even so, his reputation for every imaginable kind of debauchery was soon made. His quick intelligence and his changeability earned him a nickname: the Man of Mercury or Mercurialis. This has an interesting double meaning – was he as slippery as quicksilver, as deadly as the rank and poisonous *Mercurialis perennis*, the herb known as 'Bad Henry', or as benevolent and useful as 'Good Henry', *Chenopodium bonus-henricus*? Of course, he was both.

Harry blamed his excesses on his hothouse upbringing, which had so effectively taught him to be ambitious. 'I was ambitious, and of all success – success in pleasure, success in fame. To wean me from the former, my friends persuaded me to marry; they chose my wife for her connections and her fortune, and I gained these advantages at the expense of what was better than either – happiness!'[42]

This arranged marriage took place in the early summer of Henrietta's second year, on 22 May 1701. Harry was married to Frances Winchcombe of Bucklebury in Berkshire at Wren's City church St Dunstan in the East. The wedding party drove back to Chelsea, where they took boats to cross the river to Battersea stairs for the reception at the manor house, where the shy bride was subjected to the full force of the assembled St Johns. Apparently she took refuge with the least intimidating of them all, Henrietta, who amused her; 'this charming little person whom Harry petted and teased'.[43] That Harry made such a fuss of Henrietta, even on his wedding day, reveals the bond of affection already formed between them, but also suggests that he was less than mesmerised by his new bride. It was, after all, a business affair; his glamour and prospects allied to Frances Winchcombe's fortune and estate – though for her part, sadly, Frances was in love.

The newly-weds spent that June and part of July *en famille* at Battersea whilst their new house in Golden Square was made ready. This closeness seemed to seal Henrietta's babyish adoration of her half-brother, for Harry was to be the Apollo of her childhood, far more important to her than her parents. He was arguably the man she was always to love most, for good or ill.

CHAPTER TWO

'My Darling Heriott'

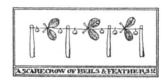

O N THE NIGHT OF 26 November 1703 a great storm raged
over southern England, a phenomenon of weather exactly
matched in our memories, press reports and television news footage
of the great storm of the early hours of 16 October 1987. In the face
of such elemental furies, Henrietta's distant, and more fragile, world
comes close to ours. In 1987 the Channel ferries all scurried to port
as their radios picked up unbelievable immediate weather warnings.
In 1703 the winds blew from the south-west, 'resembling thunder
at a distance and being attended with terrible flashes of lightning'.[1]
All along the Channel and round to Gunfleet Bank, off Clacton,
hundreds of seamen were drowned, warships and an unlisted fleet
of little ships were lost. The Eddystone lighthouse, along with its
crew and builder 'the ingenious Mr Winstanley' who happened to
be visiting, disappeared altogether.[2] In 1987, the storm growled and
crashed its way from Dorset to Norfolk in four or so hours. Some
thought it was a nuclear attack, many could not believe their eyes
as tree trunks and garden sheds whirled about their heads. In 1703
the sea invaded the land, washing into the sherry vaults of Bristol,
and boats were rowed across fields to rescue stranded families. The
devilish wind wrought havoc, roofs were lifted off and chimneys
fell in their thousands, avalanches of bricks and wet soot ruining
many a cosy parlour, and worse, for some unfortunates with the

largest chimneys were killed in their beds. Walls crumbled, hayricks were unmade and their straw left hanging in the trees, boats were flung out of river-beds, and carriages were thrown over hedges.[3] In 1987, when salt-spray could be tasted in north Surrey, garden and street trees, trees in parks, whole woods were decimated, and views unseen for 200 years were opened to astonished eyes. In 1703 groves were uprooted and great woods felled – 'Wood Town no longer,' moaned old John Evelyn, the author of 'Sylva', at his beloved Wotton estate in the Surrey hills, and in London Queen Anne watched at the window of her palace as more than a hundred of the most venerable elms in St James's Park came tumbling down.[4]

Somewhere between St James's and Evelyn's Wotton, Henrietta was in the St Johns' old house by the river at Battersea, which took the full force of the south-westerly as it stood on the Surrey bank of the Thames, here flowing north to south in its great meander. The family wing was sheltered, but the little community, which was really a port beside the sprawling, busy river, had plenty of clearing up and mending to do and the mudlarks, the old women and urchins who trawled the flotsam for anything of use, made good livings.

Henrietta regarded Battersea as her real home. When the weather was kind the house and the village were bathed in the glorious sunsets that fired the golden river, and it seemed quite a little paradise. For travellers on land it was off the beaten track, for the main roads had long avoided the river meadows. Celia Fiennes had 'passed the end of [Wandsworth] and Clapham and part of Lambeth – so thro' Southwark [and] over London Bridge' on her ten-mile journey from Kingston to the City.[5] Daniel Defoe, as so many others, passed by on the other bank of the Thames, through Kensington, Chelsea, Fulham, Hammersmith and Twickenham when he wanted to see what the 'country affords' west of London. Once he supposed 'you take your view from the little rising hills about Clapham' but failed to mention Battersea, and let his eyes slide off to Peckham and Camberwell and 'the most glorious sight without exception', the whole City of London.[6] It was a time when everyone was dazzled by London, and gravitated of necessity to London Bridge, the only bridge until the wooden viaduct was built between Fulham and Putney in 1727–9, followed by old Westminster Bridge in 1738.

Upriver was rather a separate world. Although the St Johns' Battersea was comfortable and noteworthy it was hardly spectacular when compared to the cavalcade of riverside palaces about which Defoe was so lyrical. He thought the river journey from Hampton Court to Westminster's limit at Somerset House in the Strand, passing Ham, Richmond, Kew, Syon, Fulham and Lambeth and so many fine mansions and lawns, displayed a 'distant glory'. 'There is a beauty of these things at a distance,' he mused picturesquely, 'taking them en passant, and in perspective, which few people value, and fewer understand; and yet here they are more truly great, than in all their private beauties whatsoever', and surpassed anything that the rivers Danube, Seine or Po could muster.[7] When the riverboat levelled with Battersea stairs the sated travellers' eyes were turned to the opposite bank, to Wren's palatial Royal Hospital, incongruously situated amidst the hayfields of Chelsea.

Richard Steele, 'Mr Spectator', on the other hand, taking a boat from Richmond one fine August dawn, reported a more workaday river:

> [W]e soon fell in with a Fleet of Gardiners bound for the several Market-ports of London; and it was the most pleasing Scene imaginable to see the Chearfulness with which those industrious People ply'd their Way to a certain Sale of their Goods. The Banks on each Side are as well peopled, and beautified with as agreeable Plantations, as any Spot on the Earth; but the Thames itself, loaded with the Product of each Shore, added very much to the Landskip.

It was an uneventful trip. They put in at Nine Elms, just downstream from Battersea, for a load of melons for Covent Garden, then landed with 'Ten Sail of Apricock Boats' near Somerset House.[8]

Melons, apricots, the lavender and vegetable fields of Battersea, the hayfields of Chelsea: it is hard to imagine this early eighteenth-century river flowing like a cornucopia, but it was so in Henrietta's day. Salmon and eels were caught by the Battersea fishermen, teal and snipe were shot on the marshes to fill pies, and the untouchable royal swans were so numerous that by dint of accidental deaths there were swan roasts. The village was a clustering of cottages around the jetty and Battersea stairs, the wooden structure that stood in the river and was supposedly the St Johns' private landing place. There were two inns, the Castle and the Raven, St Mary's church and Sir Walter St John's school. The river, which dominated all life, was enormously wide, tidal and sprawled unembanked to Chelsea, often lost in the morning mists, on the other side.*

At Battersea – 'Batrichsey with Waynesworth' as it was antiquely called – no less than Lydiard, Henrietta was a country child. Hers was not some tall town house where the work was hidden in attics and basements, and the ladies were isolated in between with nothing to do but sew and sigh. As Dean Patrick had volunteered, there was a great deal of love and consequent contentment amongst the extended 'family' community. The house was rambling and im-mensely ancient, its origins lost in constant rebuilding, but with some fragments of Jacobean grandeur in the carved oak staircase with wide, well-worn treads, and ceilings of decorative plaster strap-work. One small parlour was curiously panelled in scented cedar-wood cut with diamond motifs.[9] In the walled and sheltered garden courts the lady Johanna grew the yellow Austrian briar, *Rosa lutea*, which was known to the Saracens and Moors and named because Clusius had found it in Austria and brought it to England over a hundred years earlier (1585). There were larkspurs, the double-flowered kinds grown by Gerard and Parkinson, honeysuckles and hollyhocks and many other blooms. There were fruits trained against the walls – the lady Johanna and later Henrietta's mother Angelique grew their own apricots, peaches, melons and possibly

---

* Old Battersea wooden bridge, painted by Whistler, was built 1771–2.

even pineapples – as well as more ordinary apples and pears, salads and vegetables. Lastly there were the vital herbs – sweet cicely, borage, pennyroyal, parsley, sages, lavender, rosemary and others – all necessary for the lady Johanna's preciously guarded 'receipts'.*

The benefits of this bounty are evident in Henrietta's first portrait, in which she appears to be four or five years old. In the convention of the time she is shown as a miniature woman, infant-plump with wide-apart dark eyes, a snub nose and pertly dimpled mouth, the very child that Harry loved to tease. Her abundant hair, dark and curly, is more or less governed by a lace cap; her dress is loose, a gathered gown in the manner of a house-dress, and one bare foot peeps from her skirts, where a black and white spaniel puppy nestles in her lap. The painting is an unskilled likeness, she would hardly have sat still long enough to be properly portrayed, and the head has an air of detachment, a china-doll's head on a rag body. She is no blushing English rose (unless it is Pliny's vivid red *Rosa rubra*, the rose of Lancaster) and most unlike the peaches-and-cream beauties of her day, but the portrait is a lively image of a cheerful little girl. She invites the idea that, as soon as she could walk, her grandmother Johanna would have taken her around the garden gathering sweet plums, or into the church to see Sir Walter's heraldic golden falcon[10], or perhaps to her closet, where she kept the great family Bible, where she would have taught Henrietta to put her fat little hands together in prayer. With growing independence did she escape from her nurse and governess Mademoiselle Haillé (who had been Harry's and George's governess, too) to scurry out with the kitchenmaid to collect the warm brown eggs, or follow the garden boy sent to water the wondrous Portugal melon beds?

As to her education, her mother Angelique and Mademoiselle Haillé between them made her as good with conversational and

---

* Family tradition had it that Lady Margaret Beaufort's great-grandmother, Queen Philippa, a keen and scientific gardener, had reintroduced rosemary to Britain when the Roman introductions had been lost, by bringing cuttings from her garden in Flanders.

written French as she was with English, and she soon read well and
widely. Perhaps she was as forward as her young kinswoman, Lucy
Hutchinson, who described her own cleverness so charmingly:

> By the time I was four years old I read English perfectly, and
> having a great memory, I was carried to sermons; and while I
> was very young could remember and repeat them exactly, and
> being caressed, the love of praise tickled me, and made me
> attend more heedfully. When I was about seven years of age, I
> remember I had at one time eight tutors in several qualities,
> languages, music, dancing, writing and needlework; but my
> genius was quite averse from all but my book, and that I was so
> eager of every moment I could steal from my play I would
> employ in any book I could find, when my own were locked
> from me.*[10]

When Henrietta was five and a half, in the middle of January
1705, her grandmother Johanna died at Battersea, though in her
'owne house', the pretty brick house a short walk from the manor
house, which she and Sir Walter had recently built to give them
some peace in their final years.[11] They had been married for fifty-six
years. She left instructions for her funeral: 'I would have an exhor-
tation to my children & grandchildren to be made by Mr Gower in
my owne house before my being carried out of the house on that
solemn occasion.' She trusted to Sir Walter's 'discretion' to arrange
this.†[12]

The family gathering on that gloomy January morning was made
up of Henry and Angelique St John with their children, Johanna's
eldest grandson Harry and his wife Frances, Johanna's own daughters, Anne Cholmondeley and Johanna Chute, with their daughters,
'young' (though she must have been approaching fifty) Johanna's

---

* The Royalist Lucy Hutchinson, born Lucy Apsley, was the daughter of Lucy St John,
one of the daughters of Sir John St John (d. 1594) and his wife Lucy Hungerford portrayed
in the triptych in Lydiard church.
† 'Mr Gower' was her chaplain, Nathaniel Gower, who was vicar of Battersea and a master
at Sir Walter's free school in the village; he was married to Johanna Ffoote, the daughter
of Sir Walter's steward William and his wife Susannah, who had long been the lady
Johanna's housekeeper.

husband George Chute and the bachelor William St John. Henrietta encountered for the first time Aunt 'Chumley's' daughter, yet another Johanna, who was to become her dearest friend in long after years. The Chutes' daughter married Sir Peter Soame, and their son, also Sir Peter, was to be another lifelong friend.

After the funeral, at the reading of her will, the Lady Johanna dispensed her treasures: 'To my old and deare friend the Countess of Lindsay I leave my gold cupp which Mrs Drax left me for a Legacy and wish I would leave her a friend may love her as much and have more power to serve her than myself.' There was £100 for her servant Alice James for life, then the money was to be invested and used 'to apprentice a poor girle or Boy of Battersea'; Johanna's 'Booke of Receipts for Cookery' and the 'preserves in the dining room' were for her granddaughter Joana Soame; all her clothes, linen and furniture, her silver porringer and spoon, 'the basin I wash in & the cupp I drinke my chocolate in' plus her silver skillet were for her 'old and honest' housekeeper, Susannah Ffoote. Her pictures and trinkets were divided between her granddaughters, another 'receipt' book and a cross-stitched skreen were for Anne Cholmondeley, and for Henrietta's father – whom she knew so well needed to repair his soul – she left the Great Bible, with pictures of the four Apostles, Matthew, Mark, Luke and John.[13]

Johanna's death quietened the Battersea households. Sir Walter retired to his own house and busied himself with the building of a gallery in the church, reached by an outside stair, for his school-children. His free school, for twenty poor boys, was his favourite charity.* In the manor house Henrietta's mother Angelique came into her own as mistress without fear of contradiction. Her earlier uncertainties disappeared, and Angelique blossomed with pride in her housekeeping skills, even if she was rather empty-headed and frivolous. She was undoubtedly pretty, with a sweet face, long nose and rosebud lips with deep smile lines at the corners of her mouth

---

* The school in Battersea today still bears his name.

which Henrietta inherited. Angelique is still as elegant as she was as a bride, even though she is now in her late thirties and the mother of George, Henrietta and John. Her last child, a fat little boy named Holles of whom Henrietta was particularly fond, was to be born in five years' time, in 1710. Henrietta's relationship with her mother was never to sparkle, it was correct rather than closely affectionate. Angelique gave her French conversation and some of her French taste in clothes and pretty things, she dutifully presented her at Court and took her to Bath when the time came, but otherwise the gentle French mother found her only daughter's impetuosity – which came largely from a thwarted or at least unchannelled intelligence – just too much to bear.* With her disaffected and self-centred father, and her elder brother George being groomed in pomposity and fecklessness, Henrietta was practically orphaned in the years after her grandmother's death.

Consequently as she grew so did her worshipping affection for her glorious Harry. Harry St John brought the high game of life as a whirlwind through the sleepy rooms of Battersea. At first he was the bringer of sweetmeats, the boisterous, handsome, gorgeously attired brother who swung her on to his shoulders and carried her around the house singing. But with the years his influence deepened, making 'half a scholar of her'[14], bringing her poetry to read, adding the classics and Italian to her appetite for French and English literature, and teaching her to demand more than the domesticity for her life. Whether from Harry, or her parents or other visitors, the street wisdom of the coffee shops and news-sheets reached her ears. In truth it was Harry's own doings that were all the gossip – just being his adored little sister was an education in itself.

Perhaps as he had no children of his own he liked his role as mentor. He was ever to address her, sometimes rather pompously and even when she was grown up, as 'my dear child' or 'darling

---

* At Angelique's death Harry Bolingbroke acknowledged his stepmother to have been a 'silly' and rather stupid woman, but too silly to have done any harm. Was she just jealous of Henrietta, and the attention that Harry paid to his only sister?

child'.* The unhappiness of his marriage made him restless, and though he and Frances had one of the fashionable new homes in Golden Square, a pretty terraced house on the west side, with a balcony outside the first-floor drawing room, he was hardly ever there. Frances St John was very musical (Harry was bored by music except in the theatre or opera) and she spent much of her time quietly with her musical friends and teachers.[15] Her early fascination with Henrietta was not developed into a friendship, for Frances was overwhelmed by the St Johns and hardly ever visited Battersea or Lydiard. In turn, Harry had absolutely refused to go to his wife's much-loved home at Bucklebury while Frances' fretful and blind father, Sir Henry Winchcombe, was alive. The old man had died at the end of 1703 and the estate was shared between Frances and her sisters Betty and Mary. Frances immediately made her share over to Harry. When the plump and companionable Betty Winchcombe died swiftly of 'a most malignant sort' of smallpox in early September 1705, Harry netted Frances' half-share of Betty's inheritance as well. Later that month Harry, too, became feverishly ill, and Frances patiently nursed him back to health.[16]

Harry's relationship with his father worsened dramatically three years later, when old Sir Walter St John died in 1708 and it was revealed that he had passed over his son (who had clearly not been forgiven for the Escot affair) and left Lydiard and Battersea to his grandson Harry. Harry, having Bucklebury as a country retreat, was happy to leave things as they were, with the family living at Battersea and spending summers at Lydiard in their customary way, but a further sense of insecurity crept into Henrietta's home life. Nothing, however, could stop Henry St John inheriting the baronetcy, and thus armed he announced that he would be a Whig candidate for the Wootton Bassett seat which the brilliant Harry had held in the

* Of course, there was just the possibility that she was his child, for he was just twenty when she was conceived, and fast making his reputation for 'every kind of debauchery' which might well have included seducing his rather lonely and adoring stepmother. This rather wild hypothesis is perhaps supported by Angelique's coolness towards Henrietta, let alone Harry's worsening relationship with his father.

Tory interest for seven years. At the general election that year the good pocket burghers of Wootton preferred their old Whig ways, as under Sir Walter, and they contributed to the narrow Whig majority. Then Harry, despite frantic efforts to find himself a seat, was out of the House of Commons. 'My father makes a scandalous figure,' he wrote in disgust to Robert Harley, 'neglected by all the gentlemen, and sure of miscarrying where his family always were reverenced.'[17]

He retired, to spend two years in the political wilderness at Bucklebury, where Henrietta saw and realised that a gardening passion could obsess her hero. Bucklebury was a romantic Elizabethan brick house with a great Tudor doorway, set in a park and estate just north of the Great West road near Newbury (and so en route to Lydiard) in Berkshire. The village of Bucklebury is in the River Pang valley, but the house was on higher ground, surrounded by oakwoods and the sandy, picturesque – by dint of the re-entrant contours – Bucklebury Common. Harry had enthusiastically planted an avenue of oaks, his Blenheim Avenue, to celebrate his hero Marlborough's victory of 1704, for which he, as Secretary at War and controller of the army's purse strings, felt he had some credit. But now he was turning against Marlborough's expensive wars and siding with the landed interest who had shouldered 'the whole burthen of this charge' without 'having served in the Fleets nor armies, nor meddled in the public funds and management of the Treasury'. These innocent, 'poor and dispirited' landed countrymen were at the mercy of the 'meddlers', i.e. those who made money out of wars, who with their new fortunes were distorting rural prices, disrupting rural contentments.[18] As Harry St John inspected the planting of his new groves, admired his new-built pavilion and summerhouse and pottered in his greenhouse, one of the earliest of its kind which Frances had given him as a present, he conceived the idea that gardening in itself might be a useful political symbol in the Tory cause.

Not that he behaved himself whilst in the Bucklebury wilderness. His frequent assertions that this was the life and he would retire altogether prompted Jonathan Swift to propose a motto for the summerhouse:

> From business and the noisy world retired,
> Nor vexed by love, nor by ambition fired,
> Gently I wait the call of Charon's boat
> Still drinking like a fish and —— like a goat![19]

Whether the demure Frances St John knew of this I do not know. Harry's chief gardening and whoring companion at the time was pretty Tom Coke of Melbourne in Derbyshire, who was Vice-Chamberlain to Queen Anne:

> Sir Plume of amber snuff-box justly vain
> And the nice conduct of a clouded cane;
> With earnest eyes and round unthinking face,
> He first the snuff-box opens, then the case.[20]

Coke had made his lovely garden of walks and arbours round an oval pool at Melbourne Hall (which survives to this day) from the inspiration of Het Loo (where he had spent much of his youth) and of his father-in-law Lord Chesterfield's splendid garden at Bretby.[21] After the death of his wife, Lady Mary, Tom Coke was distraught enough to return to the escapades of a man about town, finding every encouragement with Harry – whom everyone at Melbourne naturally concluded was equally without a wife. In London they spent lavishly on snuff, chocolates and their wig-maker's bills, let alone clothes, and they made assignations:

Dear Tom,
I go tomorrow morning to Bucklebury and shall be back on Saturday, on which day it would be a great pleasure to meet you in town . . . As to whores, dear friend, I am very unable to help thee. I have heard of a certain housemaid that is very handsome: if she can be got ready against your arrival, she shall serve you for your first meal.
Adieu, ever yours most entirely,
Harry.[22]

Gossip had it that Harry had 'a blackguard girle' called Belle Chuck in 'high keeping'. He was known to pay the 'highest price for the greatest pleasure' and the lovely, dangerously tell-all Sally Salisbury, 'famed for her rare and wonderful beauty, her wit and fun', was one of his favourites.[23]

There is still at Melbourne a room so little changed that it is possible to imagine these two rakes, their gorgeous wigs discarded and in their own hair, carousing over their conquests, sprawled across the high-backed Jacobean chairs that surround the table in the panelled dining room. This colourful period was not to last, however, and was never absolute. Tom Coke was soon and easily enough steered, by the Queen's court ladies, into another marriage, to Mary Hale, and he became a model of respectability once more. And Harry (whose solemn biographers are uniformly harsh on his sexual adventures) was too much the politician to run short of reasons or any justification. His favourite was that Lord Rochester was his hero, and Graham Greene, Rochester's more sympathetic biographer, throws an interesting sidelight. Sir Walter St John's sister Ann had married the Royalist leader Henry Wilmot, 1st earl of Rochester, and so their son, the licentious poet and Harry's hero, was also his kinsman. Rochester the Royalist died in exile in 1658, and when mother and son were able to return to England, to their home at Ditchley in Oxfordshire, the boy quite simply fell in love with the English countryside.

In *Lord Rochester's Monkey*, Greene imagines the 10-year-old wandering in the gardens and park at Ditchley and opines on this influence: 'the country establishing a hold on John Wilmot's affections that the city was never completely to eradicate. The city was to mean the clouded merriment of drink, the intrigues of the theatre, the half-hearted friendships with professional poets, affairs of love and lust', whereas 'the country was to be peace, even a kind of purity, finally the place to die in'. Rochester himself is remembered saying that 'when he came to Brentford the devil entered into him and never left him till he came to [Oxfordshire] again'.[24] Henrietta, it must be remembered, only ever saw Harry in his 'country' guise. How much or how little she knew of his double life – even if as she grew older she heard the gossip, too – would not have made one jot of difference to her adoration. It might have added to it.

With the election of 1710 the Tories were returned to power and Robert Harley made Harry Secretary of State for the North, chief minister for half the land. After the attempt on Harley's life in March 1711 (Harley only saved by his thickly embroidered waistcoat from death by Guiscard's knife), Harry tasted the glory of leading the House of Commons. Swift, who knew only too well the strenuous life that Harry was leading, commented, 'if he lives & has his health [he] will I believe be one day at the Head of Affairs'.[25] But Harry's lightning ascendancy was not to continue. The following summer, when Queen Anne handed out earldoms and Garters, Harry was excluded. He was made Lord Lieutenant of Essex, and he was furious. Hearing of the death of a distant cousin Paulet St John, Earl of Bolingbroke (he died unmarried on 5 October 1711 and the earldom became extinct), he asked the Queen for what he felt was his due. In truth, Shakespeare's words were in his head: 'Harry Bolingbroke' ringing down the years, 'proud Bolingbroke', 'jaunting Bolingbroke', 'King Bolingbroke' who claimed his throne as Henry IV taking his name from his birthplace, John of Gaunt's castle of red-brown carstone on the edge of the Lincolnshire Wolds. Was not Gaunt – Shakespeare's 'time-honoured Lancaster' – his ancestor too, a Gandalfian hero with his song for England?

> This other Eden, demi-paradise,
> This fortress built by Nature for herself
> Against infection and the hand of war,
> This happy breed of men, this little world,
> This precious stone set in a silver sea . . .[26]

This at least was his birthright, the source of all his beliefs, the reason that his most famous philosophies and dreams of a Patriot King were running in his head. (Not, of course, that he intended to live at Bolingbroke, a bleak outpost standing sentinel over fifty miles of fen and marsh where the geese and mallard screamed, with, on a clear day, a view of Boston Stump; though it was still habitable, just, at that time.) The Queen, prompted by Harry's enemies, was not so moved. She offered him a viscountcy. Harry was even more furious: 'I am given, not this earldom, which, as belonging to my house, would alone have induced me to consent to a removal from [the House of Commons] where my enemies allow I had greater influence than any single commoner in the kingdom – I am given,' he sputtered, 'not this but a miserable compromise of distinction – a new and inferior rank.'[27]

At Battersea they drank a toast to 'Viscount Bolingbroke' – or at least Henrietta and her mother did. Her father remarked to his son, 'Ah, Harry, I ever said you would be hanged, but now I find you will be beheaded.'[28]

Harry did not give up his politician's head entirely however. He played his part in the negotiations for the longed-for Peace of Utrecht and he found Henrietta's brother, George, a job with the British delegation. When the treaty (which brought Gibraltar, Minorca, Newfoundland, Hudson Bay, Nova Scotia and St Kitts under British sovereignty) was signed, it was George St John who carried it to London on Good Friday 1713. There was joy in the streets, and a great national peace thanksgiving, with Queen Anne driving in state to St Paul's. Tiered viewing stands were set up all along the Strand for thousands of guests to see, wave and cheer. It was a proud day for the St Johns. But, the Peace digested, the next crisis concerned the Queen's failing health and the succession. Harry spoke rashly about the overtures he had made to the Jacobites in France, partly on his own account but partly in league with the government's 'official' spy Matt Prior, for the return of James Edward Stuart, the Old Pretender. Harry really believed in a Stuart king – a Patriot King who could make himself 'the vital centre of politics, the father of his people'[29] – rather than an imported Hanoverian. His own religious flexibility (in reaction to the

Presbyterian lectures of his youth?) led him to underestimate James Edward's Catholicism, which he imagined he could control as the new king's chief minister. This, despite the Act of Settlement passed by his own kind of Tory gentry, stating that any Catholic or Catholic's spouse was 'forever incapable' of possessing the crown. He underestimated the power of the alternative. The formidable Robert Walpole and the Whigs had their connections to George Lewis of Hanover all set up: 'George Lewis' was, writes Linda Colley, 'a German with only a smattering of the English language, a plain, middle-aged, un-charismatic man, with no great appeal except the essential one. He was a Lutheran, not Catholic.'[30] When the Queen died on 1 August 1714, Harry – so his friends said – hesitated, and lost.

A month later he was back at Bucklebury, pretending to be a farmer: 'They tell me you have a very good crop of wheat, but the barley is bad,' wrote Dean Swift enigmatically from Dublin. 'Hay will certainly be dear, unless we have an open winter. I hope you found your hounds in good condition, I imagine you now smoking with your humdrum squire, I forget his name, who can go home at midnight, and open a dozen gates when he is drunk.'[31] It was all a charade, for Harry was more likely riding hard across the Berkshire Downs to Ashdown House, a hunting-box 'consecrated' to Elizabeth, the Winter queen of Bohemia (and great-aunt of James Edward Stuart), by her devoted William, 1st Earl of Craven, to meet Jacobite envoys. His romanticism took him over; it was the perfect setting for illegal and dangerous trysts (though his sharp perception may have noted that Ashdown was virtually the twin of Thorpe Hall, from where his great-grandfather had been hounded to exile for treason). After a quiet winter his own spies were slipping him 'certain and repeated information' that, as he later recalled, 'a resolution was taken by those who have power to execute it to pursue me to the scaffold'.[32] He was not going to give them the pleasure. On the evening of Friday, 26 March 1715, he made an ostentatious appearance in his box at Drury Lane Theatre, paying generously at the curtain call, choosing the play to be performed the following evening and promising loudly that he would be there. On the Saturday evening he slipped out of his house in Golden Square into his waiting coach, which already contained Louis XIV's envoy, La Vigne, and they made for Dover, where a Captain Morgan took them to Calais. Harry travelled as La Vigne's valet, wearing a dark riding coat buttoned up over his face and a black wig. His belongings were stuffed into two large leather bags and he had a small fortune in banknotes, which his loyal wife Frances had sewn into his waistcoat.

In London on the Monday morning it was learned that he was in Paris, lying low but in touch with friends. For Henrietta it was a time she chose never to recall; nothing could have saved her from the shocking news, the arguments and tears and the gossip. In the August the dreaded Bill of Attainder was passed in Parliament, Harry was impeached for the 'most treacherous confederacy' and sentenced to death. All his belongings were confiscated, which included Battersea and Lydiard. Fortunately no steps were seemingly taken to seize either estate. It was a long summer of alarms, invasion fever ran at large throughout the country. The Jacobites' greatest supporter King Louis XIV died on 1 September, but he had already funded the Pretender's invasion, or invasions, as troops were marched westwards and northwards to counter his supporters' landings and gatherings. James Edward himself was late in coming, however, and when he left Scotland for France in early February, the '1715' rebellion sputtered to its close. Later in 1716 Harry Bolingbroke was offered a pardon, on condition that he returned to lead the Tories into harmony with the Whigs, and betray the Pretender's secrets, so belittling the cause in English and Scottish eyes. He refused, saying he might achieve the former (which would have been no small miracle), but to betray such confidences 'would cover me with perpetual infamy'.[33]

So, there he was lost in France, at least to Henrietta. Her beloved brother had become public property, and a traitor in everyone else's eyes. She was not to hear from him for over two years. It was best that she retire to Lydiard to bury herself with the books and poetry they had shared. She certainly learned the harsh lesson that tragedies that could not be helped had to be endured and overcome. Fortunately, at about this time she found a new friend in Frances Hertford, whom she could confide in, for there was little comfort for her at home. Her father had been assiduously plying the Hanoverian king George I with suppers of Lydiard venison and brandied peaches, and had been rewarded with the title Viscount St John of Battersea, and he had successfully claimed back the estates of Lydiard and Battersea. He also acquired a town house in Albemarle Street off Piccadilly. Angelique, now Lady St John, had found herself a royal duty and was often at Court, as Henrietta later recalled. The king had taken a special fancy to her brandied peaches:

> and ever after, till his death, my mamma furnished him with a sufficient quantity to last the year round (he eating two every night). This little present he took kindly; but one season proved fatal to fruit-trees, and she could present his Majesty but with half the usual quantity, desiring him to use economy, for they would barely serve him the year at one each night. Being thus forced by necessity to retrench, he said he would then eat two every other night; and valued himself upon having mortified himself less, than if he had yielded to their regulation of one each night; which I suppose may be called a compromise between economy and epicurism'.[34]

By the time she recounted this story she had mellowed; as a passionate young woman she must have cried with fury at this pandering to Harry's tormentors, disbelieving that by such trifles some favours were bought. Perhaps she took it so far as to refuse to be presented at the hated Hanoverian Court, for she was always to feel herself an outsider, and be glad of it.

How much she knew of the feelings of her estranged and equally suffering sister-in-law is unclear. Frances Bolingbroke was holding her little fort in Golden Square without the help of her in-laws, for, she felt, 'those few friends I meet with now, are worth a thousand relations, that I found long ago'.[35] Harry had returned his interest in the Bucklebury estate to trustees on her behalf before he left, and she struggled to raise money to send to him. One of her 'few friends' was Jonathan Swift, who wrote to comfort her. She replied:

> Mr Dean,
> your letter came in very good time to me, when I was full of vexation and trouble, which all vanishes, finding that you were so good to remember me under my afflictions, which have not been greater than you can think, but much greater than I can express.[36]

Much against her will she stayed in London, hoping for the chance to plead for clemency. Her health was poor, her temper 'insipid and dull' except 'in some places [Albemarle Street and Battersea], and there I am a little fury, especially if they dare mention my dear Lord without respect'. August 1716 was especially hot and London was more unbearable than ever. She longed for the cool of the country but hung on hoping that 'one time or another his Majesty will find my Lord had been misrepresented, and by that means, he may be restored to his country once more with honour'; or else, she had confided to Swift, 'however harsh it may sound out of my mouth, I had rather wear black'.[37] When Harry refused his offered pardon she retired to Bucklebury to fade away.

Not so Henrietta, whose natural energies restored her to the widening world of pleasures that was the lot of girls of her class and time. In the midst of pleasures came the best surprise of all. In the spring of 1718 she received a letter from Harry. It came from France; it was not much of a letter, perhaps only the fragment that the censors had left, little more than a string of endearments that ended 'you are I suppose now att London where I wish you all imaginable satisfaction, adieu my dear girl, from one who loves you entirely . . .'.[38]

It might have been on the tail of a business letter to her father, for 'att London' indicates Albermarle Street, and 'all imaginable satisfaction' that she was about to be having a good time with the shopping, theatre visits, concerts and parties that made up the season. Albemarle Street was then almost exactly as it is now, developed as a block of town houses between the great Piccadilly mansions of Burlington and Berkeley and their spacious gardens. A short walk down St James's Street – except, of course, ladies of consequence never walked – led to St James's Palace, and the perfumiers, watchmakers, hatters, lacemakers, booksellers and cheesemongers of German (Jermyn) Street and Bond Street, and the interlacing alleys and yards that supplied every luxury the heart could desire. She loved all these things, but Harry's recall to her life eclipsed them all. She replied, over and over again, with gusto, with questions and requests for his likeness, so that he was soon making excuses for his slow responses, and chiding her 'you are a punctual correspondent!'[39]

From the surviving letters, which she kept carefully for the rest of her life, Harry's conscience appeared to trouble him, he longed to know what she thought of him and repeatedly expressed his concern for her, and his gratitude for her loyalty, which became his perennial theme:

> Ma chère enfant, que je parle de vous avec tendresse, ne vous trompent point et je parle comme je pense; car quoyque vous soyez fort aimable à ce que les personnes ne vous connoissent pas par un si bel endroit que moi. Je vous connois par la bonte du coeur et la constance des sentiments. Vous ne m'avez jamais manqué un moment dans toute la variété de mauvaise fortune quie j'ai en à essuyer.[40]

The 'mauvaise fortune' had climaxed with his disillusioned and final break with the Old Pretender, after which he had been very low and unwell, a refugee in mysterious French châteaux, Ablon and Marcilly, at the whim of equally mysterious and undoubtedly beautiful comtesses and mesdames, whom he had found fascinating. He shared his secret: 'C'est à une personne qui vous aime beaucoup sans vous connoître, par tout de que je luy ay dit en pas tout ce que luy est revenu de vous. Adieu, ma chère Henriette. Je vous embrassé de tout mon coeur.'[41]

Frances Bolingbroke, who had pined away at Bucklebury, though never forgetting to keep Harry supplied with money, died quietly on a Friday morning, 24 October 1718.[42] Now he was free for his new love. However, the name of this magical 'personne' was kept secret for a while longer, but Henrietta had guessed the implication: 'I have long taken it kindly of you that I never found any variation in your sentiments for me, and I never will forget it,' he assured her, 'for it is an excellent character as well as a rare one. I thank you for the joy which you express att my good luck. It is really such, for I sought it not. If I can return to you, it will be great satisfaction to me.'[43]

Still with no name, there was an excursion into dressmaking, clearly beyond him: 'I don't know whether you will be half so pleased to wear the stuff which is making for you, as the person who has ordered it will be pleased in sending it to you – she expects your picture, and hopes you will sit still that it may be well drawn. She bids me assure you that she loves you extremely.'[44] Finally, needing Henrietta's measurements and favourite colours 'la personne' revealed herself with her own postcripts. She was Harry's (fairly) new and lasting love, Marie-Claire Deschamps de Marcilly, Marquise de Villette. Henrietta was drawn into their evident happiness, eager to love Marie-Claire in return. Her Paris gown was delivered to Lydiard in the summer by Harry's long-time secretary, John Brinsden (who had gone into exile with him). When the sober Brinsden is drawn into a country dance he does not tell, but Henrietta does and her description of the 'country jollity' opens Harry's eyes to Brinsden's being 'so great a Beau' for he 'made but a scurvy stock-jobber here'.[45]

A few days before her twentieth birthday, 15 July 1719, a stranger arrived at Lydiard with another package from France; this time it was 'a little toilette', an exquisite Parisian-made dressing-case, with brushes, combs, powder-boxes, rouge pots, bottles of perfume and all attendant trifles, a perfect delight. She wrote her thanks in a shower of affections, to which Harry returned the compliment, having always observed in her 'ye symptom of a good heart & [I] have always loved you, for sentiment in my opinion is preferable to wit & you have both'.[46]

The woman who was to transform Harry Bolingbroke's life was to be Henrietta's friend and confidante. Marie-Claire de Marcilly was petite, fair and doll-like, with a piquant wit and clever mind. She was born at the Château Marcilly (near Nogent-sur-Seine about 50 kilometres east of Paris), the 'wrong side of the blanket' but eligible for Madame de Maintenon's school at St Cyr on the edge of Versailles' park, which was under the king's patronage and bestowed the widest and most excellent education. She had starred in a celebrated performance of Racine's *Esther* in 1689 when she was fourteen and was courted by the Chevalier de Villette, only to be outmanoeuvred by his widower father, the Marquis de Villette-Mursay. The young marquise had charmed everyone, even her stepson and his sisters, and when the happy old marquis died after about sixteen years he left her a very rich, and beautiful, widow. She had resisted many suitors, and had met Harry Bolingbroke at the time when his spirits were at their lowest, in the spring or summer of 1716. She renounced her Catholicism and became a Protestant, they lived together for five years or so and were married at Aix-la-Chapelle in May 1722.[47] Not long after their marriage Harry told Swift of his 'infinitely more uniform and less dissipated' life, candidly adding 'that Love which I used to scatter with some Profusion among the whole Female Kind, has been these many Years devoted to One Object'.[48]

With Marie-Claire's fortune Harry immediately took to his gardening, as he had with Frances' at Bucklebury, this time buying the small château of La Source at Orleans in early 1720. He told Henrietta, I regret to say, that 'you are neither of an age nor sex to practise much philosophy'[49] – nor would he recommend it to her – and details of his 'rural philosophising' as he called his gardening were directed to Swift. La Source delighted him: 'Il n'y en a pas en France de plus pur.' He wrote:

> You must know that I am as busy about my hermitage . . . as if
> I was to pass my life in it, and if I could see you now and then,
> I should be willing enough to do it. I have in my wood the
> biggest and the clearest spring perhaps in Europe, which forms
> before it leaves the park, a more beautiful river than any which
> flows in Greek or Latin verse. I have a thousand projects about
> this spring, and among others, one which will employ some
> marble.[50]

The purity of La Source, it turned out, was to assuage his anger. Horticulturally he continued as at Bucklebury, building a green-house and growing fruits and vegetables in his family's tradition. In June 1722 he wrote to Henrietta, recalling the 'extreamly good' Battersea pickled melon: 'We are just entering into the season of that fruit, and you will oblige me and the Marquise very much if you send us the receipt for making this pickle.'[51]

The 'marble' project mentioned to Swift was altogether a darker and more male preserve, a scheme for direct confrontations between Harry's demons and the beauties of La Source. His accusations and meaningful mottoes were set up about the place carved into marble or painted on to wood. UBI BENE IBI PATRIA was over the front door, and the river-god's temple over the Loiret spring sported a dirge of his own composing:

> By the frenzies of an outrageous faction,
> On account of his unstained fidelity to his queen,
> And his strenuous endeavour to accomplish a general peace
> Having been forced to seek a new country
> Here, at the source of this sacred fountain
> Henry of Bolingbroke
> Unjustly banished,
> Lived pleasantly.[52]

In his banishment Harry had been absorbed in reading and rereading the classics, and took from Horace the motto for his 'ally' or covered way, 'fallentis semita vitae' (the untrodden paths of life), and more cheerfully for his greenhouse, 'hic ver assiduum, atque alienis mensibus aestas' (eternal spring and summer out of season), from Virgil.[53] The first-century Roman philosopher and statesman Seneca the Younger was a more unusual inspiration for a 'rural philosopher' but Seneca, too, spent time in exile (in Corsica), and Harry was taken with their similar experiences to the point of writing 'A Consolation to a Man in Exile'. This was 'so much in Seneca's style that was he living now among us one should conclude that he had written every word of it' in the opinion of Alexander Pope.[54] Seneca's 'style' of relishing the simplicity and purity of country life away from the corruption of the city was shared not only by Harry's hero Lord Rochester but, as he had discovered, by Thucydides in Thracia and Xenophon on his little farm at Scillus, both 'far from the hurry of the world'. Their extruded philosophy was that 'having paid in a public life what you owed to the present age, pay in a private life what you owe to posterity'.[55] There was a sting in the tail: the simple 'good' life of a man who lived close to the bounteous earth was infinitely superior to the profligacies of those in power.

Nothing of Harry Bolingbroke's landscape garden, nor any of his marble mottoes, survive at La Source,[56] but he could not have wished for a more elegant trio to carry his philosophy into gardening and literary history than Jonathan Swift, Alexander Pope and Voltaire.

Swift heard most about La Source whilst he was strenuously, physically gardening in Ireland, 'levelling mountains and raising stones, and fencing against inconveniencies of a scanty lodging, want of victuals, and a thievish race of people' at Thomas Sheridan's place in County Westmeath. More congenially he was also helping the Revd Patrick Delany at Delville near Dublin (in the garden that would become the delight of Mary Granville Delany in after years) and fancying some 'agreeableness' in these activities.[57] Against his tales of labours Harry's words come smugly: 'Perfect tranquillity is the general tenor of my life: good digestion, serene weather ... I am sometimes gay, but I am never sad; I have gained new friends, and have lost some old ones; my acquisitions of this kind give me a good deal of pleasure, because they have not been made lightly.'[58]

The pale and diminutive wizard Alexander Pope was a new friend. They had met briefly prior to Harry's exile, but now Pope, too, had developed a keen interest in gardening and was exhorting his frail body to labours in his new garden at Twickenham riverside. He was having 'a vast deal to do with Gardeners' in making his Great Walk, his Green and the Mount. Pope longed to visit La Source but, like Swift, did not dare; instead he imagined 'his spirit leaving his body in his own garden' and making for France:

> What pleasing frenzy steals away my soul?
> Through thy blest shades, La Source, I seem to rove;
> I see thy fountains full, thy waters roll
> And breath the Zephyrs that refresh thy Grove
> I hear what ever can delight inspire
> Villette's soft Voice and St John's silver Lyre.[59]

Voltaire was the Bolingbrokes' frequent visitor. He was euphoric about Harry's genius. He could hardly believe that this was an Englishman who spoke French with 'justice and energy', who knew Egyptian history, Virgil, Milton and French poetry, 'who can absorb everything and remember everything' and, most importantly and along with his clever wife, was 'infinitely satisfied' with his own new epic, *La Henriade*, on the legends of the thirteenth-century Henry of Navarre.[60]

There were English visitors, possibly even Lord St John his father, and certainly Henrietta's youngest brother Holles, who was sent out to be 'polished' in his teens, but without success. But what about Henrietta, who would have certainly given so much to see La Source and its owners? Harry did consider her, he had written in November 1720:

My darling Heriott,

You seem so perfectly idle in England, that if I could send an enchanted boat like that of Armida to Battersea Stairs, you should sail down the Thames, cross the sea, and up the Loire in a trice, and land in my park, where, in the most beautiful place that Nature ever adorned, you would find the tenderest welcome. This image flatters me so agreeably, that I would dwell longer upon it if I could hope to think it into reality and practice.[61]

Indeed he found the image so agreeable that he repeated it a few weeks later. Whether it was too dangerous, for he was still a condemned traitor, whether Henrietta's father forbad it as a pointless expense on a girl, or whether Henrietta or the Bolingbrokes, especially the frequently unwell Marie-Claire, became ill is unclear. More optimistically it might be supposed that Harry had glimpsed the day when he might come home. For whatever reason, Henrietta was never to make her longed-for expedition to La Source.

CHAPTER THREE

'Bright Marian'

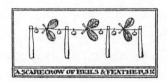

I N ENGLAND there was a place for a woman in the burgeoning
rural philosophy of the wits and the poets, the taste-makers of
that day. At least, if with a twinkle in his eye, the *Spectator*'s Joseph
Addison had introduced his Leonora, whose 'Reading has lain very
much among Romances' and had given her a very particular 'Turn
of Thinking', which was evident in her 'Country-Seat':

> which is situated in a kind of Wilderness, about an hundred
> Miles distance from London, and looks like a little enchanted
> Palace. The Rocks about here are shaped into Artificial Grottoes,
> covered with Woodbines and Jessamines. The Woods are cut
> into shady Walks, twisted into Bowers, and filled with Cages of
> Turtles. The Springs are made to run among Pebbles, and by
> that means taught to murmur very agreeably. They are likewise
> collected into a beautiful Lake, that is inhabited by a Couple of
> Swans, and empties itself by a little Rivulet which runs through
> a green Meadow, and is known in the Family by the Name of
> The Purling Stream.[1]

Lydiard was roughly a hundred miles from London, and although
Henrietta could not call it 'her country seat' and had no powers
to direct the walks or streams, it was her home. She was firmly in
the ranks of Leonoras, of a similar 'Turn of Thinking' and – whilst
Addison might smile – she, too, possessed the literary imagination

that was perfectly capable of seeing turtles and purling streams in the ordinary countryside. It was, as Addison meant it to be, all in the perception. It was this crucial turn of thinking that saw the natural beauties of early eighteenth-century England, and thought them as lovely as a garden. It was this perception that turned landscape into landscape gardening.

The historical descriptions of Lydiard suggest it was a fairly enchanted place in those summers, set amidst the marshy buttercup meadows and flowery hay pastures and developed by time and nature. Outcrops of Corallian limestones occurred, which had been quarried for building stone – 'Swindon stones', pretty, white and smooth, with a modest reputation in the seventeenth century – thought 'not inferior to Purbec grubbes, but whiter'.[2] The worked-out pits had become ivy-draped and oozing depressions, shaded by seedling elder and thorn into grotto-like glooms. The folklorist and antiquary John Aubrey, who had pottered about on the estate asking questions for his *Natural History of Wiltshire*, had been enough a curiosity himself to be well remembered in Henrietta's youth, and he had found 'a hermitage' and chalybeate spring known as 'Antiock's Well' where the waters were believed to have healing powers.[3] The well was thought to be near Toot Hill, east of the park near Mannington, not far from 'My Lord's Coachway to Swindon'. There was a mystery and controversy about these things that kept the myths alive.

Lydiard had purling streams enough, from springs that surged after rains, flowing under pleasurably rustic footbridges, their waters collected into the old fish ponds, fringed with water iris and willows. There were meadows with odd names, 'Cut and Go mead' and Prinnells, and part of the parsonage glebe near St Mary's church was called 'Hamme'. Young avenues, planted around the time Henrietta was born, marked the way from the church to Hook Street, and to the wide green at Hook, where the road ran south to Wootton Bassett and north to Purton and Cricklade. These avenues were busy green ways, for cottages and the estate workshops, including the smithy, straggled along the way to Hook, 'growing' out of the pockets of limestone from which they were built.

In her summertime wanderings Henrietta – smilingly gregarious or the happy solitary as her mood and the weather took her – encountered all kinds of country people. Chatting with the curate, watching the blacksmith shoe the chaise pony, dancing with the dairymaids at the harvest supper; these neighbours as well as her Cholmondeley and Chute cousins, perhaps the Ffootes and the Gowers from Battersea, and a scattering of Wiltshire gentry, were all part of her country commonwealth of Lydiard summers. Lazing in the trees' shade with her book or one of Harry's letters, she dreamed of the sparkling waters of La Source and how happy he was there. Thus infused with the ideal of the simple life and a garden, caught between stories and realities, her adolescent mind stored away the possibilities for her own future.

Just south-west of Lydiard house on the way to Wootton Bassett, there was an ancient moated manor house of Cistercian origins named Midgehall. For over 200 years Midgehall had belonged to the Seymours, the family of the Duke of Somerset, and it was one of the homes of Henrietta's friend, Frances, Countess of Hertford. Whether it was that they sat in church together, or that the current duke's eldest son and Frances' husband, Algernon Percy, Lord Hertford, had been one of Marlborough's aides at the Utrecht negotiations and was known to Harry and George St John, it was in 1716 (the dreadful summer of Harry's exile) that they first met. Frances was very newly married. She and Henrietta were the same age, and both tall, but Frances was fair with 'a great deal of bloom, fine teeth, and if not regularly handsome [she] had a very animated, sensible, and engaging countenance, particularly in her address and manner of speaking'. Her face 'was a little marked with smallpox, but otherwise she had a good complexion'.[4]

Frances (Fanny) and her sister Molly, were the daughters of Henry Thynne and his wife Grace Strode. Their father had died when Frances was ten, and their grandfather, Thomas Thynne,

1st Viscount Weymouth, had brought them up in his bewitching great house, Longleat, a treasury of porcelain, gilt and brocades, moon-faced portraits and Elizabethan dust. They were not the only refugees, for Lord Weymouth had a pet bishop in his attic, the endearing old Bishop Ken. Though nearly killed by a falling chimney in the great storm, he lived out his days pottering in Lord Weymouth's library. The viscount was 'a most affectionate grandfather' and he had sent his welcome to the young Frances: 'I hope we shall see you here very soon, though Longleat had never less fruit; but the gardens are pleasant, and there is room enough for you and your sister to show your good dancing.'[5] The gardens were indeed pleasant, laid out by George London and Henry Wise as the Great Parterre, four great plats edged with clipped yews and flowers with a fountain in the centre. On the east and west sides of the Parterre were huge walled gardens, their walls crowded with flowers and fruit. Indeed there was hardly a Longleat wall without its pear, apple or quince, so keen was Lord Weymouth on his fruit. His other particular interest was in his plantations of seedling Weymouth pine, *Pinus strobus*, the white pine being reared from cones brought from New England. Somewhere between the fruit walls and Heaven's Gate, amongst all the glories of Longleat, the young Frances Thynne grew into a keen gardener.

She had been married 'out of the nursery', courted by Lord Hertford's parents, the imperious Duke and Duchess of Somerset, bearing shagreen boxes full of diamonds. The marriage was arranged before the couple had even met, which Frances felt was very hard on her husband, 'a man of thirty years old, who had lived in all the gaieties of the Court and the army, for above ten years, and might at that time have chosen any unmarried woman in England would his parents have given him the liberty to do it'. Lord Hertford was very tall and lightly built, with a long face and sandy hair, and he was asthmatic. Frances, who was very honest, felt 'he was never very susceptible to love' and it was 'not likely that I should have become the object of it'.[6] One evening in London, very soon after their

marriage, he had gone out with his drinking companions, promising
to be home early. In a heartless tease they had sent him home
drunk and late. When he sobered up he had 'announced his total
separation' from the party-crowd, and soon he was in thrall to
marriage, hating to be apart from 'the best of wives'. In his conversion, having left her to come after him to London, he wrote a
timeless lover's note:

> should you not come before ten of the clock, I will go to bed,
> and will endeavour to sleep, though the fear of being so when
> you come home and by that means losing that so much longed
> for kiss, I fear will keep me awake; but should it so happen, a
> kiss from dear Fanny will recompense everything I have suffered
> by the absence of her in whom is the whole happiness of my
> life.[7]

The Hertfords' happiness had produced a baby daughter, Lady
Betty or 'Poke', when Henrietta met them, but all was not quite as
blissful as it seemed. Frances hated being in London, and her husband had his lordly duties as a Member of Parliament and Lord of
the Bedchamber to the Prince of Wales: Henrietta's new friend was
very conscious that people who did not really know her reproached
her for her 'taste for solitude' and a 'seeming melancholy and a
timidity' and even worse – a crime in Court circles – her 'sort of
savage bashfulness'. She knew that her shynesses were partly her
nature but had an equal cause in the inexplicable disapproval she
had inspired in her in-laws, the Somersets. They had no cause to
despair of a granddaughter, for there was plenty of time for a son,
so Frances was mystified as to what she had done wrong. She knew
the frostiness irritated Lord Hertford, and felt he protected her
'from the principle of honour and good nature, for I was not happy
enough to inspire him with any passion for me'.[8] The compromise,
which she told herself was better for her daughter's health, was that
they should spend as much time as possible at their country home,
Marlborough Castle. Lord Hertford seemed willing to commute up
and down the Bath road. For Henrietta it was an easy journey in

summertime from Lydiard, about fourteen miles, along the estate roads to old Swindon and Coate, then south crossing the Ridgeway and over the downs to Marlborough.

Henrietta and Frances's friendship suited them both: Frances needed Henrietta's robustly cheerful companionship during her husband's absences, and Henrietta had nothing else in particular to do. Their shared interests made them both into poetic gardeners. The template for their relationship had already been written by Frances' acquaintance Elizabeth Rowe in her early poem 'Love & Friendship', in which two shepherdesses, Amaryllis and Silvia, debate the respective merits of those two states in their Virgilian grove. At the moment when the 'propitious god of love' intervenes, Silvia maintains 'With fair Aminta's name my noblest verse shall shine' ('Amaryllis' being poetically impossible), while Amaryllis is off after her Alexis:

> Dear, lovely youth! I cry to all around:
> Dear, lovely youth! the flatt'ring vales resound.[9]

The Hertfords' Marlborough home offered the Virgilian grove. It was (and still is, as Marlborough College) at the west end of the town's 'one very large streete', beyond St Peter's church, actually in the ancient parish of Preshute, framed by the Bath road to Calne on the north and the River Kennet to the south. The castle had belonged to the Seymours since 1550. Celia Fiennes had nosed her way in in 1702 or thereabouts, reporting on 'a great rambling building but now most pulled down and newly building; they were painting it, good appartments for what is done'.[10] The result was a Queen Anne house of dark red bricks, with a sequence of airy, elegant rooms lit by large sash windows. The garden, nestling below the downs in the midst of the lush meadows beside the Kennet, had an emerald enchantment; smooth bowling greens and grass banks vied in attractiveness with the walks beside rills, and the canal and the fish pond, all leading to the wilderness walks beside the bright river. Frances and Henrietta read Pope's *Windsor Forest*, and found the Kennet included in his catalogue of Thames tributaries – 'Kennet swift, for silver Eels renown'd'.[11] Frances, alone in winter, penned her own sad song, 'Ocassion'd by Seeing the River Kennet Frozen Over':

> Poor stream! Held captive by the Frost
> Thy current numb'd, thy brightness lost;
> Compell'd thy journey to delay,
> And on these desert shores to stay,
> Thy fortune is to mine ally'd,
> Both by superior force are ty'd,
> Different captivitys we prove;
> Thou bound by cold, and I by love.[12]

Far from 'savage bashfulness' this is the gentle melancholy that many people recognised as the key to Frances' character. 'The Gentle Hertford' was the perfect foil to the impetuous Henrietta, and presumably they mollified each other's failings, as friends do.

The most curious feature of Marlborough Castle's garden was 'the Mount', as Celia Fiennes described it: 'that you ascend from the left hand by an easye ascent bounded by such quick sett hedges cut low, and soe you rise by degrees in four rounds bounded by the low cutt hedge and on the top is with [the] same hedge cutt in works, and from thence you have a prospect of the town and country round and two parishes two mile off in view'. The journey to the top, a steep climb despite the 'rounds', was rewarded with an extensive space, with room for a small formal parterre 'cutt in works' and a pavilion, and a reservoir, called 'a pond'.[13] William Stukeley, the Stamford antiquary, Aubrey's successor as chronicler of England's oddities, visited Marlborough, pronouncing the mount was a moated Roman castrum, which had been reused as a Norman motte. No one quite knows, even now, but its similarity in form to the prehistoric Silbury Hill, just five miles west along the Bath road, suggests it is even older. That one form reflected the other was noticed by, of all people, William Kent, who put both mounds, with the garden as a sylvan glade, into his illustration for 'Spring' in James Thomson's The Seasons (1730). 'Spring' was dedicated to Frances.

For the two shepherdesses theirs was at first a summer garden friendship, when Henrietta would 'holiday' at Marlborough. The Hertfords were both keen gardeners, and workers in their garden. They made a grotto at the foot of the mount, they planted lots of trees, and had great plans for introducing a cascade into the canal. Frances had a 'butterfly garden', soon 'in vast perfection', as she described it to her mother, 'only a little overstocked, having besides its usual inhabitants eleven young partridges which we have bred up from two or three days old, a hare, two lapwings, and a curlieu . . .'.[14] Henrietta was easily absorbed into their nature-loving gardening life, and her relationship with Lord Hertford was of a bantering, laughing kind, whilst she became an honorary aunt to little Poke and soon a favourite of all the household. Marlborough seemed a little island cut adrift from London and politics, where baby partridges, the flowers and the weather were the vital concerns. There was 'sad hot weather' that brought thunder and storms: 'they say there was forty sheep killed by lightning, but I hope it was a mistake,' reported the soft-hearted Frances, 'the hail fell so large about four miles off that one of the hailstones was five inches round'. She was enchanted with a present that sounds like the produce of Lydiard's gardens, 'of a basket of orange flowers and a fine nosegay with orange, myrtle, yellow roses, double stocks, and a fine melon'.[15] The early summers of their friendship were full of such delights and country wonderments.

As poetic shepherdesses, the feminine equivalents of rural philosophers, they each chose a sobriquet for their fantasy life: the fair, winsome Frances was 'Renée', and the plump and puppyish Henrietta became 'Marian'. 'Marian bright' was prompted by John Gay's dedication of *The Shepherd's Week* (1714) to Harry:

> Lo, I who erst beneath a tree
> Sung Bumkinet and Bowzybee,
> And Blouzelind and Marian bright,
> In apron blue or apron white,
> Now write my sonnets in a book,
> For my good lord of Bolingbroke.[16]

Harry's letters from France were ever exhorting Henrietta to amuse and enjoy herself while she could, but he was a chauvinist at heart and it would never have occurred to him that she could be capable of real friendships, which he regarded as a clubbable male preserve.* Henrietta's rural and unthreatened upbringing, with few demands made to toughen her character (except Harry's flight and exile) had encouraged in her an honest and trusting, perhaps naïve, nature. To be sure, none of her immediate family seemed to care enough to challenge her cheerful complacence and her mischievous confidence that shine from her portraits. She was seriously and mysteriously ill in 1721 and her mother took her to Bath to convalesce, but there is nothing in her later life to suggest that Lady St John's regard for her daughter was anything more than practical parenting of the lightest touch. Amongst her peers Henrietta, with an attainted half-brother whom everybody knew about, must have felt socially suspect at this tender time of her life. Her friendship with Frances Hertford, then, was vitally important, and it turned out to be a friendship for life. Frances, her innocence sheltered by her rank as a duke's daughter-in-law, her romanticism cherished by her husband Lord Hertford's unusually gentle disposition, had the luxury of following her own integrity and no one would question her choice. She and Henrietta were all in all to each other for twenty years (for both of them marriage was quite a different matter) and it is interesting to note that only when Henrietta was lost to her for a period of six years did Frances find another close friend and correspondent in Louisa, Countess of Pomfret. This poetic garden friendship reflected its settings, and what might appear a frivolous and light-hearted pastime was profoundly honoured in faith.

In 1723 Frances was forced out into the world; she was appointed as a Lady of the Bedchamber to the Princess of Wales, and her time for the garden at Marlborough became more limited and more

---

* At that time it could be said, his 'clubs' defined a man. Harry had been prominent in the (Tory) Brothers' Club, and with the wits of the Scriblerus Club, but neither these informal dining clubs nor the St James's establishments took any account of women.

precious. One of the shepherdesses' abiding themes was the misery of leaving the country for the town, a fair torture for the shy Renée when her 'in-waiting' time came. From her 'distant plain' at Lydiard, Marian speaks:

> To Renée decked in pomp and bright array,
> Such as becomes the business of the day,
> A rural nymph attempts in humble strain
> To pay her homage from the distant plain.
> Marian's intent is only to express
> In lowly style her love and tenderness
> And hasten to inquire of your health,
> Your journey, your reception, and your wealth,
> Your costly lace, your gems, and rare brocades,
> Fin'ry unknown in these our lonely shades.

Frances put a brave face on her court duties, the price paid for her rank, but she hated being 'stifled in the crowd' in the dusty rooms and corridors at St James's Palace, and having to listen to the Prince of Wales' jokes 'so coarse and loud'. Marian commiserates:

> Or else retired behind the Chair of State,
> Where you're compelled to praise what most you hate,
> Or listen to some idle page's prate
> Till midnight strikes, and then with aching feet
> Repair to ease your limbs, in Gro'venor Street.[17]

In their green shade the two of them giggled over Frances' experiences; 'what most you hate' is Marian's reference to the pernicious Whiggery surrounding the Princess of Wales, Robert Walpole's great ally. Naturally enough, given her disposition and her brother's tribulations, Henrietta hated Walpole. For Frances it was perhaps unwise to say too much, though being best friends with the sister of the greatest disaffected Tory of them all was hardly politic. For the first ten years at least this added a frisson of secrecy to their friendship.

With these verses, Marian, who composed her doggerel entirely for fun (and hardly ever sat down to write serious poetry), feared that her 'too many lines and yet so little sense' might disturb Renée's much-needed rest, and she'd best throw them into the fire. As it happened on this occasion Renée had not even left Marlborough for London because of a feverish cold. She replied:

> But I am far from all the noisy crowd,
> And only hear the wind that whistles loud,
> No Beaus or Belles these rural shades afford,
> Our boys run half a mile to see a Lord.

In 1725 the Hertfords' son, Lord Beauchamp, known as 'Beachy', was born. Frances had more time at home, and Henrietta shared the modest domesticity at Marlborough, as well as the affections of both children. Renée was happy:

> Retired from Courtly seats, I take my ease,
> Nor fear offending, nor aspire to please;
> (Contented with my lot in silent shades
> To nurse my children and direct my maids)
> News I have none, for 'twill be none to say
> I love you more and better every day.[18]

Henrietta was always sure of her welcome at Marlborough. As the town was where the horses were changed before or after the difficult downland road to or from Lydiard and London, it was often easy for her to stay. The quiet summer days at the castle, when both Hertfords were freed from the Court, fell into a routine not unlike a retreat: early breakfast was followed by a garden inspection before household prayers at nine o'clock:

> . . . out we rove
> Around the terraces and grove,
> Where flaunting woodbines [honeysuckles] spread around;
> We lift the branches from the ground
> And tie them to some neighbouring lime
> Round which they may securely climb;
> Or tend the roses, and divide
> The suckers from their parent side.

The rest of the morning was spent with their woolwork – though Henrietta hated needlework so it was most likely she who read aloud from a gardening book or 'sometimes an author more sublime'. Frances saw her children, then it was a plain dinner – 'no seasoned dish allures our taste' – they sat and talked, 'or trace the Mount's aspiring walk' before retiring to their own rooms to read and write letters. Supper followed evening prayers:

> . . . and with a cheerful heart
> Converse an hour and so we part.
> Now if our pleasures are not great,
> You'll own at least our life is sweet.[19]

At times Renée and Marian were joined by a third to take their strolls by the Kennet or a picnic on the mount. She was 'Philomela', Elizabeth Rowe, a published poet, and much older than Frances and Henrietta, with an interesting past, a pretty wit and a sharp tongue which cooled Marian's tendency to giddiness. Philomela had been born Elizabeth Singer, the eldest of three sisters whose mother died when they were young. Their father, an intensely godly gentleman of Nonconformist zeal, brought them up in Frome in Somerset. Elizabeth was clever, musical and artistic, and between the interminable prayer sessions of her childhood she wrote poetry and painted, resourcefully squeezing 'out the juices of herbs to serve her instead of colours'.[20] She grew into a beauty, an 'animated and dainty creature, with fine auburn hair, sparkling blue eyes' and a fair complexion, much celebrated for her hand-painted fan 'decorated with an exquisite painting of Venus in her chariot drawn by sparrows'.[21] Elizabeth was hardly twenty when Lord Weymouth at Longleat saw her poems and thought them worthy of publication; her first volume of 1696 included 'Love & Friendship'.[22]

It was for these poems that she earned the sobriquet Philomela, 'most musical, most melancholy' as Milton's nightingale. She was courted by the poet and diplomat, the charming Matt Prior, later to be Harry Bolingbroke's boon companion and secret agent on the embassy to Paris in 1712 to persuade the French into the Peace of Utrecht, 'Matt's Peace'. Concerning 'Love and Friendship' Prior asked her:

> By Silvia, if thy charming self be meant;
> If friendship be thy virgin vows extent;
> O! let me in Aminta's praises join:
> Her's my esteem shall be, my passion thine[23]

while hoping that she was Amaryllis – and he might replace her unworthy swain.

Philomela's taste had been for neither swain nor versifier, but for a prodigy she met in Bath, Thomas Rowe, returned from Leiden University with four degrees and fluency in the classical languages. He had 5,000 books in his library and had 'formed a design to compile the lives of all the illustrious persons in antiquity omitted by Plutarch' from his *Parallel Lives*, his biographies of forty-six Roman and Greek heroes. Thomas and Philomela were married in 1710 and settled in Hampstead, where she was saved from disillusion by Thomas' death in 1715.* Philomela poured her grief into poetry:

> O thou wast all my glory, all my pride!
> Thro' life's uncertain paths, my constant guide:
> Regardless of the world, to gain thy praise,
> Was all that could my just ambition raise . . .
> Why has my heart this fond engagement known?
> Or why has heav'n dissolv'd the tie so soon?[24]

With her father's and sisters' deaths she was alone in the world, and though not impoverished, nor afraid of solitude, she spent time at Longleat comforting Mrs Thynne at the death of Frances'

---

* Philomela sounds only too much like a subject for the shattered idealism of a Dorothea Casaubon. Frederick R. Karl, *Gorge Eliot: A Biography*, London: HarperCollins, 1995, pp. 457–8, says 'there is no end of speculation' on models for Dorothea and Casaubon, but this does not extend far from Eliot's circle (Dorothea has the youthful idealism of Eliot herself, or perhaps Barbara Bodichon; Casaubon has suggestions of Herbert Spencer and Frederic Harrison amongst others). Perhaps here the idealist Elizabeth Singer and the scholarly Thomas Rowe are just another example of where this present narrative leaps beyond its time, to the nineteenth century of our more well-fed imaginations.

sister, Molly, Lady Brooke. When Mrs Thynne herself died in 1725 Philomela comforted Frances, and she continued to visit. She was now fifty, a respected poet, a woman of intellect and studious habits, and hardly less than an improving influence on the two younger women. Her nature was that mix of melancholy and enchantment, sometimes she seemed an angel of death, at others a laureate of life. She still had many strings attaching her to her former, younger life and acquaintance, and a worldly-wise head on her modestly swathed shoulders. Though Frances was obviously her favourite, Philomela developed an affectionate regard for 'Mrs St John', which says something for Henrietta's growing wisdom.

It was Philomela who encouraged their study of Italian, and introduced their favourite drama, Giovanni Battista Guarini's *Il Pastor Fido* ('The Faithful Shepherd'), some of which she published in translation. This was stirring stuff, the poetic equivalent of the Italian landscapes painted by Claude Lorrain and Salvator Rosa which the grand tourists were bringing back to London for the first time in the early 1720s. It was the seed of the Italian 'craze', a symbol of happy times, which neither Frances nor Henrietta ever quite forgot. *Il Pastor Fido* was full of passionate orations; it was perfect for performing with heart-searing declamations to the skies from the top of Marlborough's mount, and a whole new purpose was found for the grotto.

> 'That I have lov'd, and lov'd three more than life,
> If still thou doubt, the fields, the conscious groves,
> The savage race can tell; and these hard rocks,
> Soften'd by my complaints, can witness too'.*[25]
> [race = purling stream]

* Mirtillo is speaking from the third act of this Arcadian love-tangle. Silvio and Amarilli are matched but Silvio prefers hunting and Mirtillo loves Amarilli. Eurilla, in love with Mirtillo and jealous, contrives a lovers' meeting in a grotto so that they may be discovered by Silvio. This happens, at the price of Silvio's spearing Dorinda, who loves him and is hiding in a nearby bush, he thinking the bush concealed a wild animal. Amarilli is sentenced to death for unfaithfulness, but Mirtillo offers himself instead. The high priest consults the goddess Diana, who forgoes a sacrifice and reveals that Mirtillo is a child of the gods. Dorinda survives and is loved by Silvio. Mirtillo, the faithful shepherd who redeems the perfidious maid, and Amarilli are united; Eurilla is forgiven.

Handel's treatment of *Il Pastor Fido*, 'an amiable piece of intimate music drama' with pretty dances, was already popular (first staged 1712) and it was performed at the Queen's Theatre in the Haymarket in 1719, where Frances and Henrietta surely saw it. (It was revived again in 1734, when they were both in London, with some new and showy arias and dances, though it was never thought so spectacular as *Rinaldo*.) Frances and Henrietta were both Handel's admirers; for Frances his music for his patroness, the Princess of Wales, provided real pleasure amidst her irksome Court duties, and for Henrietta there were long-remembered conversations with 'the great Handel' who 'told me that the hints of his very best songs have several of them been owing to the sounds in his ears of cries in the street'.[26]

In London, though they might dance till dawn, their other interests could be pursued as their energies allowed. They prided themselves in being sturdy walkers, and across Green Park (or Upper St James's Park as it was still called) from Piccadilly (Frances being in Grosvenor Street, Henrietta in Albemarle Street) was the path beaten by the beau monde to The Mall. The Duke of Buckingham's house, with half a dozen gods including Apollo and Mercury dancing on its roof, and his fabulous gardens were high on the list of the sights to be seen. The duke died in 1721 but his duchess was proud of their 'Rus in Urbe', with its lime avenue, long canal, greenhouses and the orange trees in gigantic tubs on the terrace, the little wilderness where the blackbirds and nightingales sang and Henry Wise's flower parterre filled with lavenders, roses, pinks and scented rosemary and sages.[27] Buckingham House was at the pinnacle of garden fashions, which were just about to change, under the influence of the younger gentlemen on their grand tours. In Piccadilly, Lord Burlington's house (which had splendid old-fashioned gardens, too) was being given a Palladian façade, albeit his lordship was off hunting for ideas and treasures in Italy again. At Devonshire House, which Henrietta knew well, the duke allowed visitors to see his new acquisition, the *Liber Veritatis*, a bound collection of almost 200 original drawings by Claude Lorrain, 'a virtually complete record' of the artist's work.[28] This was the fount of picturesque ideals, an almost biblical authority for an ideal landscape of contrasts (of piercing Mediterranean lights and deep shades), of surprises (an angel, god or shepherd or two, it makes little difference though they are invariably active, some placid cattle or a pretty farm building) and of 'contexts' (a tree-girt grove, secluded as in a garden, or pastoral landscape that was unthreatened by man).*

Like Alexander Pope, Frances and Henrietta certainly visited Lord Burlington's new garden at Chiswick in its early days, in or just after 1720. This was to be first amongst the pioneering landscape gardens, with a wilderness and little 'Italian' buildings, including a 'bagnio', a pagan temple and a rustic house. The famous Orange Tree Garden, the orange tree tubs encircling a pond with an obelisk in the middle, painted by Pieter Andreas Rysbrack (1728) was completed. Perhaps this was Henrietta's favourite, for it was overlooked by an Ionic temple built to a design by Inigo Jones: Isaac Ware's book of Jones' designs was her lifelong treasure. Chiswick also had a 'regular piece of water' beside the Bollo Brook and overlooked by a Tuscan temple, where a rowing boat was kept, partly for decoration ('surprise') and also for visitors' use.[31]

Henrietta and Frances were quite unaware that they were teetering on the rim of landscape gardening history, though Frances, as will become clear, was always up to the latest fashions in her gardening ideas. Henrietta was simply there – however much or little she considered she had learned at this time, in later life her ideas and perceptions (so often beyond her means) clearly sprang from these things.

In the midst of all this 'country jollity' as he called her pastimes,

---

* It seems impossible that Pope did not take the *Liber Veritatis* as his starting point for his three rules – the pictorial interplay of light and shade, the opening of vistas and placing of ornamental surprises, and the concealment of the boundaries[29] – for making a garden. With the folio volumes of Richard Earlom and Josiah Boydell in 1777 the *Liber Veritatis* initiated the Claude Lorrain craze amongst artists and William Gilpin acknowledged the picturesque formulae as the inspiration for the Picturesque.[30]

Henrietta's beloved Harry Bolingbroke at last came home. After his
refuted pardon he had sent his secretary John Brinsden with a
personal appeal to George I, which did not work. 'Had Bolingbroke
been restored,' writes historian Linda Colley, 'and been able to
re-establish his party following, or had [his friends] been able to
guarantee a contingent of Tory votes, these politicians could have
achieved both individual access to office and gradual Tory accepta-
bility by harnessing the party to governmental survival.'[32] Harry,
unable to compromise, missed his moment once again. He had been
in England briefly and secretly in 1723, and he stayed surreptitiously
with Alexander Pope at Twickenham in 1724 while his wife Marie-
Claire went to see the king's mistress the Duchess of Kendal with a
bribe, likely to have been her own money. As with previous St John
bribes, this succeeded. In the spring of 1725 Parliament gave permission for Harry to come home, restoring his estates of Battersea
and Lydiard, but denying him his seat in the House of Lords.
Politically he was now too late. Arguably George I wanted a mixed
government and a national party, and Bolingbroke – perhaps only
Bolingbroke – could have achieved this. But Harry's first interests
were in his new garden and old friends, and at the king's death in
1727 he had accomplished little of a Tory headway. The new Queen
Caroline, Robert Walpole's firm ally, persuaded her husband George
II of 'the folly and hazard of dismissing a well-established ministry
and forming a motley cabinet of Whigs and Tories'. The new king's
laziness, and Walpole's canny generosity with the Civil List for the
royal household, assured the Whigs their future in power (for, as it
turned out, fifteen years), dispatched the Tories to the wilderness
and Harry Bolingbroke to his garden.[33]

For Henrietta, this whirl of the political dice was to bring her a
closeness to her brother and sister-in-law, and perhaps the happiest
seven years of her life. She spent a great deal of time with Marie-
Claire, guiding her through the ways of English manners and English
colloquialisms, all unnerving and strange to a sophisticated lady of
the French Court who spoke little English. Harry made Lydiard over

to their younger brother John St John (George had died in Venice in 1722) but it continued to be the family's summer home until John married Anne Furnese in 1729. At Battersea the status quo remained: Harry intended it for himself and was openly impatient for their father to die (Lord St John was now 73 and was to live for another seventeen years) and their relationship grew only worse, with an antipathy that rebounded on Henrietta. Though Battersea was still truly her home she now preferred Lydiard, or Marlborough with Frances, and increasingly being with the Bolingbrokes. Harry found her like himself in many ways; she was tall and well-built (never waif-like), with glossy chestnut curls and laughing dark eyes. She had her own quick perception and a lovely, strong voice, and her long-fingered expressive hands fluttered with meanings. She had more than a little of Harry's air of authority, leaving even Frances Hertford sounding a little awestruck at times:

> To bright Marian, dearest of her friends,
> These new dull lines the faithful Renée sends.
> Who would not answer when you deign to write?
> And yet, what can a brain like mine indite?[34]

In 1725 Alexander Pope was the arbiter of taste in the garden kingdom of the Thames valley, much in the same way as Beau Nash was setting out to rule his principality of Bath. What could the Bolingbrokes do but move into the arcadia celebrated in *Windsor Forest*? Having sold La Source, they bought Dawley House, a dream estate in the fertile pasturelands of another of Pope's 'fam'd Authors' of the Thames, the River Cole (*sic*, Colne) of 'clear Streams' and 'flow'ry Islands'.[35] Dawley had belonged to the politically powerful Bennets for a hundred years, and that house-agents' handbook, *Britannia Illustrata* of 1710, showed what they were selling and the Bolingbrokes buying – a grand nine-bay house with extensive out-buildings, an orangery and gardens, woods and avenues, beside a bend in the lane, the Dawley road, leading northwards from the Bath road towards Hayes and Uxbridge. Since the engraving was made, the

Bennet grandson, Charles, 2nd Earl of Tankerville, had done considerable works, diverting the road so that travellers no longer crossed in front of the house. He had fenced the park of about 400 acres, added a herd of 750 deer and a private menagerie. It was a new-made estate for a gentleman, and the iconoclastic Harry Bolingbroke, with a smile, was pleased to demolish its selling points.[36]

Pope introduced him to James 'Jemmy' Gibbs, who had built his own villa at Twickenham. Gibbs was in his thirties, called half-teasingly, half-admiringly 'the wonder of our days', the builder of St Martin-in-the-Fields and of the Senate House and King's College Fellows' Building (universally known as the 'Gibbs' building) at Cambridge. Now he was strewing the Thames valley with smaller jewels, such as James Johnston's Octagon (now part of Orleans House Gallery), Chiswick's pagan temple and garden pavilions at the Duke of Argyll's Whitton.[37] Quite what he did at Dawley is uncertain, though it was radical enough for Henrietta, when she first saw it, to think it was being rebuilt. The result was reported as 'a two-storied house of brick with round-headed windows below a rather flat roof' – which suggests that the 'rather flat roof', and a third storey, was behind a parapet, rather as at the brick 'Palladian gem' of Kelmarsh in Northamptonshire, which Gibbs was designing at the same time.[38]

Gibbs' layouts were deceptively simple and beautiful, with entry into a high, invariably double-cubed hall, flanked by smaller corner rooms right and left, a round-arched vestibule in the centre of the house with the stair hall, and an enfilade of rooms along the garden front. The hall, Henrietta remembered, was 'painted in stone colours, with all the implements of husbandry placed in the manner one sees or might see arms and trophies in some General's hall; and it had an effect that pleased everybody'.[39] These trophies, which excited everyone's interest, were drawn in black crayon like 'charcoal figures on farmhouse walls'.[40] Pope told Swift that he had overheard Harry agreeing to pay the painter £200 for the 'Trophies of Rakes, spades, prongs etc.'[41]

The picture of Harry's Dawley survives in an anonymous poem, 'Dawley Farm', of 1731:[42]

> See! Emblem of himself, his Villa stand!
> Politely finish'd, regularly Grand!
> Frugal of Ornament, but that the best,
> And all with curious Negligence express'd.
> No gaudy Colours stain the Rural Hall,
> Blank Light and Shade discriminate the Wall:
> Here the proud trophies and the spoils of war
> Yield to the scythe, the harrow, and the car;
> To whate'er implement the rustic wields,
> Whate'er manures the garden or the fields.
> See on the figur'd Wall the stacks of corn,
> With Beauty more than theirs the room adorn,
> Young winged Cupids smiling guide the plow,
> And peasants elegantly reap and sow.[43]

Dawley had 'Satis beatus ruris honoribus' inscribed over the doorway, and Harry insisted it was now his farm:

> Himself neglects what must all others charm
> And what he built a Palace calls a Farm.[44]

It was his 'agreeable sepulchre' where he would moulder away, wielding his pen and spade: 'I am in my farm,' he announced, 'and here I shoot strong tenacious roots: I have caught hold of the earth (to use a gardener's phrase) and neither my enemies nor my friends will find it an easy matter to transplant me again.'[45] With distant memories of Harry's previous guise as an English 'farmer' at Bucklebury not entirely eradicated his friends never doubted, however, that 'this scheme of retreat is not founded upon weak appearances', and when his enemies accused him of dissembling there was Henrietta to put them in their place: 'my brother's calling it a Farm was only meant that it really was one; for he then kept [rentals of] £700 per annum in hand'.[46] Harry dis-parked, i.e. unfenced the park, sold the deer and the menagerie's occupants and returned a large portion of his land to his tenant farmers.

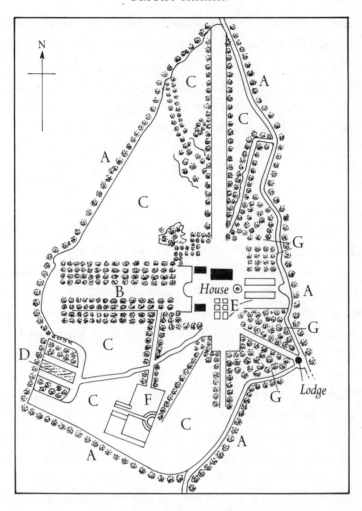

Plan of Dawley as rationalised by Charles Bridgeman for Lord Bolingbroke, the 'farm', of about 200 acres that Henrietta knew well:

A. New hedge boundary to reduced park, cutting short old formal avenues

B. Bowling green

C. Farmed areas

D. Small canal

E. Flower beds and borders

F. Site of former menagerie

G. Orchards

Again at Pope's instigation, Charles Bridgeman visited Dawley, and stamped his approval on this loosening of the corsets of the formal garden into the new and natural style, of which he was the subtle begetter.[47] Long, tree-lined walks extended to the north and west of the house, the north walk passing through meadows, the west walk doubling as a bowling green. Both walks ended in the informally hedged boundary of the house's setting, with fields beyond the hedge. Within the bounds secondary walks invited exploration from the house, a lime avenue led to the old menagerie, a serpentine path wandered through an orchard, another crossed the lime walk to the remnants of an old canal. A small formal canal and flower beds were immediately east and south of the house, with a terrace that looked westwards down the bowling green. Dawley's landscape garden melded into the larger landscape in a relaxing and civilised way. And this was eight years before the date given by the Whiggish Horace Walpole for William Kent who 'first leaped the fence and saw that all nature was a garden' at Lord Burlington's Chiswick.[48] It was after all politics by other means. Yet Henrietta's brother was a practical gardener, too. He loved to see things growing, to eat his own melons and strawberries; he loved walking through his hay meadows and chasing on horseback, with his hounds, through his own countryside. His friends thought him a little past the last. Swift wrote to Pope from Dublin on 29 September 1725, 'I am in great concern at what I am just told in some newspaper, that Lord Bolingbroke is much hurt by a fall in hunting. I am glad he has so much youth and vigour left, of which he hath not been thrifty, but I wonder he has no more discretion.'[49]

For Henrietta, Harry's court at Dawley, given grace and laughter by Marie-Claire – whom he liked to call 'the good woman of Dawley' – was an attractive place to be, and the company suited her to perfection. For a start, there was as much of her darling Harry's company as she could desire, and his energies and vigour ruled their days. For all he was twenty years older the gap seemed narrowed by his liveliness and lordliness. They were tall and stately alter egos, arguing as they strode across the lawn, in such a contrast to the dainty, fair Marie-Claire, who called Henrietta 'our Fanfan' out of their (almost) parental affections for her. Marie-Claire was less an outdoors person, less enamoured of this crazy English gardening than the other two, and the two St Johns shared their gardening memories and greenhouse practicalities to their hearts' contents. When they were not at home, there were constant schemes for garden visiting, and most frequently to their 'neighbour' Pope.

The miniature Pope, approaching forty, not five feet high, pale and stumbling from Pott's disease, a childhood tubercular infection of his spine, was Dawley's court jester, both grave and gay. It was a long time since he had made a comic turn of topiary, pricking the bubble of that fashion as well as the 'Virtuoso Gardiner who has a Turn to Sculpture', but they still laughed at 'ladies in myrtle' and 'their Husbands in Horn beam', and

> A Lavender Pig with Sage growing in his Belly.
> A Pair of Maidenheads in Firr, in great forwardness.[50]

That was Pope's first piece of gardening philosophy; the new taste, he added, was being culled from the Ancients, from Martial's rejoicing 'in the true rustic, the untrimmed farm'. There was 'something in the amiable Simplicity of unadorned Nature, that spreads over the Mind a more noble sort of Tranquility, and a loftier Sensation of Pleasure, than can be raised from the nicer Scenes of Art'.[51] His parallel thesis to nature was bounty, the ideal of fruitfulness of the garden of Alcinous, which he had found in Homer and translated for the first time: 'tall thriving Trees' of apples, pears, figs and olives were weighted with fruit, and

> The balmy Spirit of the Western Gale
> Eternal breaths on Fruits untaught to fail:
> Each dropping Pear a following Pear supplies,
> On Apples Apples, Figs on Figs arise;
> The same mild Season gives the Blooms to blow,
> The Buds to harden, and the Fruits to grow.[52]

The Bolingbroke circle treasured Pope for his gardening wit, but his wider celebrity had come for his *Windsor Forest* and *The Rape of the Lock*. His translation of Homer's *Iliad*, followed by the *Odyssey* (some saw Odysseus in Bolingbroke or vice versa), had made him money, and he was now settled into his new house by the Thames at Cross Deep, Twickenham, making his garden, but frequently at Dawley.

In September 1726 he was returning home late at night in the Bolingbrokes' coach and four, when it was upset into the River Crane just near Whitton. The windows were closed and the poet was asleep, waking to find the water reaching 'the knots of his periwig'. He could not get out, the footman was stuck in the mud and had difficulty reaching him, but fortunately did so just in time, breaking the window glass and saving Pope's life. The glass cut a deep gash across his right hand, which meant the loss of the use of two fingers. Voltaire, who was also staying at Dawley at the time, was mortified 'that those fingers which have written the "Rape of the Lock" . . . which have dressed Homer so becomingly in an English coat, should have been so barbarously treated'.[53]

The accident brought Dawley and Twickenham ever closer. Pope loved to show off his garden's progress. His villa stood in a small riverside plot, and he had leased extra land (eventually totalling five acres) back from the river, west of the villa and across the road. His imagination was undeterred by this odd arrangement, and – with permission – he had a tunnel excavated under the road, entered from the house cellar, and this cellar he glorified into a grotto. No one knows exactly where his inspiration came from, Homer's grotto of the Naiads, Virgil's seaside grotto and Calypso's cave have all been suggested[54], but it was the way he made a virtue out of inconvenience that was so inspiring. Henrietta found it so. Pope describes it himself:

> From the River Thames, you see thru' my Arch up a walk of the
> Wilderness to a kind of open Temple, wholly composed of Shells
> in the rustic manner; and from that distance under the temple

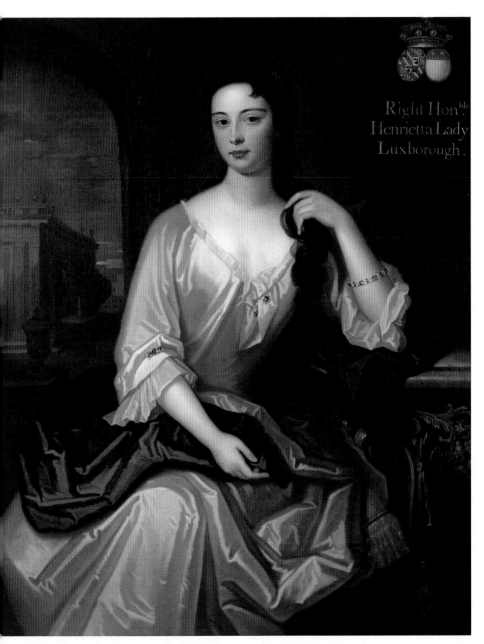

Right Hon.ble
Henrietta Lady
Luxborough.

Henrietta St John [Knight]; this portrait descended through the Knight family,
and is possibly her wedding portrait painted *c.*1727.

Left Sir Oliver St John of Thorpe Hall, Cromwell's Chief Justice and Henrietta's great-grandfather.

Above Henrietta's grandmother, Johanna St John, the Chief Justice's daughter who married Sir Walter St John of Lydiard. This is possibly her wedding portrait *c.*1651.

Below Henrietta's mother (*left*), Angelica Magdalena, Viscountess St John, and father (*right*), Henry, 1st Viscount St John.

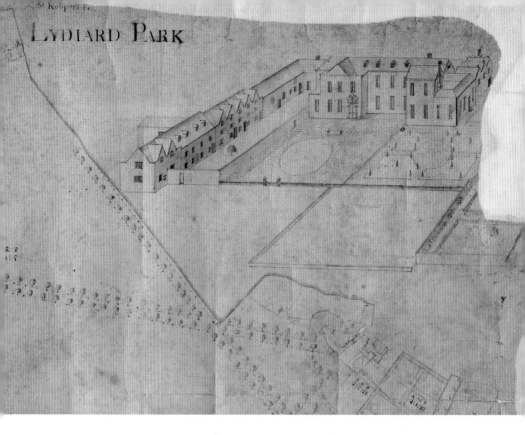

Top Lydiard Tregoze *c.*1700, the south-west front in elevation and part plan [beneath] being the only known illustration of the house of Henrietta's childhood, with the family wing, the newly-planted avenues and formal flower and fruit gardens.

Below Battersea as it was during Henrietta's lifetime, with the St Johns' house and Battersea Stairs to the left of the church, and, extreme right, the house built by her grandparents *c.*1700, now Old Battersea House.

Left Henrietta St John as a child in *c.* 1703.

Below left Sir Thomas Coke of Melbourne, Vice-Chamberlain to Queen Anne and the boon companion of Harry Bolingbroke's rake's progress.

Below Frances Winchcombe, 1st wife of Harry, who died in 1718.

Henry St John, 1st Viscount Bolingbroke, Henrietta's half-brother and the golden Harry
of her childhood.

Right Henrietta in 1719 in possibly her debut portrait, which remained in the St John family until modern times.

Below Robert Knight, later Baron Luxborough, Earl of Catherlough, the young man that Henrietta married in 1727.

Below right Elizabeth Rowe: 'Philomela' the distinguished poet and friend of the Countess of Hertford and Henrietta.

Above Frances, Countess of Hertford, Henrietta's lifelong friend and correspondent.

Below Marlborough Castle and its gardens: a bird's eye view dated 29th June 1723 of the playground of Henrietta's youthful friendship with Frances Hertford.

Above William Kent's illustration for 'Spring' in James Thomson's *The Seasons*, 1730, showing in fanciful pastorale the mount and grotto at Marlborough Castle, with Silbury Hill in the background.

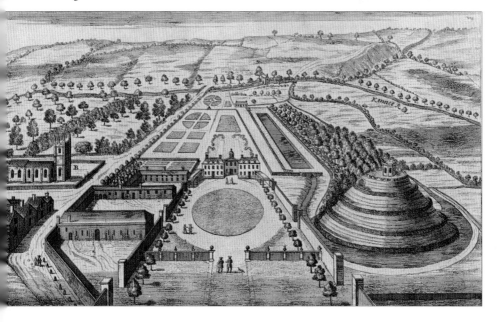

Alexander Pope's Thames–side villa and garden at Twickenham, which Henrietta visited in its earliest years.

William Kent's illustration of the Shell grotto in Pope's upper garden, showing, between the rusticated 'legs', the arch of the tunnel leading to the basement grotto and the riverbank, with a boat on the river.

you look down thru' a sloping arcade of trees, and see the Sails on the River passing suddenly and vanishing, as thru' a perspective Glass. When you shut the Doors of this Grotto, it becomes on the instant, from a luminous room, a Camera Obscura, on the walls of which all the objects of the River, Hills, Woods, and Boats, are forming a moving Picture in their visible radiations.[55]

The walls of the grotto were stuck with shells and slivers of looking-glass for maximum glitter when a lamp 'of a thousand pointed Rays' was lit. The floor was pebbles, but Pope planned for pearly cockleshells, a plentiful commodity from the Thames fishermen, but needing rolling and watering for a smooth surface, as the legendary luxurious surface of The Mall for Charles II's 'Pell Mell'. Was it here, or at Marlborough, that Henrietta had her first lesson in grotto decoration, in the patient making of shell patterns in wet mortar? What is certain is that there were long discussions over the 'camera obscura' effect in the cellar/grotto, where the movements on the luminescent water were 'projected' on to the glistening walls by the concentration of the light from the river. A real camera obscura to produce this effect (and almost certainly Pope's inspiration) was an attraction at the Royal Observatory at Greenwich, which Addison had visited for his *Spectator* piece on 'The Pleasures of the Imagination' (1712), finding 'the prettiest landskip I ever saw' drawn on the walls of a dark room.[56] Though Pope's villa itself, or the basement level, acted as a camera box, there was, of course, no lens. From the Shell Temple in the upper garden, however, the tunnel focused the image to give a similar effect, the likeness of a miniature boat on the river, clearly shown in William Kent's drawing of the Shell Temple. The conversations around this phenomenon are exciting to contemplate. Telescopes, microscopes and optical devices were then on sale at London instrument makers, notably John Marshall's in Ludgate Street, near St Paul's churchyard,[57] but the camera obscura was still an object of experimentation for its ability to enlarge or reduce the size of objects, and 'compose'

picturesque views. Was it Pope's 'camera obscura' that gave Jonathan
Swift his visions of Gulliver's Lilliput, where 'the country round
appeared like a continued garden; and the inclosed fields, which
were generally forty feet square, resembled so many beds of flowers',
and equally the view of his land of monsters, Brobdingnag?[58] As for
Henrietta, she saw the complete effect at an opportune moment, or
moments, in the late 1720s, for the Shell Temple fell down a few
years later. However, the whole idea of a camera obscura and a
perspective glass remained in her mind.

When Pope discovered an enthusiasm for geology and minerals,
and supplies came from the kindly Ralph Allen's quarries on
Coombe Down at Bath, his garden works became ever more elaborate. Lord Peterborough, another of their circle who specialised in
exotic fruits and flowers at Parsons Green, planted him a vineyard
and sent pineapple plants for his stove house, and there was his
'little Bridgemannic theatre' made by some of Bridgeman's gardeners
sent over from the Prince of Wales' garden at Richmond.[59] But
Henrietta only saw all this in its first guise; Pope's garden went on
to become celebrated without her, perhaps all the more reason that
it remained such a bright vision in her memory.

Next door at Whitton she saw another gardening legend being
fostered, with the young John Stuart, later 3rd Earl of Bute (for
whom *Stewartia*, syn. *Stuartia* was named), spending his half-
holidays from Eton helping his uncle, Lord Islay (3rd Duke of Argyll
in 1743), to plant up part of Hounslow Heath. Their seedling pines,
oaks and birches were soon to be joined by more exotic varieties,
the honey locust (acacia), thorns, magnolias, maples and rhododendrons raised from the first seeds brought from the American
colonies.[60]

When sated by Dawley, Whitton and Pope's villa, the Dawley
coterie invaded Mrs Henrietta Howard 'next door', a mile downstream at Marble Hill. She was, like Frances Hertford, a lady-in-
waiting to the Princess of Wales, but Mrs Howard was also the
Prince of Wales' mistress. Looking towards her retirement she had

in 1723 secretly arranged with the architect Roger Morris that he would build her a house, on land Lord Islay had helped her to buy.[61] Secrecy, especially for those included in it, added a piquancy to Mrs Howard's dream house. When George I died suddenly on 12 June 1727 at Osnabruck, en route to Hanover, she wondered at her fate. While she wondered, Dean Swift, who was over from Dublin and staying at Dawley, wrote his 'Pastoral Dialogue between Richmond Lodge [belonging to the Prince of Wales] and Marble Hill'. It begins with Marble Hill fearing that Mrs Howard might be forced to sell:

> Some South Sea Broker from the City,
> Will purchase me, the more's the Pity,
> Lay all my fine Plantations waste,
> To fit them to his Vulgar Taste;
> Chang'd for the worse in ev'ry part,
> My Master Pope will break his Heart.

Pope had designed the garden, albeit a simple lawn flanked by groves of trees, set back to channel the eyes and feet towards the ready-made ornamental canal, the Thames. Richmond Lodge was confident of keeping royal favour:

> I then will turn a Courtier too,
> And serve the Times as others do.
> Plain Loyalty not built on Hope,
> I leave to your Contriver, Pope:
> None loves his King and Country better,
> Yet none was ever less their Debtor.

Then came Mrs Howard's good news that she was not only still the favourite of the new king, George II, but he had increased her allowance. Marble Hill grows silly with doggerel, vaunting her charms:

> Then, let him [Pope] come and take a Nap,
> In Summer, on my verdant Lap:
> Prefer our Villaes where the Thames is,
> To Kensington, or hot St James's.

(Pope and plump Johnny Gay, his *Beggar's Opera* almost ready for the stage, were intimates at Marble Hill, forever wisecracking, and eating and drinking, at the good-natured Mrs Howard's expense.) Marble Hill prattles on,

> Nor shall I dull in Silence sit;
> For, 'tis to me he owes his Wit;
> My Groves, my Ecchoes, and my Birds,
> Have taught him his poetick Words.
> We Gardens, and you Wildernesses,
> Assist all Poets in Distresses,
> Him twice a Week I here expect,
> To rattle Moody for Neglect;
> An idle Rogue, who spends his Quartridge
> In tipling at the Dog and Partridge;
> And I can hardly get him down
> Three times a Week to brush my Gown.[62]

Fêtes at Dawley, picnics at Marble Hill, and undoubtedly a trip to Stowe in Buckinghamshire to see Jemmy Gibbs's works there, it was all a charmed life. En route to Stowe, about four miles from Dawley, there was more amusement with Harry Bolingbroke's Tory ally Lord 'Batty' Bathurst at Richings, or Riskins as they first called it. Bathurst, the fourth of Pope's epistolatory lords (Burlington, Cobham, Bathurst and Bolingbroke), was 'a carefree creature who swam through life' helping his friends (and he lived to be ninety-one).[63] Now he was in his vivacious – it was a word often applied to him – forties, eager to show off his improvements at Richings – for what are improvements unless they are shown? It was by nature a lovely place, by 'Coln's clear stream and flowr'y banks', a retreat they called a little French farm, an 'extravagante bergerie',

> Of Love and Gaiety the destin'd seat
> Where maids of honour might with pleasure rove
> Amongst the lab'rinths of the gloomy grove;
> Where statesmen might forget the nation's cares,
> And find a refuge from perplex'd affairs.[64]

These words are Frances Hertford's, for she was amongst the courtiers who escaped from Windsor Castle to Richings for some fresh air. Frances was so taken with Richings that the Hertfords bought it from Lord Bathurst (who concentrated his garden-making on Cirencester Park) and Henrietta was to know and love it better than ever. Frances recalls what it was like in those Dawley days:

> These arbours he for other guests had plann'd:
> Where wits might muse, or politics be scann'd,
> He stretch'd the lawn: and cut the smooth canal,
> Where Cleopatra's gilded bark might sail;
> Or nymphs more modern might admire the scene,
> Float on the wave, or dance upon the green![65]

At Richings Lord Bathurst's villa was on the site of a former chapel dedicated to St Leonard, the patron saint of Windsor Forest. Around the house he had made wide terraces, four square and of the proportions of a cloister, framed in a double row of beech hedges which were high enough to protect a secluded cloister walk. On the south side the cloister walk was broken by wide steps leading down to a large green lawn and to the canal with its flanking lawns. Otherwise the whole garden was a wilderness, or labyrinth, of trees and shrubs with paths leading to the menagerie, the kitchen garden, or any number of rond-points – open groves with an ornament of some kind. 'Batty' liked his company to meet in one of these groves, where Windsor chairs would be set in a circle. Imagine them, the Dawley set, warm from wilderness walks on a summer after-noon, the cooling drinks being served – Lord Bathurst, Marie-Claire Bolingbroke, Harry, Henrietta, the little Pope and cheerful Gay, the more sober Dean Swift, Mrs Howard, the Hertfords, perhaps Harry Bolingbroke's friend Brook Taylor – only one more is needed for a round dozen so bring in the rural gardener's favourite oracle Stephen Switzer. Switzer was devoted to Lord Bathurst whom he had helped with Richings, thinking him 'the best of Masters and the best of Friends'.[66] Switzer (though I think him Henrietta's preference) vied with Kent for seeing all nature as a garden. He decreed the demolishing of garden walls (or not building them in the first place) so that 'wherever Liberty will allow, [I] would throw my Garden open to all View to the unbounded Felicities of distant Prospect, and the expansive volumes of Nature herself'. This, you will understand, was the pleasure garden, for even in a land as yet innocent of a plague of wild rabbits, most of the edible and precious fruits and flowers would remain safely inside walls. Switzer understood the virtues of some enclosures, of preserving 'private Walks and Cabinets of Retirement, some select Places of Recess for Reading and Contemplation' but proposed that 'all the neighbouring Fields, Paddocks, etc., shall make an additional Beauty to the Garden, and by an easy unaffected manner of Fencing, shall appear to be part of it, and look as if the adjacent Country were all a Garden'.[67]

Switzer's books had great authority, and were certainly open on the tables at Dawley; *The Nobleman, Gentleman and Gardener's Recreation* of 1715 was enlarged into the two volumes of *Ichnographia Rustica*, as the handbooks to the landscape gardening revolution. But Switzer was also a practical gardener – his *Practical Husbandman and Planter* was most likely what Frances Hertford called the 'Gardener's Toil', sometimes required loud reading whilst she was at her woolwork – and he owned a nursery and seed supply shop. He was a very modern entrepreneur, and whether it was politic or no, he was on the same band of the rainbow as his rural philosophers, for 'it will not be unpleasant for [the owner] to fall into natural Coppices, Paddocks, Corn Fields, and a little Gravel or Sand Walk . . . for whatever some may think of Magnificence, there is an inexpressible Pleasure in these Natural Twinings, and private Walks to a quiet, thoughtful, studious Mind'.[68]

He acknowledged the influence of the ancients, of Homer, Virgil and Ovid, for 'from these three . . . the ingenious Designer as well as Poet, may collect noble Thoughts, and Ideas of things, from the first what is Great, from the second what is Beautiful, and from the

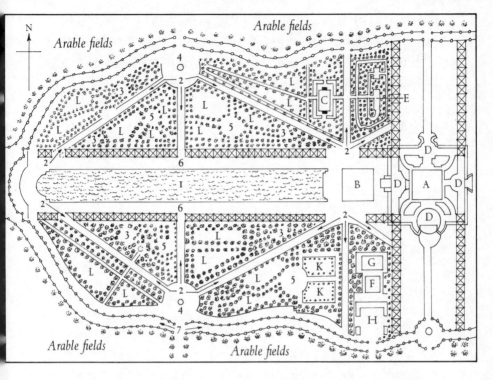

Plan of Richings adapted from Stephen Switzer's Ichnographia Rustica
*(1792): this stylised representation is more likely Switzer's ideal rather than the
exact reality of his work for Lord Bathurst, but it gives a good idea of what the
Hertfords bought, and re-named Percy Lodge, and the garden that Henrietta knew
and which featured in Lady Hertford's letters:*

A. The House
B. A formal parterre
C. The Menagerie
D. The terraces
E. The Labyrinth
F. The Gardener's House
G. Melonry and Frame yard
H. Stables
K. Kitchen Gardens
L. [many] Lawns and Groves

1. The Canal
2. Formal grass paths
3. Wildernesses or labyrinths
4. *Rond-points* with statues
5. Fountains
6. Lawn borders beside the canal
7. Common Road Right of Way

Note the coach or chaise road for driving right round the garden, and the
'Common Road or Right of Way' along the south-side; on the north boundary
Lord Hertford planted the flower walk which merged with the fields of corn,
so loving described to Henrietta by Frances.

last what is Strange'.[69] As for Henrietta, with the bright evidences of all these things round her at Dawley, at Pope's villa, at Marble Hill and Richings, she carried her store of images and memories away, until such time as she would need them.

CHAPTER FOUR

The Honourable Mrs Knight

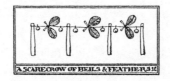

FOR ALL HER brilliant gardening company, none of it was very marriageable, and at twenty-seven Henrietta was fretting for love. So much talked about, so little known? She may have had proposals, just possibly one from Harry's brilliant mathematical friend Brook Taylor, the cleverest of men, whose young wife had died in childbirth in 1723.[1] But Taylor at forty, when he might have proposed, absorbed in his calculus and catenaries, which did not quite have the fascination of the camera obscura, was hardly 'the faithful shepherd' or pretty swain of her expectations. There was another 'éclat', as Harry would call it, when he wrote furiously saying that he would never see her 'thrown away' to a 'man of narrow fortune, a mean birth and bad character', though this rogue never acquired a name.[2] To be sure she was fussy, for as the astute Elizabeth Rowe commented to Frances, 'I should have thought nothing but an Adonis would have pleased [her] temper . . .'.[3]

At some time in 1724 Harry had made the acquaintance in Paris of a young man named Robert Knight, who was working in the English banking community and acting as a courier to England for all the most private and valuable transactions. Harry mischievously mentioned this 'pretty youth' in a letter to his sister, and inevitably Robert Knight turned up at Dawley, either by invitation or on business, to be introduced to her by Harry, with a twinkle in his eye. To give her manipulative brother the benefit of the doubt, he genuinely wanted married happiness for his sister and Henrietta was getting dangerously 'mature'. Robert Knight was from an old Warwickshire family, he had an extremely rich father, and he seemed a good-natured and pleasant young man, with political ambitions, so this was far from throwing her away. At twenty-five he was two years younger than Henrietta, but tall enough and elegant enough, with fair colouring and a lovely smile, which undoubtedly detracted from his rather overly prominent nose and his supercilious way of looking down it. Did Henrietta love him? Given the happy circumstances of life at Dawley in the spring of 1727, she was probably head over heels. In looks he just enough resembled Harry as a young man, the Harry of her childhood, to match her dreams. And like Harry, Knight was brought up in London, had been to Oxford, and had spent time on the Continent after an exciting flight into exile. Henrietta could also determine that his future was now rosy. There was hardly time for more, though perhaps Frances Hertford had expressed some doubts to the worldly Elizabeth Rowe, to extract the assurance that Henrietta's 'gentle disposition and good sense will make her happy'.[4]

It was not a long engagement; they were married on 10 June 1727 at the fashionable St George's church in Hanover Square. St George's had 'select vestry' status, meaning that it was virtually controlled in the way they liked by the parishioners resident in the large Mayfair houses, of which Lord St John, with his house in Albemarle Street, was one. Nothing is known of the wedding party and who was there; few Knights were likely to have been present, and we know with absolute certainty that Robert's father was absent. Afterwards it would have been perfectly usual for Robert and Henrietta to have joined the household at Battersea, or at Dawley, or perhaps at Lydiard as it was summer, for they had no home of their own. Harry had a friend wanting to sell his house in Dover Street but 'he will not take less than 5,000 guineas',[5] which Harry thought exorbitant. Henrietta liked the idea of Dover Street and, with Robert apparently willing to pay 'a great price', she begged Harry to try again, but it came to naught. Her father had found them a possible country house, Harry found one that proved impossible, but soon all these discussions were shelved because it was decided that they should go to Paris to live with Robert's parents. Paris, at last. It was ironic that having so longed to go to France to see Harry and his friends, she was now to be placed amongst strangers, and uncongenial strangers at that. Harry had to support her acquiescence very soon after she and Robert arrived there at the end of November: 'you are surely very much in the right to comply with Mr Knight's desire, and I am hopeful you will receive the benefit you expect from change of air'. With his own renewed hopes for office under the new king, George II, keeping him firmly in England, Harry had the grace to add, 'I wish for many reasons I was still in France, where I should be glad to receive you and to take my part in doing the honours of the country to you.'[6]

Henrietta found herself in the Knights' overstuffed and gloomy mansion, Le Roule, on the Faubourg St Honoré, near the church of Saint Philippe du Roule, a good mile from Les Tuileries in a north-westerly direction. Paris, or this newly developed part of it, seemed bleak in midwinter, with enormous distances to walk, which she found strange after the intimacy of Piccadilly and St James's. Her father-in-law was welcoming enough, but his second wife Anne was less so. Robert was ill with a prolonged fever in the New Year which was dispiriting, but at least they were together. As soon as he was better he resumed his travelling on business, and she realised that she would see little of him. Her circumstances were really no different from most brides of her kind, whose marriages took them off to remote and strange houses full of eccentrics. Harry, the only person to whom she expressed doubts, assured her that 'it will grow pleasant as the Spring advances' to be able to walk to the Elysée and Les Tuileries. He, at least, was certain of Robert's worth: 'I should reckon upon his friendship if I had any occasion of employing it, and both he and you, my dear, may be assured that mine shall never fail you.'[7]

Why these doubts? Why were the assurances needed? Henrietta was just six months married but already somehow unhappy and sensing some dark secrets held within the opulent mansion on the Faubourg St Honoré. In truth, it was not that her 'gentle disposition and good sense' had failed her entirely, it was that there was something she did not quite understand. It is likely that Henrietta never knew the full and devastating story; that her marriage was part of the fallout from the greatest financial scandal of all time.

As far back as 1711, when she was no more than twelve, and Secretary St John and Lord Treasurer Harley were still closely allied, Harley had masterminded the launch of the South Sea Company, making himself the first governor and Harry St John a politically nominated director. The company (set up by an Act of Parliament of 1 August 1711) was to have the monopoly of trade to South America and the south Pacific, where the people were hungry for – it was confidently predicted – silk handkerchiefs, woollen stockings, sealing wax, spices, clocks and watches, even Cheshire cheese.[8] The optimistic investors' monies were to support a government shortfall of some £9 million, and the company shares were 'given' in return for this diverted cash, so that the company literally 'floated' on hot air and propaganda from the outset. The company's Chief Cashier was clearly a critical appointment, and Harley thought he had just the man in the person of the general manager of the Sword Blade Bank, Mr Robert Knight – known to everyone as Bob. The only obstacle was that the manager's father-in-law, Jeremiah Powell, was about to become governor of the rival Bank of England. Eventually, with Harry St John's compliance, Harley set the question to his protégé. If Bob Knight were to be the Chief Cashier of the South Sea Company, would that make difficulties at home? Knight replied that he hardly spoke to his father-in-law, and his discretion could be relied upon, and so he got the job.[9]

In 1711 Bob Knight was a mathematical wizard in his late thirties; he was thought amiable and charming, admired for his innovation and ingenuity, all valued qualities in the hothouse atmosphere of

City reputations. He was well known, for his father was a prosperous sugar baker living in Bread Street, a City ward councillor and sometime Master of the Grocers' Company. It was he, a younger brother, who had left the Knight family's country estate, Barrells, in a remote and pretty corner of Warwickshire, just west of Henley-in-Arden, to seek his fortune in London town.

Bob Knight had grown up in the family's tall house in Bread Street, the narrow thoroughfare connecting Cheapside and Cannon Street, just east of St Paul's. The house was next to Wren's St Mildred's church,* which the family treated almost as their chapel, gathering beneath the ornately gilded and domed ceiling for their baptisms, weddings and funerals, as well as Sunday prayers. There was only a small skeleton residing in the family cupboard with talk of Bob's uncle, John Knight, who was expelled from the House of Commons in 1698 for forging endorsements on Exchequer bills.[10]

Bob Knight's brilliance with figures dated from his schooldays. He always wanted to work in finance rather than sugar baking, and he started as a lowly clerk at the Sword Blade Bank. On 2 February 1701 he married Martha Powell, daughter and co-heiress of Jeremiah Powell of Edenhope in Shropshire, and brought her to the Bread Street home. Their first child, Robert, was born on 17 December, and duly baptised in St Mildred's. A daughter Catherine was born in 1704, and Margaretta was the latecomer in 1713. Young Robert Knight's childhood was as nearly perfect as early eighteenth-century London could offer, he was comfortably housed, well educated, and presumably well loved – if not actually spoilt as a 'pretty youth' in a household of women. As a schoolboy he watched his father's steady climb to success, and his installation in his office at the impressive South Sea House, an easy walk from Bread Street, along Cheapside and Poultry, to the far end of Threadneedle Street (the opposite end to the Bank of England). South Sea House boasted an

---

* Built 1677–83, destroyed 1941.

enviable boardroom with thirty gilt and ebony directors' chairs (one for Harry St John) around a splendid table, but the Chief Cashier's office was pleasingly modest, as was his salary of £200 a year. He was rather left to his own devices, which included making his own quiet fortune.

In 1715 old Knight the sugar baker died and was duly laid to rest in St Mildred's vault. Bob Knight decided to sell the Bread Street home and find something newer in the City, as well as a house in the country. The ways of City property dealing were familiar to him, but for the country he began in the way others did, by asking his nephew Robert Surman (whom he had helped to a post at the Sword Blade) to look into the bank's books to see who was in financial difficulties. The name that emerged was that of John Wroth, a debtor for a £5,000 mortgage on an Essex estate of 180 acres called Luxborough. The Wroths, an ancient family of fading grandeur, had other houses, but Luxborough was ripe in that it was not entailed, nor marked for an heir. Bob Knight made a reconnaissance trip to Chigwell and along Luxborough Lane, where he found a tumbledown Elizabethan manor on a lovely site with the River Roding flowing through the grounds. On making enquiries he further found that the glamorous-sounding name was soberly rooted, along with nearby Loughton, in a fourteenth-century William de Loughteburg, or one John Luctebourg, which was a local name in 1404. In 1435 Richard Riche, Citizen of London, was lord of the manor of 'Lucburgh' or 'Lugburgh', and the Elizabethan house was even less prettily named 'Lugsborow'. Gloriana and her entourage had stayed there for two days in May 1591 with the widow Anne Stonerde. Robert Wroth, a City grandee praised at length by Ben Jonson[11] for his love of country life, had married the Stonerdes' daughter, and the family had become the great landowners of the Roding Valley.[12]

A pedigree and a pretty setting; it was just what Bob Knight wanted, and he bought Luxborough for £10,000. He was in a hurry: he had the Elizabethan remains pulled down and his new house built quickly, of brick with stone facings – or perhaps it was just rendered and painted to look good – a squarish house with a pillared portico on the entrance front. He commissioned the doyen of decorative painters, Sir James Thornhill, to paint his hall in grandiloquent classical style – Thornhill was a little passé, some people said, and Bob Knight who did not pretend to know about such things fell into the 'vulgar taste' of Swift's 'South Sea broker from the City'.[13] Like so many arrivistes, he upset the locals by trying to divert Luxborough Lane – a route well used by fishermen to reach the Roding – and failing to do so, and by bullying his way into a private pew in Chigwell parish church, after an acrimonious correspondence with the churchwardens.[14]

Bob Knight moved his family into Luxborough at some time in 1717, when Robert was an impressionable teenager. Martha Knight, still ailing as she had been since the birth of Margaretta in 1713, found that the damp airs of the Roding valley did not suit her. After a few months the Knight family all returned to London and it seems that they never lived at Luxborough again, though perhaps they visited it briefly in fine summers. Mystery surrounds Martha Knight's death, doubly recorded as in early 1718[15] and, on a memorial in Wootton Wawen church (in Warwickshire) set up by Robert many years later, as 1723, at the age of thirty-seven.[16] The later date seems most likely, but if so, Martha would have lived her last years in a state of worry and heartbreak.

The 'Bubble' year of 1720 opened with a steady beat of optimism, for the Knights and everyone else. As the South Sea Company flaunted its prospects for trade rights in Africa, for carrying slaves to the West Indies, for taking over part of the National Debt, the share value rose from £128 in January to £300 in March, and £500 in May, and continued rising.[17] In his quiet office Chief Cashier Bob Knight was diverting his assets, sending large sums of money abroad and legally tying up his London properties in the names of relatives he could trust. In his Company green books he was carefully disguising the entries to tell quite another story to that which was taking place – with manipulations of such ingenuity that to this day they have not been fully understood.[18] On the streets of London at least one, anonymous, pamphleteer was scorning the loss of 'all sense and reason', and as 'a set of crafty men having undertaken to delude the world with an opinion that they can by a little hocus-pocus management, make a single unit become a good ten', predicting it would surely all end in disaster.[19] Few bought his line, the many were intoxicated – credit was the new alchemy. Fifty companies arose in two months, including the Bleaching of Hair Company, a company for the transmutation of quicksilver, one to insure marriage from divorce, another to design an air pump for the brain, and very popularly, a company to plant mulberry trees and breed silkworms in Chelsea Park. Perhaps these fantastical ideas do not seem so outlandish in today's age – how far have we sunk into gullibility? – and the last had actually been tried a century earlier by James I in the Mulberry Garden at St James's, now part of the grounds of Buckingham Palace.[20]

Some canny people sold their South Sea shares in May, including the astute Sarah, Duchess of Marlborough, and old Thomas Guy, who built his hospital out of his South Sea fortune, said to have been £234,000.[21] News of such profits just fired the fever of further speculation, gentlemen of fortune were 'hatched' overnight, the streets sported new coaches, embroidered coats and the glint of gold jewellery. None of this euphoria, however, permeated into the quiet of Bob Knight's Cashier's office, and even when the Bubble burst and the crowds were clamouring for their money at the front of South Sea House on that hot August day, the Cashier quietly closed his green book and, leaving by the side door, went home to his dinner. To an experienced City man like Bob Knight the whole affair was clearly ridiculous; it was only right that the Company had protested about the upstart ventures, so closing them down and precipitating the 'burst' as shareholders demanded their South Sea money in order to pay other debts. The crowds continued their clamour through September, it was reported that 'Exchange Alley' was a sorry sight, with coaches, coats and gold watches on quick sale – 'all corners of the town are filled with the groans of the afflicted'.[22]

Chief Cashier Knight, perhaps muttering 'easy come, easy go', merely washed his hands and wondered, with some justification on the evidence of his day, how they could think he had done anything wrong. For four months he cavilled at accusations so effectively that he was thought a casualty of the bursting Bubble himself. The Duchess of Marlborough's card-playing companion Lady Lechmere, the Earl of Carlisle's daughter, wrote, 'I am really very sorry for him, for in all appearances he was a fair, obliging man.'[23] The Duke of Chandos reported to Harry Bolingbroke at La Source in October:

'I have seen a great variety of fortunes, but in all my life I never saw so universal a sense of misery as I did last week; the distress mankind was in was inconceivable and a general Bankruptcy was apprehended. God be thanked the ruine that threatened the Publick is pretty well blown over, but the destruction the fall of stocks and the loss of credit hath brought upon private families is never to be retrieved and the number of families of all degrees have suffered accordingly.[24]

If the Christmas atmosphere was edgy in the Knights' house, we do not know, but when the House of Commons inquiry opened on 14 January 1721 it was 'the talk of the town' that the culprits would be hanged. Bob Knight continued to justify himself. 'If I should disclose all I know,' he is often quoted as saying, 'it would open such a scene as the world would be surprised at.'[25] He protested that he was acting under orders, that he was loath to betray the Company's secrets, or friends, but on Saturday 21 January he was summoned for questioning. One day was enough, and that evening he left London, gathering up his son Robert (who was enjoying a well-funded life as an Oxford undergraduate) and taking the Dover road and ship for France. On that chill Sunday evening, in

a harbourside inn at Dover, he penned a letter to the House of
Commons inquiry:

> Gentlemen, though self-preservation has obliged me to with-
> draw myself from the resentment against the directors and
> myself, yet I am not conscious of having done anything that I
> can reproach myself for.
>
> I have taken with me but a little more than a sufficiency to
> maintain myself, and the effects left will more than answer for
> all deficiencies.
>
> I have withdrawn myself only to avoid the weight of the
> inquiry, which I found too heavy for me; I am sensible that it
> would have been impossible for me to have avoided the appear-
> ance and charge of prevarication and perjury, not from my own
> intention to do so, but from the nature and largeness of the
> transactions . . .

He goes on to apologise for adding to their 'difficulties' and to
deplore the way he was questioned, ending: 'I am pressed for time,
so can only assure you that I am, with all respect, in inclination,
though not in power, Gentlemen, your most obedient humble
servant, Robert Knight.'[26]

The letter was delivered on the Monday morning by Robert
Surman (now Deputy Cashier, who had probably gone as far as
Dover with his mentor) and it sparked a furore. Government officers
raided South Sea House and the Sword Blade Bank, the directors
were arrested and stripped of their public offices, and Knight's
reachable assets, about £300,000 and including Luxborough, were
seized. A reward of £2,000 was offered for his capture, but there
was gossip that he had been allowed to escape because he knew too
much.

For Bob Knight and Robert their adventures were only just beginning. After ten days on the run they were identified in Brussels
by a smart secretary from the British Legation, but tipped off to
make their escape. The secretary, Edward Gaudot, gathered sixteen
dragoons and gave chase. At Leuven, twenty-six kilometres west

of Brussels, he found the inn they had stopped at, and with the four best riders and fresh horses he caught up with the Knights at Tienen, nineteen kilometres farther on. They were taken to prison in Antwerp Citadel, and in the House of Commons there were cheers at the news.[27] Now the great game started. The Commons had quickly passed an Act forbidding the South Sea culprits leaving the country, but Bob Knight had left before the Act became law, so he was immune, and Robert had committed no crimes. Secretary Gaudot had found Knight carrying 'incriminating papers', but these mysteriously disappeared. Did they really want Knight back? With the great 'Skreen Master' Robert Walpole organising the cover-up that would keep him in prime ministerial comforts for the next twenty years, the trial of Bob Knight might reveal far too much. He was much more conveniently made a scapegoat, the 'sole author of the mischiefs done to the nation'.[28] There was a great deal of bluster about extradition to the Austrian authorities who controlled his Antwerp prison, counteracted by secret instructions.[29] Then, on a warm night in the spring of 1721, the Knights, father and son, were spirited away whilst the charade of their still being confined was kept up, until a hole in the prison wall and a rope (if not actually a ladder) were 'discovered', and not a single witness to their 'escape'. They had been set free on an Ardennes mountainside, and after a little wandering they reached Paris.[30]

Bob Knight was soon comfortably established in Paris with the funds he had carefully salted away. It was said, however, that he was so miserable about his exile that every year he would travel to Calais, to gaze at the white cliffs of Dover, and groan.

And what of his son? Did he regard his adventures as an interesting variation on the grand tour, which he would laugh about with his friends? Robert stayed with his father until they settled in Paris in the autumn of 1721, and then returned to Oxford to finish his studies. Unfortunately, Robert's was not a nature to treat the escapade lightly; his father had spoiled him, given him grandiose notions of his place in the world, sent him to Oxford for the gentleman's education he had not had himself, and Robert had become a rather pompous young man. His life had run so smoothly that he was habitually inflexible, and perhaps rather humourless. He more likely regarded his father's experience as an affront to family dignity, which it was his duty to repair. But the hurt was raw, and although his father had purchased the parliamentary seat of Great Grimsby for him, he could not face his father's accusers, and chose to work as a go-between to confidential clients in Paris and England, rather than expose himself in the political arena. Bob Knight's squirrelled-away fortune was considerable – that 'little more than a sufficiency to maintain myself' – and he was soon making a great deal from his Paris enterprises. He was a very clever, if unhappy, man. The Great Grimsby seat was kept in the family, going to John Page, originally a South Sea Company clerk, now married to Robert's sister Catherine.[31]

Robert Knight, just down from Oxford, had first met Harry Bolingbroke in Paris in 1724, sometime after the Bolingbrokes came back from their exploratory trip to London to arrange Harry's pardon and permanent return the following year. Robert, like everyone else, must have been charmed by the elder statesman, quite justifiably seeing him as a means of his own political advancement. Perhaps their meeting came about because Harry was doing business with Bob Knight. If their paths had crossed again between 1724 and late 1725 or early 1726 it would explain why Harry seemed to know Robert rather better than Henrietta did when she married him – to the extent of being able to 'reckon upon his friendship' and so easily include the new bridegroom in his assurances of never failing affections.

Henrietta's concerns in that rather miserable January of 1728 in Paris sprang, it transpired, from an encounter she had – or perhaps a conversation she overheard – on the Channel packet boat to Calais. She had met Thomas Coke, Lord Lovel (Baron Lovel of Minster Lovel and not to be confused with Harry's old friend Tom Coke of Melbourne, who had died in 1727), and a man called Harrison. They recognised her and Robert, and – Lovel having been almost ruined by the South Sea collapse, and being a supporter of Robert Walpole, as well as eccentrically outspoken and cruel – it can be imagined that they were hurtful and rude. Whether Robert was involved is not clear, for it was to Harry that she confided her hurt. Perhaps they made vicious remarks as to how much Bob Knight, using the South Sea shareholders' money, had 'paid' for her. Lovel, known for a buffoon, might have suggested he would like his share. She pleaded with Harry to quell the gossip, and he replied, 'You do me great justice in believing that I could not be negligent of you or of the family to which you now belong. As I have a true esteem for them and a true affection for you, so you shall find me all my life a steady, sincere friend, and to the best of my power a grateful one.'[32] He supposed it was the kind of story 'carried about by the understrappers of a set of men who live by lyes', he thought that their father Lord St John 'should oblige Lord Lovel to disavow it and even Harrison himself if it can be fixed on Harrison', but in the end she should treat it with 'a due contempt' so that 'an idle story without proof ought to drop when you give the lye to it'. Lord St John, of course, did nothing, though there is no evidence that Henrietta ever wrote to him. The nasty taste remained, she was unconvinced by Harry's prevarications and she still referred to it in April, although she had reasoned for herself that jealousy of the Knights' prosperity may have been the cause, and Harry concurred: 'you will find as long as you live that prosperity turns more heads than adversity' and he dismissed Lord Lovel as a 'stranger to delicacy and decency'.[33]

Was Harry's 'true esteem' based on the experiences he and Bob Knight had in common, of their flights to France and a mutual hatred of Prime Minister Walpole? It is unclear what he had to be thankful for when he wrote 'you shall find me all my life a steady, sincere friend, and to the best of my power a grateful one'. It is more than possible that Harry was in the Knights' debt for his own pardon price – or, if all Marie-Claire's money including the proceeds

from the sale of La Source had paid for his pardon, that Bob Knight
had subsequently put up the money for Dawley. And Henrietta's
bride-price was the staggering sum of £40,000; Lord St John
gave her a dowry of just £6,000 invested, the capital to be paid
three months after his death, so it is unclear where this vast amount
was lodged.

Spring in Paris did lighten Henrietta's mood. She found
Mademoiselle Haillé, Harry's old governess and hers, and she made
contact with some of his friends, including Madame de Ferriol. She
settled into the Knight household, where Bob Knight developed a
very fond regard for her, and she liked him. But his second wife
Anne, to whom Henrietta found she was supposed to be a kind of
companion and translator of French language and manners, was
inclined to be querulous and difficult. Their friends were appallingly
dull by Henrietta's standards, not at all the kind of people to hold
her interest. So it was an important letter that greeted the ailing
Bolingbrokes on their return to Dawley in early June, having spent
six weeks in Bath. Harry replied, 'I congratulate you both on the
contents of it. This being the case you are surely much in the right
to think of coming over at the end of the summer, before you are
too far gone.'[34]

The question of where the Knights might live in England had
been rumbling along; Harry, whose mind ran easily on political
philosophy but snagged on the cunning and deception of property
dealers, had given up on the Chetwynd house in Dover Street, much
to Henrietta's disappointment, as well as on a country house he had
in mind. He longed to find her a home 'such as you might like and
like always' which has 'real conveniency and advantages, not barely
those which strike at first sight, and have little more than the glare
of novelty'.[35] He wanted her to have a garden, 'I wish I could find
such a farm for you as would please me in every respect', but, as
there was now some urgency in the matter, he added, 'meanwhile
there is a poor farm in the county of Middlesex at which you and
yours will always be welcome, whenever you return to this

country'.[36] His secretary and Henrietta's old friend, John Brinsden, was almost her last visitor at Le Roule before she set out – he was on an errand to find some decent French burgundy at a reasonable price, because the clarets sent to England proved 'more generally than ever bad'.[37]

Robert and Henrietta at last arrived safely in England in mid-September. Bob Knight had done some mortgage-juggling, surreptitiously retrieving his assets; it transpired that Robert was the owner of a small estate called Ruckholts, between Leyton and Wanstead in Essex – ironically much sought-after South Sea fortune territory – and conveniently on the road to Luxborough. They visited Ruckholts, staying several days, but apparently did not like it, for it was soon sold to the Wanstead estate and played no further part in Henrietta's life.

She was happily at Dawley for her confinement. Her son was born on Christmas Day 1728; he was named Henry, though immediately called Harry.

Soon after Harry's birth Henrietta and Robert went to live in Grosvenor Street, where her beloved Hertfords were their neighbours. These new town houses were all very similar to each other, and Frances had described hers: 'In a street which turns out of New Bond Street and has five rooms on the 1st floor and four upon the 2nd, one of which is 30 feet × 17 feet with five sash windows in it and a little light closet and stairs at the farther end of it. We have good light back stairs besides and 4 rooms up the 2nd and 3rd stairs.' The kitchen was 'away from the house' at the back, with a small garden or yard and the mews for a coach and horses. The rent was £65 a year.[38]

Henrietta rather cleverly became pregnant again in the spring after Harry's birth so there was no question of her returning to Paris. She found the prospect of decorating and furnishing at Grosvenor Street interesting, but between her morning sickness and expanding waistline she did not achieve a great deal. With little Harry she spent some happy weeks at Marlborough in the summer, catching up on Frances' garden-making, and her newest pastime, the collecting and saving of poets. Philomela, Elizabeth Rowe, had told her of the publication, for 1s., of James Thomson's 'Winter', first of *The Seasons*, and she had been so enchanted that she invited the poet to Marlborough, to stay as long as he liked as a kind of 'poet in residence'. The result was, as all the world knows, 'Spring', dedicated to Frances:

> Oh Hertford! fitted or to shine in Courts
> With unaffected Grace, or walk the Plain,
> With innocence, and Meditation join'd
> In soft assemblage, listen to my Song,
> Which thy own Season paints, when Nature all
> Is blooming and benevolent, like Thee.[39]

There was also the celebrated affair of rescuing Richard Savage, the romantically illegitimate lordling author of *The Tragedy of Sir Thomas Overbury*, who was condemned for murder after a tavern brawl. Frances' intercession, which proved his alibi, saved him to write – with his friend Aaron Hill – his best remembered work, *The Wanderer*, in praise of nature and the landscape.[40] Another 'pet' was Stephen Duck, a Wiltshire farm labourer and the forerunner to John Clare and George Crabbe in rural realism. Frances' praise of his work to Queen Caroline had earned him a pension and a home, the picturesque Duck Cottage built for him on the island in St James's Park lake.[41]

The summer weeks at Marlborough for the two young mothers must have been unremittingly happy, and they were at their closest as friends. Henrietta returned to Grosvenor Street when Robert came back from his travels, and her daughter, named Madelaine Henrietta, was born on 21 November 1729.

Quite what she thought when the Knights demanded she return to Paris when her baby was five months old, and little Harry was a year and a half, can only be imagined. Her own childhood had been one of timeless nursery routines blessed with the freedom of a large and loving household, and for years she had watched Frances' fond attachment to her children, and their affection for her in return. She had not imagined that her own children would have anything different. She was adamant that they could not be subjected to the rigours of a journey to Paris, nor did she think they would be welcomed in that airless house full of impatient adults on the Faubourg St Honoré. It was to no avail; Robert and her father-in-law insisted she had to go. She agreed on condition that her children were left with the Hertfords, whom she trusted absolutely, and who agreed to look after them, with Harry Bolingbroke taking on a 'guardian's' role. It was such a tense and anxious time; Frances Hertford was pregnant herself and miscarried in the spring, being gravely ill for a time.

Henrietta returned to Paris in May 1730, having said goodbye to her children, whom she was not to see for over two years. At least they were safe and in a loving household – Henrietta herself was plunged into an extraordinary existence, one which was to develop into a recurring nightmare. The Knights kept open house, on a strictly business footing, for the swarms of wealthy young Englishmen on their grand tours, and their 'bear leaders' or 'governors', and they all dined *en famille*. These visitors were so numerous that Henrietta, even 'bright Marian' who loved conversing with people so much, could not keep up with their names and identities. She was treated as a mix of social prize – Lord St John's daughter, the Honourable Mrs Robert Knight, everyone knowing whose sister she was – and a professional hostess. It was all too clear that the Knights wanted their money's worth, and the feeling that she was being exploited, and even cheapened, sank into her soul. She knew now that Harry would have little sympathy for these feminine feelings. Frances was her most frequent correspondent, and their matter-of-fact letters on the children's welfare have not survived, but Frances carefully kept Henrietta's agonised exposé of her 'manner of life'. She told Frances, ' 'tis just what the family pleases'. She rose at nine, breakfasted at ten in her own room, then presented herself in Mrs Knight's room, where she did the duties of companion-drudge-secretary, and where 'sometimes tradespeople come in, and we talk to them of what we want'. Then they each retired to dress, this being her only time to read her letters and write, before the dinner hour at 1 o'clock, when 'we dine with a multitude of English young men and their governors, several of whom we don't know the names of; after that we have coffee, and then we sit down to cards, if they choose it, for we are not to leave them [for five hours]. At 7 we walk for about an hour with them in the garden, and then we return to cards or supper.' Others then came in the evening ... and 'so we go to our respective bedchambers about two in the morning'. She made an unmistakable point of the 're-spective' bedrooms. The days had little variation, she felt completely imprisoned (she had very little opportunity for fresh air by her standards) by this stream of spotty and arrogantly importuning young men and their overbearing minders, who, as they were in a money-man's house, seemed only interested in talking of money. The trap closed even tighter when the family moved to La Planchette, the Knights' summer home at Bercy, near the Bois de Vincennes. From there it was a five-kilometre coach journey to anywhere, and the only places they went were the homes of the Knights' friends, dusty dowagers and starchy ambassadors – not at all the people Henrietta wanted to meet. To Frances she moaned 'you cannot expect an account of anything concerning the polite, or fashionable world; and as I converse with nobody (for so I may call conversing with everybody) I cannot learn what passes in the learned part of the world; so you must be contented with what you will ever find in my heart'.[42]

It transpired that she was needed to play hostess especially in 1731 because her step-mother-in-law, Anne Knight, gave birth to a son, William.[43] This did nothing for Mrs Knight's temper, and was disastrous for Robert's already tetchy relationship with his 56-year-old father. Anxious to secure something of his own inheritance, Robert had decided to buy Barrells, the Warwickshire estate of his great-grandparents, which two of Bob's spinster cousins of the senior branch of the family were willing to sell. Bob Knight, yearning for his pardon, dearly wanted to regain Luxborough and begrudged the money for Barrells, but gave way. Robert, who knew how things were in England, thought his father would never be pardoned and allowed home, and cruelly told him so.

An insight into this unhappy household comes from a celebrated source, the notorious 'Memoirs of a Lady of Quality' by Fanny Vane, which found their way into Tobias Smollett's *Peregrine Pickle*. In about 1731, Robert's youngest sister Margaretta Knight was married to Morgan Vane, whose brother Gilbert had succeeded to the title of Lord Barnard in 1723. Gilbert had married Fanny Hawes, the daughter of a South Sea Company director, who lived at Purley, beside the Thames. Fanny described herself as 'an odd whimsical girl' forever a prey to undesirable men, who, having run away and finding herself penniless in Paris, appealed to 'M. K——, who had been formerly intimate with my father' and whom she knew to be kind. Bob Knight, for it was he, assured her that she 'should always be welcome at his table, and want for nothing'. The capricious Fanny was urged to lodge with a friend of the Knights and so gain respectability, which she did, passing her time 'very agreeably in several English and some French families' for free, until she was inevitably lured away by the charming Prince of C—— or bewitching Earl B——. Poor Lord Barnard (Lord B—— of the saga) was trying to extricate himself from his disastrous marriage and marry the woman he loved.[44] With this motley society of the 'Quality of England' and French Princes of the Blood, Bob Knight was desperately trying to buy his way back into favour. Harry Bolingbroke understood perfectly: 'I wish for his sake, as well as yours, that you had less company and fewer feasts,' he told Henrietta. 'To speak to you in the same confidence you use with me, the good offices of those he treats in France will never do him much service at home, and I am sure that the frequent reports, perhaps exaggerated, of the expense he makes there, do him great hurt here.'[45]

The 'feasts' reached the ears of Alexander Pope, who wrote a vicious passage in his *Dunciad*:

> What cannot copious Sacrifice attone?
> Thy Treufles, Perigord! Thy Hams, Bayonne!
> With French Libation, and Italian Strain,
> Wash Bladen white, and expiate Hays's stain.
> Knight lifts the head, for what are crowds undone
> To three essential Partridges in one?[46]

For Henrietta, however conscious she was of the 'crowds un-done' and the casualties of the 'Bubble', they were in the grey distance of her private woes, her dawning realisation that her marriage was a trap into which, in her innocent dizziness, she had stumbled. Many brides had troubles with their in-laws (even Frances Hertford) but the wise kept their distances. Here was she, embroiled in the Knights' horrid schemes. Of the 'three essential' partridges (those birds that Frances had reared in her butterfly garden) now brought to her table, two having been dissolved into a 'quintessence' as a sauce for the third, she had feelings of sympathy as a sacrificial fourth. With her dreams of La Source behind her, had she imagined a Boucher, or Watteau, or Nicolas Lancret kind of life, not exactly *Girl on a Swing* or *Tasse de chocolat*, but an outdoor life, with friends and her children playing round, with poetry and music in the evenings? She would have enjoyed her ordinary duties, she had been brought up in well-managed kitchen gardens and butteries, and she loved arranging meals: all of this if only there had been food for her mind as well. If she had known of the famous monthly concerts held in Pierre Crozat's house on the rue de Richelieu, or at Montmorency his country home, she would have cried to have been excluded. The Le Roule feasts, the ham, truffles and wines, fed only her tendency to put on weight, and she had no time for her habitual long walks, which she loved, let alone Blindman's Buff energetically played with friends in Les Tuileries. 'I don't find many minutes to think and fewer to write,' she told Frances, 'the pleasures of the mind are denied me, and my body is whirled (whether I will or no) from one crowd to another, where I see nothing but eating and play, among people I'm not acquainted with, nor that are acquainted with one another.'[47]

In over four and a half years, from the spring of 1730 until the autumn of 1734, Henrietta spent two short spells in England, in the late summer of 1732 and the spring of 1734. At this most critical time of their lives she saw her (fortunately healthy) children for about two months at each time, when they were toddlers, Harry three and a half, little Henrietta two and a half, and then when they were five and four. If her children's image of her was that of a lovely lady who brings presents, then her own relationship with Robert was hardly more close, as he continued to travel on Bob Knight's errands in France and in England. Any love between them, based upon physical attraction, had withered since they were so much apart. While Robert was in England he had seen much more of his children than his wife ever could, spending time with the Hertfords, and the Bolingbrokes, and making himself pleasant so that they all, they told her, had a high opinion of him. Once, with infuriating irony, the Bolingbrokes were in France, at Fontainebleau, when Henrietta was in England; the Knights, including Fanny Vane, were all invited to 'an entertainment', which, Fanny reported, 'was in all respects delightful, elegant and refined – the rendezvous of the best company in France!'[48] Henrietta felt ostracised, as though she had committed some nameless crime; she realised that, despite Harry's protestations, none of their friends came near her in the Knights' home. Where was the dashing Lord Essex, whom Marie-Claire called 'mon fils' out of affection, who was always in Paris, but never near Henrietta? What of Marie-Claire's French stepdaughters or Bolingbroke's friendly Voltaire? Of Henrietta's own mother's relations whom Harry had seen in France? By that spring of 1734 it became apparent that she had no hope of a happy awakening. Her marriage of less than seven years had become as stale a ritual as a Le Roule banquet.

In early March Henrietta and Robert arrived in Grosvenor Street from Paris. It was the day after a serious fire at Devonshire House in Piccadilly.* The next day – 'Tuesday 1 o'clock' – found Henrietta in a flurry, surrounded with carpenters and upholsterers 'whom I follow about in order to get rid of them as soon as possible'. This in itself was a confession of her neurotic state, for previously she would be happily involved in every detail of such schemes. Henrietta's lost world was not waiting to be picked up again that day like a mislaid glove. In particular, the Hertfords were missing from their house farther along the street. And so, with Robert gone round to Devonshire House to see if he could give a home to some of the rescued treasures (Claude Lorrain's *Liber Veritatis* was saved), she sat down to dash off a note to Frances:

> though you were so barbarous as to let me meet with so great a disappointment as that of not finding you at London when I depended upon it, and so inhuman as not to write me a line to comfort me, and so cruel as not to inquire whether I was living or dead when you saw Mama at Hampton Court – mia amabile bench crudele Principessa – I cannot withold my hand from asking how you do . . .

Then she realised that Frances must be 'in a great hurry preparing for the wedding', the much-delayed (because of the bridegroom's indisposition) and extraordinarily lavish wedding of the Princess Royal and Prince William of Orange. This was to take place at the Chapel Royal at St James's Palace on 14 March, but Henrietta was more concerned with the large celebration planned for Hampton Court, for which Robert had already bought his outfit. Her self-doubts crept in; they would probably not attend because they had nowhere to stay nearby, it was too late 'to get what is handsome' for herself. The occasion demanded more than the silk or satin 'sack' which she habitually wore, rather a Court dress, a mantua (a

---

* The fire was so serious that the house had to be rebuilt by William Kent.

boned bodice extended into a train at the back) with hooped petticoats, all of flower-embroidered silk brocade. Henrietta knew 'that it was better not to attempt it without doing it as it ought to be'.[49] All London was talking of the wedding, or rather of the person of the malformed Prince of Orange – 'ce monstre pour coucher avec ma fille' as Queen Caroline told Lord Hervey.[50] Henrietta knew that her mother, Lady St John, and the Hertfords, all as regulars at Court, had their roles to play, but she concluded 'as I have not the honour of belonging to the Court, I shall not be missed in a crowd of so much good company'.[51] By nature she was not the least interested in the Court but the sense of isolation was extreme. To add to her gloom, the Dawley 'farm' was dust-sheeted and quiet, its glories fast fading, as Harry – after nine years there – was becoming restless. Again he was in France, accompanying Marie-Claire in search of a cure for her many ills. She spent some time at Sens, where her stepdaughter was abbess, while he stayed nearby finding the peace to think and write.

In April, with Robert away completing the purchase of Barrells, which he felt to be his hereditary home, Henrietta set off to see Frances, and was surprised that she did not have to travel so far as Marlborough, for the Hertfords, who had eyes for such things, had found an arcadian spot near Windsor. They had leased St Leonard's Hill, on the western edge of the Great Park, an ancient sanctuary dedicated to the saint of Windsor Forest, and clearly marked on John Norden's *Survey of the Honor of Windsor* of 1607. Frances called it her hermitage, 'a paradise'. It was a romantically unkempt house with ill-fitting windows and a leaky roof, a summerhouse, with a view out over the undulating greens of the Forest (which then stretched from Egham and Chobham in the east, to Wokingham and Bray in the west) to the winding Thames and the royal standard flying on the Round Tower at Windsor.[52] It was a magical island, a Camelot in green, and enchanting. The 'dusty crowded streets' of London are forsaken, for where:

> . . . nature spreads a Carpet Green
> And Opens all her Rural Sweets.
> Around us thousand Odors rise
> Or wildly breathe beneath our Feet
> The lofty Elms ascend the Sky's
> While Oaks w'th am'rous branches meet.[53]

Henrietta could not believe her assaulted senses. She was welcomed with open arms and laughter, it was all so overwhelmingly beautiful, her old life returned as if by the wave of a magician's wand. All so intoxicating that she slipped back into her 'bright Marian' persona, and Frances became Renée once more – even though they were now matrons of thirty-five. How easy it was for Henrietta's hurt soul to revive in a household of old friends. Sad to say, but without the dampening weight of Robert's presence, she was livelier than ever, perhaps even euphoric.

It is possible that her sudden cure was wrought by more than old friends, however dear they were. The 'Oaks w'th am'rous branches' were noted by a handsome young poet, John Dalton, a 25-year-old graduate from Oxford just appointed as tutor to the Hertfords' 9-year-old son, Lord Beauchamp. Frances, not wanting her precious Beachy plunged too harshly into his Latin and Greek, gave the young tutor plenty of leisure time, and he was working on his adaptation of Milton's *Comus* for a stage performance. His health was none too good, for his adolescent growth had been cramped in Oxford garrets for nearly ten years. Though he was destined for the Church, he was enjoying a well-earned freedom, his poetic susceptibilities easily charmed by two lively ladies' teasing. Whereas Frances, 'heav'nly Renée', was used to poetic adoration, Henrietta's unhappy head of chestnut curls was turned. A poetic game began between St Leonard's Hill, Henrietta's house in Grosvenor Street, and Oxford, where Dalton went to receive his MA in May. From there he imagined the 'native innocence' of St Leonard's Hill:

> While Philomel from yonder Spray
> So sweetly pours her warbling Throat

Yes, the virtuous Elizabeth Rowe was there too, only Henrietta was wanting:

> One charm I own remains behind
> Till Marian w'th each Muse comes down
> With Cupid Monarch of mankind
> I pity then the empty Town.[54]

Henrietta – 'Venus in Town' – was delayed by illness, but rejoined to 'Adonis at Oxford':

> How cruelly in artfull strain
> The Rural Scene you boast
> Too well I know insulting Swain
> The Happiness I've lost
> No sooner was Adonis fled
> To breathe Parnassian air
> But I with Sorrow dropp'd my head
> And tore my platted Hair.[55]

She had clearly been reading her Milton too, the Attendant Spirit's song:

> . . . Sabrina fair
> Listen where thou art sitting
> Under the glassy, cool, translucent wave,
> In twisted braids of lilies knitting
> The loose train of thy amber-dropping hair;
> Listen for dear honour's sake,
> Goddess of the silver lake,
> Listen and save![56]

Frances replied from her hermitage:

> The Sylvan Scene is vanish'd too
> And charms no more our weary sight
> Lady's sh'd still have something new
> Their wandring Fancy to delight.

'Adonis' wrote to them both from Oxford: 'For Oxford of the Fair bereft / Can scarce produce a single song', finding himself with only 'Nine dull, mute, leaden, old Maids' – the muses on the Clarendon Printing House building – for company. He returned in his thoughts to St Leonard's Hill:

> So when in Paradise the Fair
> Reclin'd beneath ye shade
> To please her was each creature's care
> And round ye brute Creation play'd
> Bear's Elephants new measures try'd
> As in ye medley Dance combin'd
> The frolick Beasts their Gambols ply'd
> Who ne'er before so brightly shin'd.

The 'brute Creation' was not imaginary, for the royal menagerie was at Sandpit Gate, beside the drive up to the Hertfords' house. Henrietta mentioned 'elephants seem'd just arriv'd from France', so they may have all gone to look at the animals together. Or, was her 'elephant' the heavy-footed Robert, for she is wary:

> The Muses anger too I justly fear
> For as their Judgement's just; it is severe
> Witness the Phrygian whom they flay'd alive
> For daring with Apollo once to strive.

She diverted her rhyming 'to express the Homage yet I owe, / To Friendship such as none but she bestow' to Frances, who responded by removing herself from the competition to be young Dalton's muse:

> In Virtue's chace I might perhaps succeed:
> But to grow lovely were a task indeed!
> From time and illness to recall my years
> Regain my Bloom and shed my hoary Hairs.

whereas Henrietta, now happy Henrietta, whose eyes shine

> . . . with mirthfull Wit
> Such should alone his Melody inspire
> For such alone are worthy of his Lyre.[57]

Dalton's reply was clearly and openly addressed 'To the Honble. Mrs. Knight', and he portrayed himself the mooning lover:

> As in the early Morn I took my way
> And o'er the Moss-grown Walks began to stray
> Of yonder Grove whose venerable shade
> A cool retreat from Summer suns has made:
> Where thoughts of you my happy Hours employ,
> Inspire with Gratitude; inspire with Joy . . .

He plunged on in his Miltonic stride, his 'beating Breast by Turns / Now's chill'd with fear, and now with ardour burns' – and on into harmless flattery of 'my Hartford's' virtues, before returning to his addressee:

> To know the Picture Marian needs not roam
> Her kindred soul will own the same at Home
> For link'd by Me in Friendship and in Fame
> They're one soul breathing to a different name.

So, here is an ambitious young poet serenading his employer and her lively friend. He has come into the world from his Oxford retreat to find poetic spirits alive and well in the rarefied air of St Leonard's Hill. Even Elizabeth Rowe, glancing through it all quickly as befits its pace, suspected nothing more than a poetic game. But there is one more short set of verses, by Dalton, addressed to Henrietta, who is now his 'partner' in indebtedness to Lady Hertford, but he is her – Henrietta's – 'willing bard'.

> Yes, Lovely Marian, I submit,
> I bow to beauty and to witt,
> To you I bow, to whom belong
> The charms of Beauty and of song . . .
> Give me the Friendship of my fair,
> Give me that something still more Dear
> In Love's light Plumes being others drest,
> I ask no more, than to be blest.[58]

These are the last words written in the poetic game of the spring of 1734, or at least the last to survive. Frances had all the verses copied into her Commonplace Book, where – fatefully – her friends were at liberty to read them.

CHAPTER FIVE

'Poor Fat Fanfan'

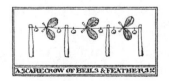

A SCARECROW OF BEILS & FEATHERS

NEITHER HENRIETTA nor the handsome tutor would have dared to compromise the Hertfords, and Dalton was to stay as tutor in their household for the next nine years, so in Frances' eyes he must have been forgiven. However, the mirthless and proud Robert discovered something – perhaps he simply glanced through Frances' Commonplace Book – that made him bundle Henrietta off back to Paris within a few weeks, at mid-summer of 1734. The period that followed was the nadir of her life; chaotic months when not even those most involved knew all of what was happening. These events can only tentatively be pieced together from papers that have survived, finding their way across the years into several different archives. Many of them were kept by Henrietta herself, so perhaps she wanted us to know.

She came back from France the following October, for her father-in-law wrote from Paris: 'It gives me a very sensible Pleasure to find by your last favour that you was then returned back to London in perfect health, and that your dear little ones were so too.' He was happy that her children (whom he had never seen) were 'little altered' for 'it's a Distemper that has spoiled many a pretty face' – so they had escaped smallpox – and Bob Knight 'should have been very much concerned, if they had had that hard fate'.[1] It is the letter of a courteous and kindly man and contains nothing more remarkable than his regards to her parents at Battersea. Letters from her father-in-law were not likely to be amongst her treasures so it is surprising that she kept this one. Perhaps she felt she could appeal to him for help in the storm she knew was coming.

It can only be imagined that when she met Robert in London they had a blazing row because his suspicions had deepened. Even though Henrietta had only just returned to her 'dear little ones' she left them again, and in some distress she fled to Marlborough where she was greeted with 'so much kindness bestowed in so pleasing a manner' as made her grateful.[2] Before long Robert sent their coachman, John Oliver, to Marlborough, with instructions to take her to his sister, Margaretta Vane, at a house in Hampshire. Robert dared not turn up at Marlborough himself for fear of coming face to face with Dalton. Henrietta's letters to Frances, which her friend kept carefully, detail the ensuing dramas of those bleak November days. On the journey to Quarley, a remote village in the downland half way between Andover and Amesbury,

> the roads were so bad some part of the way as to oblige us to have the coach held up, and to get out twice; but the horses were so good, and Mr Oliver so discreet, that we had no accident. The rest of the way was very smooth, and we came through (as I am told) the finest country in the world, for I saw nothing that pleased me. The prospect is unbounded, not one poor tree attempts to obstruct it; but I who love trees was rejoicing to see one at a distance, and when I came near it I found it was a large faggot stuck artfully upon a little mount, which was also artificial, and was I suppose, intended for the guidance of travellers as a beacon is for mariners.*

Unsurprisingly, Henrietta felt 'dragged hither' on a five-hour journey; arriving at 'the poorest village you ever saw' she asked for pen and ink to write to Frances 'but alas! I might as well have asked for wit at a punning brook; at last I got something like soot and water and a skewer with which I scribbled out the letter you said [you]

---

* In this part of Hampshire this might well have been a gibbet.

had (and to be sure could not read)'. She had sent into Andover
(about nine miles) for ink for this letter, which continues:

> I beg [Mr Dalton] may be told I do not expect nor hope to hear
> from him next post. I don't know whether I should trust your
> Ladyship or Mr Knight with my compliments to Lord Hertford;
> but as he has most reason to be jealous, I rather venture to
> assure his Lordship in this letter that I have the greatest regard
> and most inviolable attachment for him, and the greatest esteem,
> the greatest respect, and most grateful sense of his kind reception
> at Marlborough. I dare say nothing more tender, and can say
> nothing more true.

She is using 'jealous' as to mean intolerant of disloyalty, for if Lord
Hertford had dismissed Dalton it would have exposed them all to
scandal, which is presumably what they discussed.*

More cheerfully, the Quarley house that she found herself
in, with 'but one prospect' and that of the churchyard, was more
interesting than she supposed:

> First of all, know there is but one book in the house and that is
> the Farrier's Guide; there is but one picture, and that is a rose
> and crown stained upon the window; there is but one walk near,
> and that is the street of the village . . . the gentlemen are booted
> at 5 in the morning and remain so all day; they hunt or set
> whilst 'tis light, stretch themselves and yawn when 'tis dark, sup
> at 9 and to bed at 10. One of the ladies stays at home and looks
> after her family, the other does nothing at all, or rides a-shooting
> or setting. I stay at home out of complaisance and am idle

---

* This letter seems the key to the situation, and it is no coincidence that John Dalton's
Epistle to the Right Honourable the Lord Viscount Beauchamp, his pupil, which is a long
essay on good and noble behaviour, was mostly written in 1735, when it might be supposed
he was ingratiating himself back into Lord Hertford's favour. John Dalton's *Two Epistles,
the First to a Young Nobleman from his Preceptor, Written in the Year 1735–6 (The Second
to the Right Honourable the Countess of Hartford at Percy Lodge in the Year 1744)* were
published by Robert Dodsley in 1745. 'To a Young Nobleman' opens with 'What is Nobility,
you wish to know, The real substance stripp'd of all its show' and continues in praise of
Lord Beauchamp's forebears and how he may hope to emulate them. (Note: the London
Library's copy, inscribed 'B. Faussett' in copperplate and the date 1745, has had the capital
letters H from *Hartford* and L from *EPISTLE* on the title page carefully cut out = H.L.
Henrietta Luxborough?)

> through necessity . . . when I mentioned having drawn the story
> of Antiochus on a fan (which story I was obliged to inform the
> company of) I was answered 'What! A married woman employ
> herself in drawing love stories?' Upon which I immediately
> changed the discourse to a pudding.*[3]

If she had walked around the church, as she surely did, Henrietta
would have found a Venetian window – an unexpected touch of
artistry – with the inscription 'Gulielmus Benson & Henricus Hoare
F AD 1723'. So, the question arises, was her host none other than
Henry Hoare, he who 'when not on horseback, he is groaning in
an armchair' (he was only twenty-nine) from eating too much
boiled beef? Was the lady with her family Abigail Masham's daughter
Ann, whom Hoare had married about seven years earlier? Henry
Hoare bought his uncle William Benson's Wilbury House, a lovely
house in Inigo Jones' style, just over the Wiltshire border at Newton
Tony, that very year 1734. The Quarley house that they were in had
been his hunting box and 'drinking house' since he was nineteen
and had inherited his family's Fleet Street bank. So the Vanes were
buying, or leasing, the Quarley house, but the Hoares had not yet
moved to Wilbury. His uncle's cultural influence, and Wilbury in
particular, are said to have changed Hoare from a hard-riding
sportsman into a garden-maker (though we know from Harry
Bolingbroke that a man can be both!), and after a trip to Italy he
took his family to Stourhead and began his great garden. His major
planting schemes and the Temple of Flora date from the time of the
rather downtrodden Ann Hoare's death in 1743.[4] Perhaps Henrietta's
spirit in adversity played a tiny part in his conversion.

Just how long the tormented Henrietta remained at Quarley, and
indeed what happened to her for most of 1735, is a mystery; the
only certainty being that her relationship with Robert worsened, so
that at the end of the year he was keeping her a prisoner, shut up

---

* Antiochus II, King of Syria, 3rd century BC, sealed his peace treaty with Ptolemy II of
Egypt by marrying Ptolemy's daughter Berenice, having repudiated his wife Laodice. He
left Berenice and returned to Laodice, who supposedly killed him by poisoning.

in her own house in Grosvenor Street. The Bolingbrokes had left for France in July that year, and it seems impossible that she did not see them go, or that they did not say farewell to the children, but they certainly had no clue as to what was happening. Henrietta was left with the poetess Lady Chudleigh's words to her 'sisters', isolated in her female fate:

> For when that fatal knot is tied, Which nothing, nothing can divide,
> When she the word Obey has said, And man by law supreme has
> made,
> Then all that's kind is laid aside, And nothing left but state and
> pride.[5]

In January 1736, Robert, acting as a very special courier, carried Bolingbroke's *Letter on the Spirit of Patriotism* to England, to its addressee, Lord Cornbury. This was his work of complete disillusion with both the residual Tories and the discontented Whigs in their failure to unite against Walpole. The Bolingbrokes had now decided to stay in France once more, and they divided their time between the Château de Chanteloup near Amboise in Touraine and a hunting lodge at Argeville. There was no more inspiring gardening, just failing health for both of them, especially Marie-Claire, who spent a great deal of her time at the abbey of Sens. Harry needed to sell Dawley for a great deal of money (his father Lord St John, whom they called 'Old Frumps', still showing no signs of dying) in order to pay Bob Knight's 'mortgage', which no one but himself knew about, and retain something for himself and Marie-Claire to live on. He asked his friends Lord Bathurst and Sir William Wyndham to find him a buyer, he was willing to accept £23,000, the sum he had paid for it, if the buyer would also give him one or two thousand pounds a year for each year of his father's life 'not liable to run over three years'.[6] Talking 'up' this ideal figure of £30,000 or thereabouts, hoping this would become Dawley's accepted value, he also thought of persuading Bob Knight into a 'bargain' if Bob would buy Dawley (of which he already owned a part) as a home for Robert and

Henrietta. This plan was completely unknown as yet to Henrietta, and it seems unlikely that he even confided this idea to Robert. In turn, in the early spring of 1736 Harry still knew nothing of the rift between Robert and Henrietta – Robert did not intend him to know. Robert 'courted' the Bolingbrokes and Lord St John, cutting the ground from beneath Henrietta's feet, while keeping her imprisoned upstairs at Grosvenor Street, and forbidding her to write letters to any of those that loved her. That she had paper, pens and ink of good quality readily to hand was one of her obsessions for the rest of her life, the effect of this deprivation.

It was in February that the scandal broke. Had some jealous eyes seen Frances Hertford's Commonplace Book and the spread of rumour taken over? That inveterate gossip Horace Walpole heard that both Frances and Henrietta had overstepped the bounds of decorum. One noble lord confided to his diary his club talk that Robert Knight's wife had been found in bed with her 'doctor' and a London physician was named.[7] Perhaps they really meant 'the Revd Dr Dalton', or perhaps the loyal Henrietta lied to save him. There were plenty of prospective enemies, all those who blamed the Knights for their misfortunes, all the Walpolites who hated Bolingbroke and gleefully maligned his sister. Even her own brother Jack St John later told her smugly that he and his spiteful wife Anne Furnese had 'never listened willingly to these reports till they came so thick and well authorized, so exactly agreeing, all the world telling the same story' that they just had to take notice.[8] Robert, now a Member of Parliament and so jealous of the status and respect he had clawed back from the South Sea Bubble days, could not abide the gossip. Henrietta had struck him where it hurt most – she had shamed him – and his only remedy was to be rid of her. Divorce was out of the question – only obtainable by an expensive and very public Act of Parliament that would prolong his shame – and so he planned a private deed of separation. He could not bear to be in the same house with her, and gave her the alternatives, to which she replied, 'Liberty is so sweet that it is more natural for me to chuse to be in a remote cottage Free, than at home a Prisoner, But as it appears to my Friends that ye latter will be best for my family and as to ye world, I will consent to it, provided that ... [if] I should find my Confinement insupportable or ye air necessary, that I may then go to some Lodging in ye Country.'[9] Robert was adamant that he would look after the children and she had forfeited all her rights to see them, which upset her most of all. He was characteristically self-righteous, aloof and inflexible. His one concession was to allow her to go to her mama at Battersea to consider her situation.

Lady St John had but one solution, that Henrietta should plead for forgiveness, and – at least she had writing materials there – she wrote these curious 'coppy' drafts which she kept, but which have the air of the Conduct Book about them. She addressed Robert:

> my dearest Life whom I love beyond anything notwithstanding the appearances against me, for God sake let me see you and ask your pardon on my knees for as much as I have been guilty of, which I own is more than prudence or decency allows, but yet I swear the passion was platonick and is no more. Punish me in what way you please but there is nothing [worse] I can feel except that of not living with you which would be the death of yr unfortunate wife Henrietta.[10]

There was another, more personal effort:

> My dearest life for god sake consider what [effect] this parting will have and try to bring yourself to be under the same roof with me for the sake of your dear children and what Mr Knight and his wife will say – Mama is so good as to wish it you know how terrible the world's censures are. If you could pass over this you would ever find me behave as you can desire or direct. I take my solemn oath that this silly but platonick passion is the only one I have ever had and yet I now despise myself and the object of it whose face I will never see more, nor write to him. Try me for a little while ... I am in ye most terrible affliction, incapable as yet of shedding tears, if you can be molified for god's sake endeavour to hide what has passed to ye world.[11]

On second thoughts she realised that her mother-in-law, Anne Knight, would be triumphant.

The pleas were pointless, she may not even have sent them. She returned to Grosvenor Street and her gaolers who were most likely her own servants under duress. Robert set new conditions – she was still not to send letters but she could be visited by her parents and a few other carefully chosen people whom she did not particularly wish to see – but it was all clearly impossible. How could she be imprisoned in a busy London street where she was known? Her theatrical brother Holles, who was one of Robert's permitted visitors, would not keep the secret, and would not Frances Hertford (who was, of course, forbidden) not batter at the door until she was allowed to see the prisoner of Grosvenor Street? Soon there would be an even greater scandal.

By mid-April Henrietta had agreed to try a winter at Barrells. Her 'prison-house' was to be let to contribute towards an allowance of £500 a year for her, and Robert had settled that little Harry would be going to boarding school, with a tutor to look after him in the holidays, and little Henrietta would go to her grandparents at Battersea. Henrietta asked for 'a moment or two to recollect my thoughts' after he told her all this, but he left abruptly, though leaving her pen and paper on which to write to him: 'You asked me I think whether I was resolved to continue at Barrels green in case I went thither? To which I have nothing to answer but what I have already given under my hand, which is that I will go thither & endeavour to live there as you desire meaning to stick to my written consent as you do by your written resolution.' If he troubled her while she was there, or there was 'any other unforeseen accident', then she wished to live in a place of her own choosing. 'Since we are upon a topick I generally shun,' she continued,

> . . . give me leave to ask whether it might not be better [for] avoiding future misunderstandings to settle ye £500 you propose on me now [while] we are both in Town to have it done regularly; so in case I should be obliged to quit Barrells there may

be no more dispute. This I only mention to avoid any future discourse on so dreadfull a subject since you remain inexorable – any mark of tenderness or forgiveness from you would throw me at yr feet, but ye contrary gives me what degree of courage I have. May all happiness attend you! Were you to restore me to yr heart there is nothing besides that I would not sacrifice. Think what a punishment it is for my crime to be deprived of your esteem & of my children's company: the rest is not worth naming.[12]

A week later Harry wrote to tell her (though it is likely she did not see the letter for some time) that he was going to Paris to put his Dawley proposal to Bob Knight: 'it shall not be my fault if it does not succeed for I will make it such a Bargain as no man of sense and sentiment would decline – my heart is set upon it. I would have you and yours profit of my expense and not a Stranger . . .'[13] Bob Knight and Robert, being now more apart, were on better terms, and Bob had written affectionately to his son telling him that he would do all he could to obtain Dawley if that was what Robert wanted. This letter had crossed with Robert's presentation of his own case as to why he and Henrietta were to part. When Harry Bolingbroke arrived in Paris, confident of his success, Bob Knight declined, so cleverly, and parted with Harry on the best of terms and still without telling him about Henrietta's fate.[14] The old Chief Cashier had lost none of his cunning. Harry wrote to Robert regretting that the 'project I had formed, and carried as far as lay in my power, for ye sake of you and yours, and not for any convenience or advantage of my own, was not embraced, or att most was embraced in such a way as could not become effected'. He was under the impression that as the 'winter campaigne' of parliamentary doings was over 'you are going I suppose, into ye Summer quarters. Those you have in Warwickshire require to be pleasant, a dry Season, for tho' it be very long time since I was in ye country, I remember it as a dirty one.'[15]

On 10 May Harry penned Henrietta an affectionate note, of which only a fragment survives: 'I am a little surprised to hear that you sold your house, and retire into ye distant part of ye Kingdom.'[16]

Robert, having the nerve to correspond with Harry on matters of politics but still not confide his personal matters, received a sharp reply at the end of June. 'I come to a point which touches me more nearly,' wrote Bolingbroke,

> When you not only decline the offer I made you in ye warmth of my friendship for you and yours, but sell your house in Town, retire into Warwickshire, put yr Son to School att Chelsea, and yr daughter to ye worst you could have chose at Battersea, I protest to you, I am startled. You are pleased to say you suffer much in mind, because you know you must suffer much in my opinion. I do not change my opinion so easily; and of all changes, that hardest to me is thinking ill of a friend, but I am in yet some surprise att all these sudden events . . .

And yet still he does not press Robert to 'an éclaircissement', an explanation.[17]

Meanwhile, Henrietta's brother Jack had defected completely: he begged Robert to come and stay at Lydiard, adding

> Entre Nous, I must tell you my notion; which is if I had been her husband, by God I wd have dated my Ease & Happiness from ye hour she gave me a justifiable cause to part with her . . . [and, after the next swig of port] . . . I should literally have hanged myself if she wd not have play'd ye whore and given me ye occasion of Separation she has done to you . . . You'll think me mad for this Notion, but by ye Eternal god I think you now a happy man. I've never thought you so before – pray come. We insist upon it.[18]

To Henrietta, eight days later, he is soberly moralising, having heard both the gossip and now Robert's story, ending: ' 'Tis most unhappy and I feel for you, but what's blameable will be so, what is not need fear no Reflection, I flatter myself still ye latter will be your lot, that it may be is ye most sincere and hearty wish of your affectionate Brother and true friend J St. John.'[19]

Whilst Robert travelled about the country, Henrietta was kept prisoner in Grosvenor Street throughout the hot summer days.

Though she had her books she had soon realised that when only books were left, they lost their power. At times she sank into a depression, even feeling that she had not long to live. She had been sorting through the love letters she had resolved to burn, which her reason told her was the proper thing to do, but her distress – and lack of anything to write on – made her draft a letter to Robert on the back of one of these letters, which consequently survived. The fragmentary love letter, unaddressed but in Dalton's hand, was at the end of the affair:

> How different is your style already even when security permit you to speak the dictates of your heart! Pardon this reproach, perhaps my fears belie you, but I can't help remembering the time when one hour or two brought me some publick or private letter of your passionate tender sentiments wrote in your own hand; in one of the latter I find these words which I will repeat and answer
>
> 'I love you still nay more, & must ever do so unless you pour into my wounded soul the dear balm of your Compassion & teach me by gentle means to conquer it –
> pardon the present answer those words suggest to me. I have poured the balm & it has worked its effect for your passion is conquered. I expect at least thanks for the cure & might in vain ask the same Remedy in return for myself for Alas! Tis not in your power to give it since Vertue has not prevailed. Time alone can work the Cure'.[20]

These are the only glimpses into the affair that survive; there is no mention of John Dalton's name though everyone who has seen these papers and known of Henrietta's life has come to the conclusion that it was the handsome tutor. Love clearly made him ingenious in carrying on an illicit correspondence with his employer's best friend, and it is no wonder that Henrietta felt her utmost apologies were due to Lord Hertford. Her name was not spoken in that household for six years.* And, on Henrietta's account,

---

* I am loath to bring hindsight to her aid, but in after years the Reverend, later Canon, Dalton did have a 'reputation'.

was she not yearning for love in that alien life into which her marriage had plunged her? On the reverse of the paper, to Robert, she drafted 'I again repeat that ye most I ever granted to ye person I am suspected of was Compassion, which I have often accused my self of as a crime, tho' I'm now accused of worse.'[21] As Lady Chudleigh wrote on behalf of her and all others like her who had angered their husbands:

> Fierce as an eastern prince he grows,
> And all his innate rigour shows:
> Then but to look, to laugh, or speak,
> Will the nuptial contract break.
> Like mutes, she signs alone must make,
> And never any freedom take,
> But still be governed by a nod,
> And fear her husband as her god:
> Him still must serve, him still obey,
> And nothing act, and nothing say,
> But what her haughty lord thinks fit,
> Who, with the power, has all the wit.[22]

Just in time for her thirty-seventh birthday, on 15 July, Robert wrote from Kingsclere in Hampshire*[23] that: 'I will not now say anything by way of Reproach for what is past the Power of Human Nature to remedy, but this much I will say in justice to myself, that had you always thought as you now seem to think, we might both have been happy.' It was, it transpired, her spirit that angered him most; that she would argue with him, that she was not contrite in his presence, that there was 'too much talking' especially by Lady St John to the Battersea servants, and that Henrietta did not have the temperament to be quiet, to 'fear her husband as her god' nor had she ever done so. She was too much for him. He was forever 'worked into a fit of passion' over provocations, and now they came from society in general as well he felt she 'insulted him more than ever'. For that reason his birthday wish was 'that it would never be

---

* Where, if hindsight prompts me again, he was probably pursuing a mistress!

proper that we should ever meet again in this World, but be assured that I sincerely wish you happiness in the next'. Perhaps Jack St John had more than a grain of truth in his understanding, that it was not so much any person, as Henrietta's personality, that was her 'downfall'.[23]

When Henrietta at last escaped to Warwickshire in that July of 1736, to the lushness and warmth of high summer in that leafiest of countrysides, her mood changed quickly into a businesslike approach to her new challenge. Liberty was immediately sweet after her London imprisonment and the nightmares of that other 'prison' on the Faubourg St Honoré were banished for ever.

Harry found letters from Robert, who finally had the grace to explain things, waiting for him at Argeville after he had been travelling in Provence. In his reply, dated 30 August, Harry confesses himself 'stunned' with surprise. At first he hoped that 'a mistake on one side, and an indiscretion on ye other' could be overcome and 'might be conducted as to make no noise' – as it was in many marriages of his acquaintance.[24] When he read about the separation in Robert's second letter, he was puzzled that his Henrietta, whom he thought he knew better than anyone, though perhaps discounted the distance between their lives in the seven years since they were together at Dawley, 'should prostitute herself to such a low fellow'. Dalton's crime was worse in Harry's opinion, in that he was 'the dullest Poet in Christendom' – but then he judged against the genius of Alexander Pope! Had Robert really got it right, Harry implied, the evidence seemed so uncertain, even though there was apparently an intercepted love letter, which Harry suggested had been exaggerated by gossip, or – knowing Henrietta – was a 'jeu d'esprit'.[25] After that he left Henrietta for his own concerns, being particularly annoyed that Robert had let him carry on 'consorting with your Father' over Dawley in ignorance. He gave his verdict on his stepmother, Lady St John, who had just died (her end hastened by the distress of Henrietta's troubles, some said) which gave him 'neither joy nor sorrow. Silly as she was, she had not enough to be ye cause, during a long course of years, of much mischief. A wise woman would have found her account better in a contrary conduct.'[26] He would write to Jack and Holles but 'I cannot be hypocrite enough to condole'.[27] Marie-Claire added to her friend Lady Denbigh, 'Dear Lady St Jean is dead, I think it is the best thing she has done since she came into the world. They say her husband and children are no more grieved about it than I am.'[28]

Harry's deepest bitterness was reserved for his father: 'I think my writing to him att this time would gall with him, who never knew either himself or me for a desire of Reconsilement, and on ye prospect of advantage . . . I expect none, as I never received any in point of fortune from him, and from his gift, in ye whole course of my life.' Harry then cuts to the heart of his accusation to Lord St John, the 'paternal Tyranny' of his youth still rankled, and he 'could never brook any Tyranny' as a result.[29] He knew that he was speaking for Henrietta, too.

He wrote to her at Barrells on 25 September: 'I am this day [i.e. on 16 September] 58 years of age' – and he was feeling every minute of it. He had dwelt on the whole of his relationship with his father, from whom he had never had £500 'whereas he has had of my free gift some thousands besides what he forced from me by taking advantage of circumstances I was in'. He meant Lydiard, which Jack enjoyed, and Battersea, which was rightfully the home of his old age, if only old Lord St John would die. This enmity prevented Harry from ever going to Battersea while his father was alive, which – had it been possible – he said, would have stiffened their father's opposition to Robert's getting entirely his own way. He asked Henrietta to let him know immediately of 'any quicker or more remarkable decay than ordinary in him'[30] that they might both be saved. Undoubtedly Harry's return, had it happened in that autumn of 1736, would have changed her fate. She knew in her heart that her beloved brother was her ally, but his letters only confirmed her experiences, that as he roamed France wallowing in his own debts and disappointments, and in worries over Marie-Claire's health, his ability to help her in a practical way was nil. Marie-Claire, convalescing with her stepdaughter the Abbess of Sens, told Lady Denbigh, 'our poor fat Fanfan is in Warwickshire. I am sorry for her; how stupid all that is.'[31]

From the Hertfords there was a dignified silence. When Frances and Henrietta were to renew their correspondence after a space of six years Frances would confess that she had not known what to do for the best for her friend, and in her indecision, remained silent. One of the conditions of Henrietta's 'banishment' to Barrells was that she was forbidden to travel to London (and thus presumably missed her mother's funeral) or on the Bath road, which meant to St Leonard's Hill or Marlborough. Were these restrictions entirely Robert's proposals, or was he pleasing Lord Hertford, who was concerned over Henrietta's influence on Frances? For the men to side with each other was quite usual. Though Henrietta was partly protected (at least from physical violence as far as we know) by her father's status and her own, there was the parallel case of Ellen Stock, who was subjected to 'cruel usage' and appealed to her brother, who promptly worked with her husband to arrange the separation. Ellen, too, was restricted in her travelling but at least she was allowed to see her daughter three times a year.[32]

CHAPTER SIX

'Asteria'

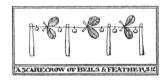

HENRIETTA'S FIRST LETTERS from Barrells were pleas for news of her children. Harry's tutor M. Gaillardy assured her that he was 'perfectly well' having clearly been instructed to impart the very minimum humanity required, and Lord St John was hardly more forthcoming. Henrietta gathered that her daughter 'behaves so as to lessen the trouble you take with her'. She added that 'M. Gaillardy mentions Mr Knight's being gone into Hampshire; wherever he goes I wish him health and happiness. I am, my Lord, Your Lordship's most dutiful daughter, H. Knight.'[1] She was anxious – even optimistic at first – that her children would be able to come to Barrells, until she was told that Harry, who would be eight at Christmas 1736, was under too strict an educational regime to travel so far. What about little Henrietta? In early December Harry wrote from Argeville to say that Robert had been to stay and 'we have had a good deal of discussion ... we spoke of your desire to see your daughter and he entered very clearly into the reasonableness of the thing, but he seemed to think, rightly enough, that it could only be for a night, whilst you continued so far out of the world, and in a place where your child could not have the necessary improvements of education.'[2] That a few days with her mother would be more beneficial than a month with a governess was not a consideration, or rather it would create a precedent that Robert did not wish to honour. Somehow, by letters and a very few meetings, Henrietta retained her daughter's affection, which was a remarkable thing as they were not to spend a night under the same roof until Maddalena Henrietta (as she was to call herself when she was older) was married. Little Henrietta hardly ever saw her brother, and though once Frances Hertford told Henrietta that he 'respected' his mother, Harry Knight became very much his father's creature.

To her first letters from Barrells Henrietta added a footnote: 'Please write to Henley-in-Arden, Arden being an old Saxon word for a wood.'[3] She 'who loved trees' had surely looked up the Duke's words in *As You Like It*:

> Are not these woods
> More free from peril than the envious court?[4]

She had looked about her and found immediate comfort in the sheltering wood. Moreover it was Shakespeare's wood, the Forest of Arden. Henley was only nine miles north of Stratford-upon-Avon, where Shakespeare had been brought up in his father's house and glover's shop on Henley Street, and less from Mary Arden's Wilmcote and Snitterfield. Shakespeare had been dead for 120 years, and though John Aubrey had started nosing out the legends in about 1680, it was still an unmarked countryside, innocent of fame, yet ripe with gleeful gossip from the locals for the literary inquisitor. Henrietta laughed at the tales: for her Will's ghost was just another vague comforting presence.[5]

Barrells – the name was derived from an early-fourteenth-century owner named Barel – was less than two miles out of Henley to the west, on the road to nowhere in particular except Worcestershire. This was a remote landscape of fields and woods and – as Harry Bolingbroke had recalled – muddy lanes; a fertile land, well watered from springs and streams flowing into the River Alne, and potentially good farmland. Henrietta would be gardening on clay, but in a clearing in old woodlands deep in leaf mould and in cow-grazed meadows. The house was set on rising ground, south of the road with an open view southwards to the ancient site of Oldberrow. It was protected by woods from the west and north-easterly winds, a home that had become well-practised at combat with the elements in this very particular place – what we would call its own micro-climate. It was a plain house of stuccoed brick, with two wings projecting forwards on the west entrance front, with a carriage sweep. It had been the home of two spinster Miss Knights and the garden was almost certainly dishevelled, as old ladies' gardens are apt to become. Henrietta made an immediate decision to turn the 'farm yard' on the east side of the house into a kitchen garden, because it would be much nicer to see from her windows.

Barrells had belonged to the Knights since 1554, a decade before Shakespeare's birth, when a Robert Knight, son of Nicholas Knight of Beoley on the Worcestershire border, had purchased it. For five generations the Knights had farmed and enlarged their estate to about 400 acres, gaining respect in the area – John Knight had founded the Knights' Charity of Ullenhall in the seventeenth century.[6] His brother – another Robert – had gone to London and become the prosperous sugar baker, the father of Bob Knight, so Henrietta's husband had bought the estate from his cousin Raleigh Knight. Now, Henrietta found that most of the land was tenanted as part of Oldberrow Court Farm, but she had as much as 56 acres in hand, including her Great Meadow and her 29 acres of woods, a home field for her own cows and her garden.[7] She was proudly, though sometimes frantically, a farmer – or farmeress – as surely as Harry had been at Dawley and with the same necessity, right from the outset.

Though Robert wrote and spoke liberally to Harry of how he was willing to make the house comfortable, the reality was rather different. Henrietta's 89-year-old Aunt Cholmondeley, her stalwart and outspoken friend, 'cursed that damned wet ditch she's thrown into' – adding 'that she lives is a miracle; for when she was sent, there were not half the windows up, no doors to the house, and the roof uncovered'.[8] In fact, Francis Smith of Warwick's men were still working on the house, and their work carried on throughout the winter.[9] It was so bad that she asked permission to go to stay with the Cholmondeleys at Vale Royal in Cheshire, or with her Soame cousins, but such was Robert's tyranny that both her father and Harry advised her not to be 'troublesome' to her relatives and to stay quietly in the damp and the cold. So her first winter was spent grappling with the discomforts and it taught her fortitude, if she needed such a lesson. Her first priority was a small and warm room of her own, so she directed the workmen to convert the dairy (which would have been on the cool, north side of the house) into her library, a low-ceilinged room with bookcases and 'sixpenny' wallpaper, and an open log fire that gave her her favourite 'chimney corner'. The walls were hung with Frances Hertford's flower paintings, which she wanted 'as near me as possible that I may have the satisfaction of seeing them constantly'.[10] She told Harry of her successes, for on 20 March of her first spring, 1737, he congratulated her: 'I am rejoiced to hear that your books and your gardens amuse you so well in your Solitude.'[11]

This was her first turning point, for she believed that once 'that boisterous baneful month of March is over and the sun resumes his power' she could expect to spend more and more time in her garden.[12] How quickly she had become the proverbial countrywoman! If her mornings were for her housekeeper, the dairy, the linen closet and 'business' – 'letting leases, receiving rents, paying parish dues and [being] anxious lest a shower of rain should soil my hay' as she later listed her chores, then fine afternoons released her to the garden. This became the pattern of her days.[13]

She would accomplish the art of solitude, as she did so many other arts and crafts, and cold evenings found her clinging to her chimney corner with a favourite book. But, of course, she was not alone in her exile. Unlike the lordly Harry and certainly the pompous Robert, she had a saving grace in her ability to 'get on' with all kinds of people, especially those in her household and garden. To give him his due, Robert had been sensible on the matter of servants:

'It appears to me that Smith, the Cook, [a] laundry maid and [a] country housemaid will be necessary – I mention her because she will serve in the house & to milk one, two or even three cows, which is the most you can want ... James I take it for granted you will keep & also John who is able to drive a Coach, and the Chaise in the French manner very well which will be useful to you.' James, her London steward, the son of Alice James, her grandmother's treasured servant at Battersea, and Smith, her own maid (these were most likely her Grosvenor Street 'gaolers'), both loved her enough to brave the wilds of Warwickshire, and they stayed. The other maids were local girls, but invariably lively. John, the stableman who could drive, was not to be confused with John Oliver the coachman who had taken her on that dreadful drive across the Hampshire downs. He had brought her and her belongings to Barrells, but he was instructed to return to London at Michaelmas. Henrietta could not afford to keep a coach, at least for several years, and relied upon her chaise. There was also Pherry, the outdoors-man, who was paid £10 a year and the feed for his one cow (but he was not to eat in the house), and she was to find a gardener. James and John were paid £8 a year, with their keep all-found. 'Then,' Robert had summed up, 'your family would consist of 4 women servants, James and John and this gardener, in all seven which will be necessary and I believe as far as I can judge sufficient'.[14] It will be remembered that he was not paying their wages, which had to come out of Henrietta's allowance or her rents. She was in fact, although it did not occur to her for some time, both acting as chatelaine and estate manager, putting all her rents and her own money back into Barrells, and acting (unpaid) on Robert's behalf. Her allowance of £500 a year came from her own invested capital (managed by Robert) and from letting the Grosvenor Street house, on which the lease was in her name, secured by Lord St John as part of her wedding settlement.

But, as she repeatedly said in one way or another, money was 'a topick I generally shun'[15] and the happiness of her household was her priority. Word travelled around the neighbourhood that she was a fine person to work for, rich by local standards, and she was soon satisfied, if not actually besieged, with willing helpers. The number of cows rose from three to five, and she looked upon them 'as a peculiar blessing to me, who am indebted to them for perfect health'.[16] The dairymaid's butter and cheese became a source of pride and the envy of her visitors. Sheep and goats, and an ever-changing population of chicken, geese, ducks and even turkeys, all of which she liked to see about her, as well as the kitchen garden which she managed with local help until she could afford a trained Scottish gardener, all contributed to the soon hospitably overflowing larder. It was as if she had dug deep into herself and found the remembered spirit of her grandmother Johanna – or perhaps the more distant ghost of Lady Margaret Beaufort – which had brought all these good things to her aid.

Barrells' self-sufficiency, imposed at first by force, and then regularly by the impassibility of the muddy lanes, was soon established as a matter of pride. Even apart from Robert's restrictions on her travelling to seek out her children or to see her father or the Hertfords, Henrietta had not the means in her first years. In fine weather the light chaise could take her into Henley or Wootton Wawen, and possibly to Stratford, but hardly farther, and otherwise she walked to her neighbours or sent the farm cart for supplies. It was strange that Henrietta, who had seen so much of the great world, found this little world so comforting: her life had been marked by the freedoms to enjoy herself followed by the suffocating confinements of the Faubourg St Honoré and Grosvenor Street which she was powerless to alleviate. Here in leafy Warwickshire, within ten miles round, she rediscovered her freedom. 'Liberty is so sweet,' she had once told Robert, and here it became so, and this was no confinement at all. It took her about two years to settle in, an achievement which her redoubtable Aunt Cholmondeley reported to Frances Hertford, remarking on Henrietta's 'spirit' and that 'she finds a respect in that neighbourhood which may reproach those who abandoned her to be sent thither'.[17]

Occasionally the great world broke in, but usually with news from those she loved. Harry Bolingbroke was still negotiating for her to see her children: 'constantly you cannot because they must be in a situation of having masters to educate them & the boy especially but sometimes I should think you might'. He assured her that her allowance could not be taken away from her 'because you would find yourself backed by all your own family & even by your Father-in-law', and he was writing to Bob Knight on her behalf. Opinions were shifting. Harry reported: 'I hear from England that my Lord St John is grown very intimate with my Lady Hertford, & that he has broke with your Husband & shuts his door to him. I join these two circumstances together because I believe one to be a consequence of the other and am apprehensive that it may do hurt; good it can do none, most certainly.'[18] There were constant terms of endearment and affectionate notes from Marie-Claire, which were a great comfort. Whether Henrietta actually saw Harry is unclear. He was still struggling to sell Dawley, hoping to buy 'some little habitation such as may suit an old, retired, attainted Philosopher & Hermit to vegetate, languish and dye in' in England, but still really enjoying France: 'As I was a farmer in England, I am a huntsman in France; and am less diverted from the latter than I was from the former Employment.'[19] In early 1737 he was prepared to give Dawley away for as little as £6,000, and if that fell through he would live there 'in a very retired manner' as well as at Argeville. In the summer of 1738 he was staying with his old friend Pope at Twickenham for several months, when he surely made the effort to see Henrietta – although there is no clue in her later correspondence that he ever saw Barrells. Dawley was eventually sold the following year, to Edward Stephenson for £26,000, and so Harry's financial troubles were at last over. If Henrietta ever regretted that she was never the mistress of Dawley – there she could have made a garden as famous as Chiswick's that might have lasted until today – there is no record of her ever mentioning it.

In her little countryside Henrietta made her social breakthrough by going to church. In fine weather she took the 'rugged walk' over Mount Pleasant, a rutted and rough lane even in August, to the old chapel of St Mary's in the fields at Ullenhall. Sometimes she drove into Henley, but she soon found the attractions of going farther south on the road towards Stratford, to St Peter's at Wootton Wawen, where generations of Knights had worshipped. At St Peter's, a majestic church dating from Saxon times but not in good repair in her days, the vicar was John Reynolds. He had been there since 1730, a King's College, Cambridge man, and both he and his wife were to become her lasting, faithful friends.*

St Peter's church stands high on a windy hill, and it is one of the few places in her countryside that Henrietta would still recognise today. She must have walked up that narrow curving path between the gravestones, clutching at her hat, many times, and entered through the well-worn doorway and down two craggy stone steps – carefully down in her delicately embroidered town shoes. A curious time warp is conjured across the church, for having passed through one old door, there is another, a palimpsest in wormy wood and battered stone, a Tudor arch framing a Norman doorway – and suddenly a company of unnumbered souls floods in, the worshippers from the centuries that have gathered here. It is but a fleeting impression, but here was the comfort of the ages in her exile, and then the friendly Mr Reynolds, ever enquiring for her health and welfare. He, too, was interested in gardens, full of suggestions that she must see the Archers' Umberslade nearby, and Christopher Wren's (the son of the architect) Wroxhall, and how marvellous it would be to make an expedition to the Lytteltons' at Hagley. It was most likely John Reynolds who introduced her to the tall, fair and handsome, sixtyish Squire Somerville, the last of an ancient line living at Edstone Hall, just south of Wootton.[20]

---

* Revd John Reynolds died in 1757; he was rector at Peter's Wootton Wawen and at Somerville Aston, where William Somerville's cousin Lord Somerville lived, and where Henrietta went to visit Mr and Mrs Reynolds.

William Somerville was her first poet in the wilderness, her first encounter that made her feel that Barrells was not merely worthwhile, but had delightful compensations. Somerville was an elegant character, not blubbery with too much port or beef, but still lean and vigorous, his body honed by hunting. He had had a great success with his long poem *The Chace*, published in 1735, with its vivid description of his hunting passions and landscapes. He was not without a sense of humour, and his current work was a burlesque in blank verse *Hobbinol, or the Rural Games*, which he was going to dedicate to William Hogarth. He had been to see these 'Cotswold Olympics', a festival originally founded by a lawyer, a Captain Dover, who lived at Stanway and conducted the games for forty years, dressed as a cavalier and riding a white horse. The captain had died in 1641 but his games had been revived after Charles II's restoration, and now crowds came from sixty miles around to watch the cudgel playing, wrestling, tilting at the quintain, walking-on-hands races, a country dance of virgins, horse racing and hare coursing – the hare not to be killed – and other such wonders.*[21]

Somerville was sociable, with a great number of interesting friends ranged at greater distances than Henrietta's small circuit, and he was free to entertain her, or more or less so. His wife Mary Bethell had been dead for about seven years, and they had no children, but he did have a mother in her nineties, who was entitled to a third of his income, and demanding of her due. He was therefore in debt, and had made his Edstone estate over to a Scottish relative in return for a settlement. Somerville's life revolved around his horses, his beagles, fox and otter-hounds. Now, suddenly, in his sixties this lively woman had walked into it. For a few years (sadly, it was but three or four) he was fancy free, and a seeming contradiction in terms – a poetic hunting squire – and he found Henrietta enchanting. He rode over the fields from Edstone to Barrells to tell her so. 'Marian' was forgotten, she was newly christened 'Asteria':

* The games survived until 1852 and have recently been revived, taking place in 2005.

As o'er Asteria's fields I rove
The blissful seat of peace and love
Ten thousand beauties round me rise
And mingle pleasure with surprise.
By nature blest in every part
Adorn'd with every grace of art
This paradise of blooming joys
Each raptur'd sense, at once employs.
Who formed this fair enchanting scene?
Pardon, ye grots, ye crystal floods!
Ye breathing flowers! Ye shady woods!
Your coolness now no more invites;
No more your murmuring stream delights,
Your sweets decay, your verdure's flown,
My soul's content on her alone.[22]

This was Somerville's 'Song to Asteria' which he presented to
Henrietta. It survived amongst her papers, and she allowed it to be
published by Robert Dodsley at the end of her life. The 'blissful seat
of peace and love' and the 'paradise of blooming joys' would appear
to be Barrells, and the latter could mean her bluebell woods or the
clouds of Queen Anne's lace and buttercups that wreathed her
meadows in June, rather than suggesting she had already made her
garden. The grottoes, crystal floods and shady woods which attract
him no more are features in his friend William Shenstone's garden
at Halesowen. It is likely that Henrietta met Shenstone at Edstone,
but she did not visit his garden nor did they become friends until
after Somerville's death.

Another of Somerville's songs reveals more:

How do busy Fools employ
Ages, barren of all joy?
Pow'r & sordid gain pursuing
Proud, triumphant in undoing
At Asteria's board refin'd
Bless our ears, & charm our eyes
Who so happy, who so wise?

There is a first mention of one of Henrietta's dinner parties that were to become so celebrated for the good food and even better conversation. Somerville continues:

> Still improving, ever gay
> Can we better spend the day
> In so mild, so pure a Light
> Can we ever think it night
> Tyrant sleep, intruding pow'r
> Claim not thou this blissful hour
> Whilst we rival those above;
> Thus to learn, & thus to love![23]

These are the early glimpses of Henrietta happily at home and William, perhaps, in love. She found that 'he retained all the vivacity of youth', that he was a most agreeable neighbour 'because he was not only very obliging, but very entertaining, and was continually making some song or other piece of poetry'. Unfortunately, she is speaking in the past tense. Somerville became suddenly ill in June 1742, just after his 98-year-old mother's death. He appears to have had a stroke, for Henrietta wrote of his 'understanding' being 'much broke' and she added 'if he lives he'll not be the same man'.[24] William Somerville died in the July, mourned and memorialised as a much loved squire at Wootton.

Had Somerville had the longevity of his mother then Henrietta's life might have continued differently, for he would have brooked no impertinences from Robert Knight. She was always to remember him, but at the time of his death she was so besieged by changes in her own affairs that she had little time to mourn. Her father, 'Old Frumps', had finally died on 24 April, and so at last the Bolingbrokes could come home to Battersea. Harry would be at the heart of affairs to protect her own inheritance, which was a great relief. Robert had always threatened that Lord St John would exclude her from his will if she did not do as she was told, and live quietly and obey those restrictions on her travelling to see her children or the Hertfords. Harry had questioned lawyers on the legality of all this, which had stayed Robert's hand and perhaps convinced Lord St John that his daughter was being maltreated. Now her inheritance was safe, and she hoped it would revive her prosperity, so that she could 'gladly fly' to her 'former amusements'.[25]

Robert, as pompous and unbending as ever, informed her of 'the great change in your circumstances, since our separation (the unhappy cause whereof I shall not now mention)', pointing out that she had nobody to provide for but herself, but that he 'must maintain and give portions to my Son and Daughter'. Up to now her income had been £210 a year, which Robert had made up to £500 from her own assets. He was now prepared to allow her to benefit from the legacy from her youngest brother Holles, who had died in 1738, and from her father's legacy, on condition that she signed Articles of Separation absolving him from responsibilities for her debts and any pension due should she outlive him.[26] Holles 'Holly' St John's affairs had been settled and he had left Henrietta almost everything he had. He was her favourite, her non-judgemental, mischievously 'theatrical' brother, who had been only twenty-eight when he died.[27] He had left her £8,000 plus a share in his residual estate and some shares in Covent Garden Theatre, which yielded her £17 a year. Her total annual income from Holly's legacy, invested at 3½ per cent, was £407 a year. Her father's £1,000 a year, plus a share of his residual estate and the sale of the Albemarle Street house, invested at 3½ per cent, amounted to £625; making her an annual income of £1,032, a very respectable figure.[28] Henrietta was so relieved that at first she did not think to point out that most of this would be spent on Barrells.

In the larger world, Prime Minister Robert Walpole's resignation in early 1742 meant that Bob Knight was, after over twenty years in exile, finally offered his pardon in the summer. It cost him £10,000, and it took another and equal amount to discharge the claims that the South Sea Company stockholders felt they had on him, but at least some old grievances were mended. His return was not easy, for there were difficulties in repurchasing Luxborough, his heart's desire, which was in trust for the young son of Sir Joseph Eyles, who had bought it from the South Sea creditors. When he succeeded, the house, perhaps because it was so shoddily and speedily built, needed extensive repairs. Henrietta wrote to her father-in-law, feeling that he still thought kindly of her, but she received a sharp reply informing her that the state of her relationship with his son meant that he had nothing to say.

More important to her was her reconciliation with Frances Hertford, which came about via the Hertfords' daughter, now Lady Betty Smithson, who gathered that Henrietta had no longer the status of an outcast, and wrote to her. A letter from Frances soon followed – 'neither time nor absence have made a change in my affection toward you,'[29] she wrote, and to Henrietta this was 'an inexpressible pleasure'.[30] They were soon launched into catching up, Henrietta reporting on her six years in the country, how she was 'grown used to it so much that I should be out of my element at a Court or in a city'. For Frances there had been many changes, she had retired from the Court after Queen Caroline's death in 1737, they had given up St Leonard's Hill – reluctantly but it was so tumble-down and they would have had to buy it and rebuild it – and acquired Lord Bathurst's Richings, the 'extravagante bergerie' which they renamed Percy Lodge. Frances adored it, she thought it 'like a scene in Arcadia' which seemed a hundred miles from London. She had a greenhouse filled with oranges, myrtle, geraniums and oleander, and an 'agreeable room', a kind of loggia, for drinking tea, playing cards or sitting with a book on summer evenings. She had winding walks through her woods, a grotto hung with periwinkles and shaded by beeches and elms, and sheltered seats or arbours, laced with lilacs, honeysuckles, 'seringas' and laurels, set about in sun and shade. Though she knew full well that it was 'almost insolent' to suggest they had improved upon Lord Bathurst's handiwork – which Henrietta would remember from her Dawley days – Frances indulged herself in a description of additions 'which I flatter myself you would approve of . . .'. '[Y]ou may remember a gravel-pit on the left hand as you went from the greenhouse . . . this my Lord has formed into an oval grass-plot, with a gravel walk around it at the bottom; and upon this plot our orange trees stand in summer.' This orange-dell, of which Frances had the banks planted with shrubs and flowers, brought back memories of Lord Burlington's famous Orange Grove at Chiswick, which both Frances and Henrietta had visited. Henrietta regretted that she could never afford such a luxury as a greenhouse full of orange trees at Barrells, nor a grove to set them out in.

Lord Hertford's second addition was a hexagonal pavilion on a high site Lord Bathurst had chosen, from where vistas were cut through the trees, as the spokes of a wheel. The pavilion

> was stuccoed on the outside with rustic work, and fitted within with paper in imitation of stucco; the ceiling is of the same and appears like fret-work. He has opened a [new] prospect from it through a long narrow glade in his woods, which terminates at Windsor Castle. Over the door are the two following lines from Il Pastor Fido:
>
> > O! vie solinghe e taciturni Orrori
> > Di Riposo e di Pace Alberghi veri'.[31]
> > [Oh solitary woods and silent horrors
> > True abodes of rest and peace.]

Henrietta's correspondence with Frances, which so easily picked up where they had left off, gave her a kind of gardening partnership-by-post, for though she was far short of the Hertfords' resources, she had the same store of memories as well as her own imagination. Her own efforts were confirmed and encouraged by Frances' descriptions of the ultra-fashionable but secluded and discreet Percy Lodge. Her small Warwickshire woodland clearing was hardly the dramatic garden landscape of Windsor Forest and the Thames valley, but it was an exquisite place in itself. From the first, she had been carefully cutting winding walks through her woods, making paths of gravel or turf. She had identified a place for a cave or grotto in a shady copse, and her summer house – which might have been newly built or converted from an old building – was to be stuccoed 'with rustic work' when she could afford it, and was already home to her collection of heroes, busts of Harry Bolingbroke, Alexander Pope, Dryden, Milton, Shakespeare, Newton and Locke.

Frances had her menagerie 'which is divided into several little courts with a pond in the midst of each . . . here we have pheasants, partridges, wild ducks, guinea fowls, bantams etc which breed in great plenty; and we have bushes, large trees, and patches of wheat where they feed and shelter themselves from the sun'.[32] Henrietta had her aviary, on the north side of the house in view from her library window, where her canaries sang in summer, though in the winters they moved indoors. She had set up a fountain in the aviary enclosure; her poultry, guinea-fowl and 'turkies' had space to roam and plenty of food, but they were vulnerable – in a bad year only one guinea-fowl survived from the brood and a raiding polecat took twenty plump turkeys one night and eight more the following afternoon. She knew that she needed a 'proper poultry house', and even dreamed of a menagerie; much as she loved pineapples, she would rather have had a menagerie than a greenhouse – but she could afford neither.

One feature of Percy Lodge that Henrietta did not emulate was 'an Indian summer house all of timber' which was to be 'painted of all the tawdry colours that you have seen upon a Japan screen'. A Mr Ramsden had made the model of this; he had seen such houses 'in the East Indies' and called it a 'bungola'.[33]

Frances loves her garden and landscape descriptions, and her practised eyes give an honest account of the appearance of mid-eighteenth-century England, or at least the fifty-nine miles between Percy Lodge at Iver and Marlborough, which 'in the finest weather imaginable' was accomplished in eleven and three-quarter hours, including stops for the horses and themselves. 'I never saw such an air of plenty as appeared on both sides of the road, from the vast quantities of corn with which the fields are covered and the addition of many hop gardens that have been planted since I passed through that part of the country. These, and indeed every other beautiful appearance of nature, vanished when we came to Newbury [where] a manufactory had been set up for the digging of a peat formation.[34] 'Newbury ashes' were burnt from the peat and used for fertiliser for years, well into the nineteenth century.[35]

At Henrietta's once-beloved Marlborough there were changes too: they had made the cascades, pushing soil into the rock crevices 'so as to allow periwinkle and other greens that love the water to creep' over the rocks, and a 'flinty' Gothic arch. Frances found that Marlborough in summer, especially her terrace with its borders of pinks and a sweet-briar hedge, caught at her heart. '[W]hether it is because this was the first habitation I was mistress of, in those cheerful years when everything assumed a smiling aspect from the vivacity that attends that season of life, or because almost every little ornament has been made either by my Lord's or by my own contrivance, I cannot tell ... [but] the flowers to me appear painted with brighter colours, and the hayfields and elder bushes breathe more fragrance than the same things do any where else.'[36] Such garden talk was their shared eccentricity, now the core of their revived friendship. Frances was only too conscious that her other regular correspondent, Louisa Pomfret, who had also re-tired from the Court at the queen's death and gone travelling in France and Italy, found plants and prospects boring, and teased her unmercifully if she wrote more than half a sentence on them.

For Henrietta, who read her letters over and over again on chill evenings in her chimney corner, there could never be too much. They fell into a mood of reverie, as old friends can: 'how much joy it would give me,' wrote Frances, 'if with a wish I could sometimes transport myself to you in your solitude, since I am convinced a mind like yours must have improved itself by those hours of leisure which would have hung so heavily upon some people's hands ... '.[37] Henrietta, chastened by her experiences, was not so sure:

> the time was that you well know I preferred reading to all the gaieties of the town, the stage, and often of the Court ... you'd have thought [that reading] would have been my greatest

comfort in solitude, but I have fatally experienced that my anxious thoughts have been so far from relieved by it, that I could not settle ... nor know what I have read. I have begun history and poetry in the different languages I know, and have sought the same pleasure they used to give me when you and I have read the same books together, but I have sought in vain; for some ungrateful friend or low-minded enemy has generally furnished me with disagreeable reflections, which other more agreeable ones could not put out of my mind. For what one meets with in books, though pleasing to the imagination, are not realities, which the mortifications of life are; and if one happens to meet with (in a book) anything resembling what happens to one's self, that one can attend to – but 'tis a prejudicial though a soothing opiate; in short, I have found that books are of least use when most wanted.[38]

This revealing sentiment, however, did not deter Henrietta from avidly buying them, and stocking her library with as many new titles as she could afford.

To this depressing essay Frances applied the surer opiate of nature:

'[T]he fine weather makes a vagrant of me,' she wrote from Marlborough, 'and I am all day rambling about the lanes and commons ... or sitting ... in an arbour under some shady tree. I have a favourite elm which is in the middle of one of the lawns and faces the canal just where the serpentine rivulet falls into it. This is honoured with a rail round it at the extent of its boughs, and a white bench round its trunk with the following line from Il Pastor Fido,

Care selve beate [Dear blessed woods]

and indeed they appear such to me ... you know I have long preferred feathered and four-footed neighbours to those of a politer and more intelligent turn, who are acquainted with, and pleased to inform one of all the misfortunes, faults and follies of their contemporaries; this savage love of solitude increases with my years, and I studiously guard against it for fear of becoming absolutely unfit for the society of the world.[39]

Henrietta might have scoffed momentarily at her friend's professed 'savage love of solitude'. Was it displaying a surfeit of sensibility in a happily-married woman with two very private gardens, and a vista to Windsor Castle, and to whom the world denied little? But she remembered that Frances had protested this 'savageness' from her youth. In her own Warwickshire backwood solitude was too plentiful, and would have sparkled more in the interludes from imaginative company. She told Frances sadly of poor William Somerville, whom she had lost. Then Frances, with her own interest in Italy revived by Louisa Pomfret's vivid travelogues, sent Henrietta back to her Italian books. Henrietta found 'the softness of the Italian language has . . . something in it soothing as melancholy music to some, and the peaceful pleasures of a country-life to your Ladyship'.[40]

After a flurry of letters they had run out of things to say, but Frances' loyalty had vitally renewed Henrietta's faith in the larger world. She bought a new coach and horses for John to drive, and went travelling for the first time in six years. She went to Vale Royal in Cheshire, to her Aunt Cholmondeley, 'who at ninety-two retains all her [faculties] and also her affection for me, and desire to see me . . .',[41] where she was sure of her welcome. It was an adventure, a journey of over 100 miles, not to be taken at the spanking pace that Frances accomplished along the London to Bath road, but of at least three days. The first twenty-five miles were the slowest, through the local lanes to Crabbs Cross, then on the road, as yet unturnpiked and improved, to Bromsgrove, past Hagley and the Clent Hills to Stourbridge. Here, for the first time, the countryside was dotted with the smoking chimneys of the earliest 'manufactories', the glassworks and potteries which were to be the van of the Industrial Revolution. Then, on the second day, after passing through Enville, where there was in the making a romantic garden that she would come to know, it was miles and miles through rural Shropshire, crossing the Severn at Bridgnorth, and on to Shrewsbury. The last stretch was more directly northwards, about forty miles through Whitchurch to Northwich and Vale Royal, one of the beautiful places that the Cistercian monks had found out for themselves.

Henrietta's stay could only have been delightful, for this part of her family were her staunch supporters. Her old Aunt Cholmondeley had never wavered, and her sons and especially her daughter, Henrietta's cousin Joana, and her family were there for renewed affections. Joana was married to Sir Amos Meredith of Henbury, near Bristol, and their five lively children, especially her elder daughters Patty and Harriet and their brother William, were all artistically clever. From that moment they were amongst Henrietta's closest friends, keeping her amused with all their London doings, the plays – the theatre was their particular passion – and fads and fashions, and, especially after Sir Amos died in 1744, they were her frequent guests at Barrells where they stayed for long weeks in the summers and helped her in her garden.

Later that year, Henrietta ventured southwards, perhaps calling in at Lydiard where she was not so sure of her welcome. Her brother Jack St John who, by the grace of Harry Bolingbroke, had inherited their father's title and was 2nd Viscount St John was altering the old house she had been born in beyond recognition, encasing it in stone to look, as it does now, rather like a poor relation of Inigo Jones' Wilton House. Henrietta carried on to Battersea, where the Bolingbrokes were settled. Marie-Claire had naturally always preferred to live in France, but she realised how much her husband had yearned for England and loved him too much to deny him his inheritance when it came at last. They laughed over Lydiard, that Jack and his wife 'have made themselves a proverb in the country already for their stinginess'. They had sent Harry (who had given them both title and estate) half a buck deer – and he replied that they really should not have bothered as he had 'the best Park in England' at his disposal, which was Kent's the game dealer at Temple Bar.[42]

At Battersea she learned also that 'the dullest poet in Christendom',

John Dalton, had left the Hertfords' employment because he had been ill and was unable to accompany young Lord Beauchamp on his European tour. Dalton had in fact left for the Friary at Chichester, writing his 'Epistle the Second [in] Hopes of amusing the Noble Person to whom it was sent', Lady Hertford. Naturally, in his journey from Colnbrook, Dalton noted the interesting gardens, 'fam'd Clare-mont' where 'Poor Vanbrugh's plan is out of date' and William Kent was softening the outline of the lake and adding the Grotto. Dalton had clearly been seriously ill, riding was very tiring, and thus he was easily despondent, feeling very outcast from the Hertfords' world – especially at the gates of Esher Place (where Kent was also working) where he no longer had his accustomed entrée – the gates were shut in his face. Here, Dalton reveals Frances' flirtatious behaviour in the security of her own home:

> She, that at Percy-Lodge so late
> From morn to night was us'd to prate,
> Almost impertinent and rude,
> Unbidden wou'd herself intrude
> With tale, and epigram, and song,
> To waft the chearful [day] along,
> Whilst I, o'erjoy'd myself to view
> Alive, and with my Lord and You,
> Not once could check her merry vein,
> Her unpremeditated strain . . .[43]

This was the liveliness of the Hertfords' household (which places the versifying at St Leonard's Hill in a context that might further suggest Henrietta was not entirely to blame). Knowing that Dalton was gone, and in a euphoric mood on leaving Battersea, Henrietta suddenly decided she would call at Percy Lodge, unannounced: she could not have known just how deeply Frances was sunk into one of her solitary moods, all the more because she was self-confessedly bereft of her 17-year-old and darling son, who had left on his grand tour with his new governor, Mr Sturrock: 'I suspect you have got my chearfulness hid in some corner of your chaise, for I do not find it about the house,' she had written to 'Beachy'.[44] Perhaps Henrietta was skittish and nervy – it was their first meeting for seven years – and Frances was non-plussed. Her 'savage bashfulness' was communicated to her son, 'My lord has told you of Mrs Knight's most unexpected visit which I own to you did not give me the pleasure which it was natural to expect I should have received from seeing an old friend who has been so long a prisoner, and I am convinced upon a false accusation.' Frances expected Henrietta to be chastened, discounting the sense of freedom that her friend felt at being 'returned' to her formerly beloved world. 'I should have thought her misfortunes would have rectified everything that seemed too light and giddy in her behaviour, since they have certainly been in a great measure occasioned by it', Frances continued, from her virtuous certainty. It must have been a disaster, a nervous taking of tea, hopefully warmed by an inspection of the garden: Frances' verdict continued to be harsh – 'she is the same person she was ten, nay twenty, years ago, her dress as French, her manner as thoughtless. She inquired very kindly after you and seems to preserve the same kindness for us still that she always professed and in which I dare say she is sincere.'[45]

Perhaps Henrietta's Warwickshire farm was her true haven after all. Frances and Henrietta never saw each other again, and their correspondence was resumed in the unhappiest of circumstances, for Lord Beauchamp died of smallpox in Bologna on the evening of his nineteenth birthday in September 1744. Henrietta wrote gently consolatory notes when she heard the news, but with little response until the spring of 1747 when Frances confessed her inexcusable conduct: 'it has not been from the want of the friendship I always professed and shall ever feel for you, but an inextinguishable grief has sunk my spirits into a kind of indolent stupidity that will not allow them to act even when my inclination endeavours to animate them'. She then allowed herself the most enchanting description of their flower-fringed 'lane' at Percy Lodge, which had brought them solace. Lord Hertford had made a long narrow walk:

into the resemblance of a wild lane in the country, and made it wider or narrower just as he had in mind to take in a great tree or fill up a vacancy with flowering shrubs. On the one hand there is for about forty or fifty yards an open grove, through which you can see a corn field . . . with a turfed walk [around the grove] . . . bordered all round under the wood with roses, honeysuckles, Spanish broom, lilacs, syringas, etc.; and underneath these bushes cowslips, primroses, violets, foxgloves, with every flower that grows wild in the fields . . . but there is nothing on the side next to the corn to separate it from it.

Farther on the walk, now gravelled, continued along the edge of the woods and ran by a bank 'covered with rosebushes, pinks, stocks of all sorts and all colours, Sweet Williams, blue and white campanulas, rose campions, chrysanthemums, lupins, and fifty things; this leads you by the side of a nursery and another corn field . . . with a hedge of sweet-briar, and the rest is a mixture of all manner of sweet shrubs. I am afraid I have tired you with this long description of our works,' Frances concluded, 'but the life I lead here keeps me in perfect ignorance of everything which passes in the sociable world.'[46]

For us, the Hertfords' flower walk disproves the belief that landscape gardening was flowerless – the planting of perennials at the wood's margin was trumpeted in the late nineteenth century by William Robinson as being a new idea – and for Henrietta it gave her the pattern for her new Long Walk. Having travelled back to her old life, and found it not so completely thornless however lovely the remembered rose, she warmed afresh to her home and garden.

As Frances had collected poets, Henrietta now collected clerics. Word seemed to have got around the vestries of Warwickshire country churches that this lady of wit and generosity was invariably to be found at home. Along with the genial John Reynolds at Wootton, there was a duo of Parson Hall, called by her (but not to his face) 'the little round fat oily Man of God', and Mr, sometime Captain, Outing, sometimes engaged as a curate. These two liked to travel together, 'for safety and pleasure', but neither was rich – sometimes one or the other was without a horse, so they had to make do with one, and were glad of a shelter from the storm or a night's lodging. In return they carried letters and fetched parcels. In time, Captain Outing, whom she dubbed 'the eldest son of Archimago' – Spenser's great enchanter from *The Faerie Queene* – became indispensable as her legal adviser, travelling to London for negotiations with Robert, as well as part of the Barrells' circle. Parson and Mrs Holyoake – wives were not forbidden though Henrietta found that they were often too 'immured in mince pies' for her liking – at Oldberrow were her good neighbours. They had three sons, the eldest a surgeon, the second an apothecary and the youngest, Franky, who worked at Matthew Boulton's 'toyshop'; that is, the precision engineers on Snow Hill in Birmingham.* Franky Holyoake carried her letters, too, and took her orders to Birmingham workshops. Then there was Thomas Allen, parson of Spernall, a village to the south-west on the road to Alcester, who became a regular friend. He in turn once brought a Mr William Perks, vicar of Coughton, 'whom I never saw but twice,' exclaimed Henrietta, amazed that he had the temerity to publish a 'Pastoral Elegy Humbly Imitated', poor smitten man, dedicated to her. His couplets, of the 'Here fragrant flow'rs refresh the musing fair, / Whilst zephyrs waft their odours thro' the air . . .' variety, do give some idea of her garden. 'Warbling songsters' and 'bees laborious' are followed by a glimpse into her summer house:

> . . . new objects strike the wond'ring eye,
> And strokes of sculpture with the pencil vye.
> Here breathing shadows each apartment grace,
> And meagre bustoes shew their marble face.

We know about the 'bustoes', including 'the robed peer' Harry Bolingbroke, but were the pencil strokes the charcoal sketches of the trophies of rakes and scythes that she remembered from Dawley? Mr Perks is rather wildly lyrical on the idea of her grotto:

---

* This was Boulton senior, though the younger Matthew, of Boulton & Watt fame, was just starting work for his father.

See heaps of shells, old Ocean's glossy store,
Have left their briny cells, and weep no more;
Beneath the rolling wave no longer sleep,
Swept from the rocks and caverns of the deep:
Some skilful hand the pleasing task pursue,
And add new lustre to their native hue.
The grotto's pride, when gayl'y interchang'd,
They shine, in regular confusion rang'd.[47]

Here is a picture of Henrietta's 'skilful hand', as she knelt in
her wood on a fine afternoon, pressing shells into wet mortar,
grotto-making. She had no prehistoric mound as at Marlborough
in which to hollow out a cave, nor an obliging basement as Pope
had at Twickenham, so hers was of her own making, an open-
fronted brick arbour, perhaps built around a spring, the site of
which she had identified early in her garden walking. Her materials
were mussel, oyster and clam shells from her own kitchen, and
scraps of coral and mother-of-pearl, perhaps a conch and scallops,
bought from Boulton's buckle and button workshop.[48] She could
not go rushing to the seashore as other grotto-makers did; even as
she was kneeling in her woods, Pope was rejoicing in fresh supplies
of spars and fossils from Ralph Allen's quarries at Bath, and crystal
curiosities sent him from Cornish mines.[49] Henrietta was working
in a grotto 'desert' and hers was a strange conceit to local eyes –
though at least Mr Perks had some imagination. 1740 was the beginning of a great grotto-making decade, but the contemporary ones
at Goodwood, Mereworth, Oatlands and Painshill, and those by
William Kent and Thomas Wright, were all in scale and distance far
out of her reach.[50] With her grotto, as most everything else, she was
working from her memories and imagination, and this gave her
garden its freshness and enchantment.

She was making a landscape garden in miniature, a brand new
concept only ever applied to great parks like Hagley or Stowe. No
one would ever have chosen Barrells for a landscape garden, for it
had neither hills nor vales, no rocks nor any features – nothing even

in the way of purling streams as at Lydiard – merely little hillocks and ancient woods, surrounded by hayfields. Barrells house, her 'cottage' as she called it, was at the end of the drive from Barrells Green. It faced west to the entrance sweep, with the most open aspect to the south, where the Great Parlour had a view across the meadow to Oldberrow. On this south front she made a bowling green, which was supported by a ha-ha – which she wrote as 'Ha! Ha!' – made in the summer of 1749 to preserve the view and keep the cows out of the garden. The ha-ha was also a newly fashionable idea. Charles Bridgeman had probably introduced one at Dawley, both he and Bolingbroke being familiar with the source of the idea in Dezallier d'Argenville's *La Théorie et la pratique du jardinage* (1709), and Henrietta may have seen the sunken walls at Blenheim and the early ha-ha at Hagley. At Barrells her ha-ha was extended round to the south-west boundary of the garden, where the whole aspect was of a semi-open area of flowering shrubs planted as specimens in grass, which she called her 'shrubbery'. She may well have been the first to do so, for the concept of 'shrubs' was still new, though known to Frances Hertford, and nurserymen called them 'flowering plants', whether soft or woody-stemmed.

The nursery trade, though thriving, had not yet reached her area. According to John Harvey's *Early Nurserymen*, the earliest Birmingham nurseries of John Pope and Brunton & Forbes were not established until the 1770s, and even then 'there was little serious competition within a radius of thirty miles' which included Barrells.[51] So she found her plants in the way gardeners do: by begging and bargaining. She had been far-sighted enough to bring some of her favourites from Battersea; her grandmother's Austrian briar roses, and 'mock orange', *Philadelphus coronarius* (which she called 'seringas'). Her shrubbery also had Portugal and bay laurels, myrtle, various thorns, many lilacs, wild cherry and hazels. She could also have had Jerusalem sage, laburnums and the 'smoke bush', *Cotinus coggygria*, which would have attracted her – it all depended upon what she could beg from a cottage garden or buy from a gardener at a large house. Lord Archer's head gardener at Umberslade supplied her with hundreds of sapling trees, and the attraction of visiting a place like Hagley or Enville was to see what the gardener had available.

Spring in the garden was important. Close to the house, in her shrubbery and along the margins of her wood, she had 'the beauties of childhood': snowdrops, primroses, polyanthus and violets. 'The embroidery Nature bestows upon my Coppice in Spring' was a constant surprise and pleasure, 'a great variety of cowslips, prim-roses, ragged-robins, wild hyacinths both white and blue' and ever more violets. She treasured all her scented plants, writing from her chimney corner on a chilly June Sunday that she had braved the cold and wet to find that 'in the Shrubbery the finest ornament is the large bush of Whitsun roses, which are still in blow and give one an idea of snow-balls this cold weather'. She meant *Viburnum opulus*, the 'snowball' tree. Henrietta also noted that the 'lilac is over and has given place to seringa of which I have enough to perfume the place with the help of the sweet-briar; and several of my roses are in blow'.[52]

But for its immediate surroundings – the open south aspect, the shrubbery, the kitchen garden on the east side and the aviary on the north – Barrells was really a (five-bedroomed) 'cottage' in the woods. These woods were a tangle of chestnut coppice with a few oaks: Henrietta had, as Gertrude Jekyll was to do almost exactly 100 years later and in faraway Surrey, walked her woods unceasingly, marking good and bad trees, and other possibilities. She made her paths gradually by going to favourite views or sunny clearings, and, as Gertrude Jekyll was able to find a double-stemmed pine rejected by the timbermen and take it as a good omen and a garden feature, so Henrietta found a double-stemmed oak. Around it she cleared a glade, a pleasant place to take a book in the afternoon or sit and dream at sunset on a warm evening.

So, there Henrietta Knight is, in her wood on a July evening somewhere about the time of her forty-sixth birthday, nine years into her banishment, in 1745. For all her busy days, her adoring household and admiring visitors, she still misses the 'entertaining' William Somerville, indeed she has been musing over a design for a memorial urn in her garden to their friendship. Though she is usually so full of ingenuity in matching most of her schemes for her house and garden to her means, the practical difficulties of achieving this are bewildering. In London it would be simple enough – she had arranged for the sculptor Peter Scheemakers to make Holly's elegant marble casket and urn in St Mary's at Battersea – but here, in the wilds of Warwickshire, where should she begin? What Henrietta needed was a knowledgeable friend, with Taste . . .

CHAPTER SEVEN

Lady Luxborough

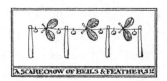

THE 'FLAWED BUT TALENTED' old Chief Cashier Bob Knight had died in bitterness and disappointment on 1 November 1744, the day after he signed his will.[1] Most of his riches went to his wife Anne and their son William, who both spent the rest of their lives in France.[2] For his young granddaughter Henrietta there was a derisory £100, but Harry Knight, now aged sixteen, benefited from an annual 6,000 livres (francs) invested on his behalf by Robert. Robert himself had the customary £100 for his mourning clothes, but also the Luxborough estate and a house in Bloomsbury for his lifetime, with a reversionary interest to Harry. As neither of them wanted either house they were sold when Harry became of age five years later. Robert did keep his promise to his father that he would call himself Lord Luxborough, which he did when a barony came his way in August 1745. He had given up his Great Grimsby seat and ostensibly retired to his estate in Somerset, but two years later he was returned to the House of Commons for Sir Robert Walpole's old seat of Castle Rising in Norfolk – Robert had joined the Whigs when he realised Harry Bolingbroke had no political future – which he kept until 1754.

Henrietta found herself with the name of a house that she had certainly never lived in, and had possibly seen once only. In the accompanying relief that her son Harry was well provided for, she was amused to call herself Lady Luxborough. She did not need it for herself, but in her Warwickshire countryside the gossip was gleefully about visiting or working for 'her ladyship' and it did her no harm. It might even do some good. Another of her poetical, clerical admirers, the Revd Richard Jago at Bishop's Itchington – about eight miles south-east of Warwick – had introduced her to his friend William Shenstone of Halesowen, across Warwickshire westwards and just over the Shropshire border. In September 1747 Jago proposed himself on a visit to Shenstone, who replied that he would be pleased to see him; he had many visitors, and was in 'daily expectation' of George Lyttelton, his neighbour from Hagley Hall. Shenstone added apropos of nothing particularly relevant, 'that a coach with a coronet is a pretty kind of phaenomenon at my door', indeed, there were 'few things prettier'.[3] It was Henrietta, in her newly coroneted coach, who had been to see Shenstone's garden for the first time on 4 August. He was undoubtedly already her captive, humble servant, but it has to be confessed that he had a partiality for duchesses and their like, and so her being 'The Honourable Lady Luxborough' sweetened their burgeoning friendship.

Shenstone was a rare bird, 'a significant figure for those who are able to see what signifies'. He was a large man, ungainly and untidy, disdainful of fashion, especially of wigs, and at the age of thirty-three already well middle-aged, if not older. He was all politeness and melancholy, 'too considerate as well as too lazy to be unkind or pressing on his tenants and so always on the point of hopeless debt', vulnerable and without defences 'against Spleen, Vapours, Megrium, Discontent, and a numerous train of such sort of beings which plague me to death', once the summers and his friends had left him.[4] In short, he was a man of Taste.

As a boy he had discovered his panacea in poetry, at sixteen he wrote an 'Ode to Health' because his was elusive. He had gone up to Pembroke College at Oxford, where he met Richard Jago and Richard Graves, and all three became lifelong friends. On a visit to Graves at his home at Mickleton Manor in Gloucestershire, where

Graves' elder brother Morgan was master and habitually surrounded by a lively crowd of young neighbours, Shenstone is said to have fallen in love with a mysterious Miss 'G', and, afterwards, with the Mickleton curate's daughter, the clever and literary Utrecia Smith. Typically Shenstone never pursued either and Utrecia was later jilted by Richard Graves, and she died tragically young, apparently of a broken heart.[5]

Whilst Graves and Jago went into the church, Shenstone – never actually leaving Oxford but simply failing to return there – spent some time in Cheltenham (falling in love again) and then some lively months in London, the farthest of his travels. He was deeply affected by the deaths of his parents and his elder brother, leaving him with a young brother Joseph to care for, and their grandmother's estate with an income of £300 a year. The estate was The Leasowes (a common name for a Midlands' holding), a well-watered grazing farm of about 150 acres of undulating meadows, just south of Mucklow Hill on the outskirts of Halesowen. His natural affinities moulded him into such a lover of his own home, that he wished for nowhere else. He wrote:

> When I ride in my chair around the neighbourhood I am as much stared and wondered at, as a giant would be that should walk through Pall-mall. My vehicle is at least as uncommon hereabouts as a blazing comet. My chief pleasure lies in finding out a thousand roads and delightful little haunts near home; where I can as effectually lose myself within a mile of home, as if I were benighted in the deserts of Arabia.[6]

It was but a short step to dabbling in his own scenery. He had the inspiration of Lord Lyttelton four miles to the west, who was avowedly fascinated by the sublime qualities of rugged nature, inspired by the dramatic contours of his own park at Hagley in the Clent Hills, which he was ornamenting with Palladian temples and picturesque 'ruins'. Shenstone also remembered that Graves' late father at Mickleton had tried his own hand at picturesque features in a more modest way, and it was really in this vein that he had found a gravel pit in a corner of one of his fields, 'scooped out a sort of cave, stuck a little cross of wood over the door and called it a hermitage'.[7]

Shenstone chose to 'loiter' amidst his fields and the familiarities of home, he and Joseph ably cared for by their redoubtable house-keeper Mrs Arnold (a passionate and skilled rearer of poultry and all domestic birds) and his trusty Tom, his gardener. Dr Johnson put it rather sweetly: Shenstone 'excited his delight in rural pleasures and his ambition of rural elegance [and] he began from this time to point his prospects, to diversify his surfaces, to entangle his walks, and to wind his waters, which he did with such judgement and such fancy as made his little domain the envy of the great and the admiration of the skilful'.[8] The dramatic domesticity of The Leasowes' landscape was ripe for such 'improvements' with the modest house sitting on high ground in the middle of the estate, surrounded by undulating fields and deepish valleys that – at least in wet weather – ran with streams. While Shenstone's cows and sheep still grazed his fields, he planted the stream courses with evergreens for contrast, he planned a series of reservoirs to feed the water to his cascades, and devised a circuit of drives and walks that allowed the best views and presented a pageant of surprises.

Next door, Hagley's 'spacious and opulent' empire looked 'with disdain on the petty state that appeared',[9] but The Leasowes' fame emerged from the curiosity of visitors to Hagley. The poet James Thomson, whom Shenstone worshipped, had come in 1746, ushered in by William Lyttelton 'the wrong way', because he knew it annoyed Shenstone. 'Mr William Lyttelton and Mr Thomson, Author of The Seasons, found me reading a pamphlet in one of my niches,' Shenstone recorded. Thomson burst out in praise of the countryside 'and appeared particularly struck with the valley and the brook by which he had passed, as they came the foot way from Hales Owen'. From the lawn behind the house Thomson remarked that he 'wished the garden to be extended, so as to include the valley'. Shenstone rather grumpily replied that by 'garden' he 'meant no regular garden, but to embellish my whole farm. The French, it appears, have their

Parque ornée; and why is not Ferme ornée as good an expression?'
The threesome moved on, admiring the Upper Pool and Farmer's
Hill then, being limited in time 'and conscious of an hare upon the
spit at Hagley', Thomson gave his parting advice: 'You have nothing
to do but to dress Nature. Her robe is ready made; you have only
to caress her; love her; kiss her; and then, descend into the valley.'
Standing in the court before the front of the house he observed
'Clent and Waw-ton [Walton] Hill as the two bubbies of Nature:
then Mr [Lyttelton] observed the nipple, and then Thomson the
fringe of Uphmore wood', till the *double entendre* worked up to
such a point that they gave way to laughter.

The hare must have been burnt to a cinder for they continued
to bait Shenstone, ridiculing his precious concept of Virgil's
Grove:

> Thomson asked if I had seen many places laid out in the modern
> way? No.
> Asked if I had seen Chiswick? Yes. He mentioned it as a
> sublime thing in the true Venetian taste. He supposed me often
> to come to town; and desired to wait upon me at Richmond,
> Mr [Lyttelton] commending Richmond prospects, he said they
> were only too rich in villas. He begged a pinch of snuff; and
> on passing by the Abeles [white poplars] near the Mill Pool,
> mentioned that Pope had [at least until Pope died in 1744] a
> scheme of planting trees to resemble a Gothic Cathedral. Hear-
> ing the Dam there was made by the Monks, O! says he, this is
> God-dam, the wit of which I could not see.[10]

Henrietta, sensitive to Shenstone's foibles, was rapturous in her
praise of The Leasowes, talking of nothing but its beauties, compared
to the meanness of her own garden. It was to become the sounding
board for all her future efforts. She had the imagination, for she
had seen Chiswick (and Pope's villa and the extravagante bergerie
of Richings/Percy Lodge), to appreciate Shenstone's ingenuity, and
the intelligence to realise the gap in resources and money expended
that yawned between other fashionable gardens and The Leasowes.

She understood the subtleties of nature, of lights and seasons: 'your woods will afford a different scenery when they are embrowned by the shade of the evening or when the moon glimmers through the leaves,' she wrote by way of thanks.[11] Was there a hint of teasing here, for The Leasowes really was a farmhouse and though comfortable enough for two bachelors it was ill-equipped for entertaining. She hardly ever stayed overnight, and it was a rambling thirty miles each way so her visits really were expeditions, starting at dawn, and always with company. On that first visit she had Mr Reynolds and Captain Outing for company and she regaled Shenstone with the story of their journey home. Picture the three of them in a scene worthy of Smollett or Fielding, having had 'one upset' in the dark on the road south of Birmingham. At eleven o'clock they stop at an inn at Shirley, hammering on the closed door and peering in the windows 'only to see a good fire in the kitchen and a maid who was sitting by it, who took her candle and went to bed' leaving them knocking. So they carry on home. '[T]he stars took pity on us, and appeared just as our hostess disappeared, and guided us in a friendly manner.' They reached Barrells at just past 1 o'clock.[12]

Shenstone visited Barrells in August 1748 (haymaking being over for both farmers and farmeresses), and Henrietta went to The Leasowes after harvest. This visit was marked by their going to see Hagley Park, and hearing there the news that James Thomson had died (on 27 August) 'which Mr Lyttelton was grieving at under one Tree and Mr Shenstone under another as we walk'd in the Gloomy part of the Park'.[13] Shenstone decided he would 'raise an Urn' to Thomson in his lower grove, and liked some 'pretty' lines from *The Castle of Indolence*, which had been published just a few weeks before Thomson died:

> I care not, Fortune, what Thou canst deny;
> Thou canst not rob me of Free Nature's grace;
> Thou canst not shut ye Windows of ye Sky,
> From whence Aurora shews her radiant Face.[14]

His understanding was better in his poetry than on his garden
visiting.

The next year on her August visit Henrietta – who always professed herself 'no Poetess' – put her thoughts on The Leasowes into
verse:

> 'Tis Nature here bids pleasing scenes arise,
> And wisely gives them Shenstone to revise;
> To veil each blemish, brighten ev'ry grace;
> Yet still preserve the lovely parent's face.
> How well the Bard obeys, each object tells;
> These lucid meads, gay lawns, and mossy cells;
> Where modest Art in silence lurks conceal'd,
> While Nature shines so gracefully reveal'd;
> That She triumphant claims the total plan
> And, with fresh pride, adopts the work of man.[15]

She had given some thought to Shenstone's calling it a *ferme
ornée*. She felt that though Dawley had been her brother's 'farm' –
and rather exceptional with the 'farmhouse' by Gibbs and the 'farmyard' designed by Charles Bridgeman – that the welfare of the
animals, crops and garden produce had been uppermost. The
'environs were not ornamented', nor, in the flat of the Thames
valley, were 'its prospects good'.[16] But the idea of 'pretty farming'
had been taken up by Philip Southcote at Woburn Farm near Chert-
sey (who may well have taken the idea from Dawley). Southcote
had some 140 acres (57.5 ha) with his flower garden and pavilions
on the middle high ground and sand-walks around 'for convenience
as well as pleasure [so that] from my garden I could see what was
doing in the grounds, and by the walk could have a pleasing access
to either of them where I might be wanted'.[17] The effect was of a
pretty landscape with trees and small buildings set about, the spaces
in between ornamented with contented cattle and well-behaved
sheep. Barrells, though a miniature, was not so far removed from
this. Henrietta wrote to Shenstone 'you will see me next Monday,
the 7th instant at your Ferme ornée, and I hope to bring you on

1. The Birmingham to Bewdley road; ½ mile short of Halesowen turn left onto a Green Lane, and descend into the valley.
2. The Green Lane where 'the Company should properly begin their walk',
3. Or, drive up to the House.
4. Gate at the bottom of the Lawn leads into a 'narrow dingle', passing the Root House, where a tablet reads:
   'Here in cool grot, and mossy cell,
   We rural lays and fairies dwell;
   Tho' rarely seen by mortal eye,
   When the pale moon, ascending high,
   Darts thro' yon limes her quiv'ring beams,
   We friskit near those crystal streams . . .
   [and on for 3 more verses].
5. The Priory Gate beside the Cascade, with view of Halesowen church steeple.
6. Seat beside old priory wall.
7. Walk down the valley with occasional seats.
8. Lake fed by rivulet, former Priory fish pond.
9. Ruins of Priory buildings.
10. Another bench with view over Lake.
11. Seat beneath a large oak tree; seat inscribed *Huc ades, O Melibae! Super tibi Salvus et haedi; Et Si quid cessore potes, requiessec sub umbra.* The seat looks onto a lawn, with the statue of the Piping Faun amongst shrubs, all shaded by large oaks. Between 11 and 12 one passes the URN dedicated to William Somerville, *Ingenio et amicitae* and a Root House inscribed to the Earl of Stamford.
12. Pool with cascade.
13. A grove of oak trees, with a circular glade dedicated to *Mr Dodsley.*
14. Statue of the Piping Faun which can be seen from the House.
15. Seat, with a view back to the Priory ruins.
16. Bench [with an inscription from Horace] beneath tall beeches and firs.
17. Gothic seat with a view.
18. Octagonal seat dedicated dedicated *To all Friends round the Wrekin* which can be seen, though thirty miles away.
19. Another Seat.
20. A Gothic Alcove.

21. Gate.
22. Seat with views of the House and of Lord Stamford's Enville ten miles to the west and the Clee Hills.

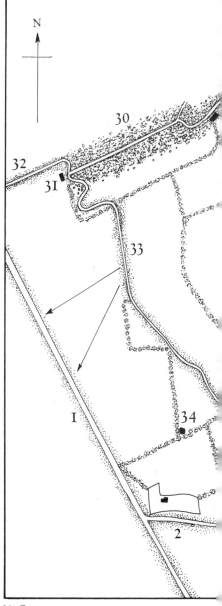

contd overleaf

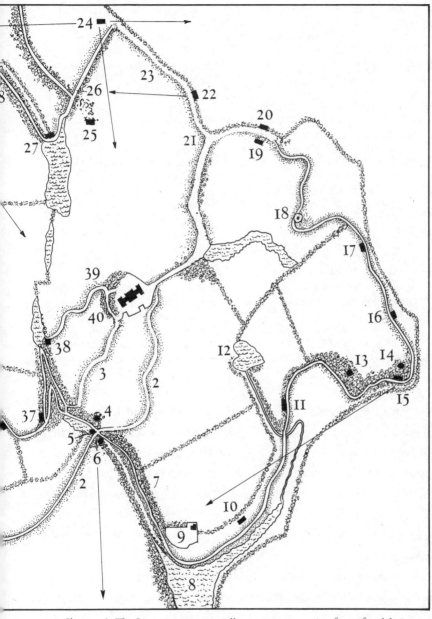

*Shenstone's The Leasowes was essentially an 150 acre grazing farm of undulating
ground with open fields and planted valleys. The highest land was on the northern
boundary, the general slope of the ground was to the south, and the central valley or
dingle, was occupied by a series of lakes and cascades which he had constructed.*

23. Grassy bank.
24. Seat with views.
25. Seat inscribed in memory of Joseph Spence.
26. The Lovers' Walk.
27. The Assignation Seat, beneath a spreading beech.
28. Urn in memory of Miss Maria Dolman [who died of smallpox aged 21].
29. Seat, overlooking broken and furzy ground, which gives way to a 'swelling lawn' and the House seen amongst its trees.
30. An avenue walk through the hanging wood with occasional views outwards, ending in
31. A rustic pavilion 'a slight and cheap edifice of rough stone' called the Temple of Pan.
32. A high natural terrace with a seat offering the 'most magnificent' views to the Clee Hills, the Wrekin, and the Welsh mountains.
33. This walk affords more varied scenery, including a view of Hagley Park.
34. 'A handsome Gothic screen' backed with firs.
35. A seat inscribed to Lord Lyttelton.
36. A seat.
37. Another seat which allows a prospect of the 'beautifully gloomy' Virgil's Grove, a small deep valley, its sides clothed in hazels and other shrubs, and the whole shaded by tall trees.
38. Is the seat dedicated to the memory of the poet James Thomson, a watery spot near the cascade and with 'dripping fountains'.
39. The walk from Virgil's Grove to the House passes Shenstone's grotto dedicated to Venus, 'To Venus, Venus here retired', and memorials to Richard Graves and Richard Jago, these all at the edge of the House shrubbery.
40. The flowers of The Leasowes were essentially the wild flowers of woods and wet places. At the House [though not indicated on the plan] there were flower borders, a kitchen garden and frame yard, which made the household self-sufficient in vegetables and fruits.

the 8th to my Ferme negligée, for that you will find it!'*[18] She was not in the same league as the 'modern' gardeners, who were all men. Her garden was her solace and comfort, not a showpiece, but a pleasure for her friends. And she had much more to do. With Shenstone ever more flattered and absorbed by his increasing flow of summer visitors, they only ever saw each other once or twice a year, but she valued his criticism and advice above all others, on matters of design in her house and garden.

The 'entertaining' William Somerville had been dead for all of seven years but in Henrietta's mind his presence lingered. He was

---

* It was such a brilliantly feminine appellation; she had been laying turf, which had dried out and shrunk, her pavilion was being dismantled and the roses were all faded 'and give an ugly aspect to my Shrubbery'.[19] Hence 'negligée'. But her quip was not, it seems, widely applauded, being beyond the wit of bachelors and clerics (who had not tasted the delights of Paris?).

an unquiet ghost whose virtues multiplied, and she really was still determined he should have a garden memorial. Her regard for Sir Thomas Browne's *Urn Burial* and *The Garden of Cyrus*[20] had decided her upon an urn, as she told Shenstone: 'I should like the whole to be as plain as possible: that is to say, as far as is consistent with expressing my friendship for Mr Somerville, and his poetical genius.' And: 'Neither would I have it expensive (for more reasons than barely that of having money) but I would express with as much simplicity as possible my respect for his memory, without flattery or pomp; and that it was my friendship only which made me raise this memorandum of him.'[21]

In response to this tall order Shenstone was perfectly willing to spend the November evenings with his books: 'I have been of late so conversant with Lists & Astragals; Plinths & Cymatia; yet your Ladyship will have good Fortune if I entertain you with anything besides.' At least, when she had considered his sketches and suggestions, their taste coincided: 'Yet of all ye Urns & Pedestals I have drawn within this Fortnight, I like none so well as ye sort you seem to prefer.'[22] Shenstone broke off his researches to visit his friend Sanderson Miller at Radway Grange, south-east of Stratford and beyond Kineton, in the January snows. He stopped at Barrells on his way home, walking the garden to agree a site for Somerville's Urn beneath the double-stemmed oak. At home Shenstone wrote his thanks for Barrells' hospitality – good company around the fire on a bitterly cold evening – and thought Henrietta would be interested in his opinion of Miller's house, nothing special 'but a couple of bow windows built in ye Gothic taste which are really delightful'.[23] To which Henrietta retorted: 'Many a man can sketch out a bow-window or heavy castle, who is unacquainted with the beauties of a genteel urn!'[24]

Next came the question of ornament. She knew what she did not like. 'I have a strange dislike to strawberries, acorns, artichokes or any vegetable that I have hitherto seen, for the handle of any vase or urn', nor did she like acanthus wreathings, and 'I cannot like

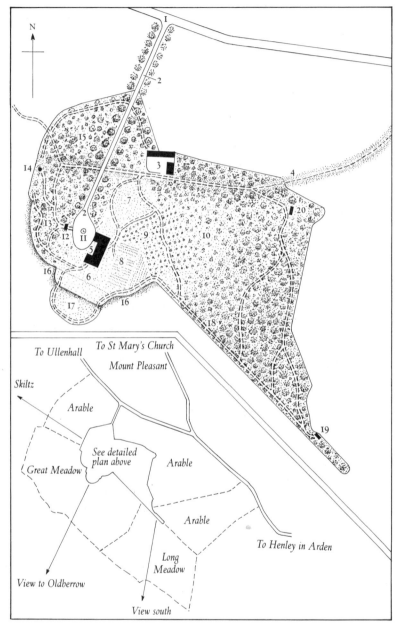

N

1
2
15
14
3
4
7
20
2
13
9
10
12 II
5
8
16
6
16
17
16
18
19

To Ullenhall
To St Mary's Church
Mount Pleasant
Skiltz
Arable
See detailed
plan above
Great Meadow
Arable
Arable
To Henley in Arden
View to Oldberrow
Long
Meadow
View south

Plan of Henrietta's garden at Barrells 1736–56 drawn chiefly from information in her Letters to William Shenstone. Her ferme negligée including her hay meadows and cornfields covered some 56 acres, and was therefore about one-third of the size of The Leasowes

1. Entrance from Henley to Ullenhall
   road.
2. Drive through tall trees to carriage
   sweep on west of House.
3. Stables and stable yard.
4. The Right of Way, a green road, which
   was banked and edged with trees.
5. Barrells House.
6. The South terrace, a planted
   pavement bordered with flowers and
   the bowling green.
7. Aviary and aviary garden with seed
   and fruit bearing plants for the
   domestic and wild birds.
8. Kitchen and herb gardens and
   Melonry.
9. Orchard and shrubbery area leading
   to Chestnut Coppice.
10. Chestnut Coppice carpeted with wild
    flowers.
11. Sundial in centre of carriage sweep.
12. Grotto, which became the Temple of
    Venus.
13. The Upper garden, mainly shrubs
    planted beneath trees, with gravelled
    paths winding their ways to
14. the double-stemmed oak with
    Somerville's Urn and the seat with a
    view to Skiltz.
15. Copse and nursery ground.
16. The Ha-Ha!
17. The Lower Garden, with spring
    flowers and roses.
18. The Long Walk, edged with shrubs
    and arching trees allowing glimpses of
    the view southward, until
19. the seat placed for a distant view 'to a
    little bit of a Gloucestershire hill'.
20. The Hermitage in its primrose dell.

lyres or even masks on an urn, I mean anything that projects so much on the sides; it takes off that roundness which is the beauty.'[25] He tested her opinions on a hunting horn and Pan's pipes, and eventually, after many more wordy suggestions on his behalf, they settled on a French horn suspended from a laurel wreath by a riband. He did not mind that she rejected so many of his researches, 'I have no Fame in Building, at present, to lose; And I wou'd give all I shall ever acquire to see this Urn both plan'd & situated so as to appear very solemn & venerable; infusing an agreeable Melancholy into all Bosoms [that] respected Mr Somerville.'[26] It only remained for the urn to be made.

In the meantime Henrietta had realised that her countryside was not such a wilderness for arts and crafts as she imagined, but within the realm of 'our honest builder Mr Smith of Warwick'.[27] Smith's men had been working for Robert on Barrells when she arrived, but at the time she had been too preoccupied to appreciate their worth. Francis or Frank Smith, originally a mason, had earned his good name for his part in the rebuilding of Warwick town after a great fire in 1694. He had married Mary Morteboys of Tanworth (about five miles through the lanes north of Barrells), whom he met whilst he was working at Umberslade for Thomas Archer, and he set up his home and business in Warwick. The Smith firm's craftsmen had built and decorated great local houses such as Stoneleigh Abbey and Farnborough Hall, and smaller ones (Studley Manor, Baginton Hall) as well as farm houses and rectories. Francis Smith had worked at Melbourne for Harry Bolingbroke's old friend Tom Coke in the mid-1720s, and the firm's pride, James Gibbs' Radcliffe Camera in Oxford, along with a trio of exquisite Northamptonshire houses, Kelmarsh, Lamport and Cottesbrooke and Stanford Hall in Leicestershire, had sealed their fame. The genial Francis Smith had died suddenly in April 1738, though his reputation, his workmen and the firm, managed by his son William, were well alive.[28] It was amongst Smith's travelling craftsmen, who were mostly contracted for individual jobs, that word soon spread of the lady with fine taste and fashionable ideas living at Barrells. Rather like the clerics, a willing band of carpenters, plasterers and decorative painters were drawn to Henrietta's service, to work for her and carry her messages and letters. So it was that the interior of Barrells, as well as its exterior, was given new life under her direction. It started with 'my friend Williams', a decorative painter who told her that he had worked on the ceilings at Shugborough and on the Chinese pavilion there. For her low-ceilinged book room he painted her a 'chimney piece' and devised and painted an architectural frieze, allowing that there was 'but five inches' to spare above Pope's head, whose bust had the place of honour. Williams used stone colours 'pretty strongly shaded so as to look like carving'[29] (as Henrietta remembered from the Dawley trophies, though he was probably paid nowhere near £200!) and he took a great deal of trouble to achieve the right effect. Williams was based in New Street in Birmingham but his family lived at Henley-in-Arden so he happily combined jobs at Barrells with his trips home. He also painted her south-facing Great Parlour in the fashionable flake-white.

Robert Moore, the stuccoist, who worked at Hagley Hall and on the fabulous plasterwork at Stoneleigh (usually credited to Francesco Vassalli), decorated her bedroom ceiling and 'mended my figure of Milton so well, though it was broke in a thousand pieces and a hand and arm lost'.[30] John Wright, another stuccoist and one of Smith's principal craftsmen, told Henrietta that 'he employs an Italian under him' when 'more elegance' is required (the status of the Italians in the eyes of the 'locals' being rather different). Wright had worked for Lord Brooke at Warwick Castle, at Warwick Priory (the home of the family of retired Royal Master Gardener Henry Wise, who had died in 1738) and on Lord Archer's temple at Umberslade. He decorated the interior of Henrietta's summer-house.[31]

Thomas Hands the carpenter, whom William Shenstone knew and who had worked on Smith's contract at Badminton House*, also built bookcases for Henrietta and helped with her garden projects. However, he took one look at the drawing for Somerville's Urn – for which she had considered painted wood – and declared it 'beyond him'. Hands said it was a job for Smith's Marble Yard in Theatre Street in Warwick. Shenstone felt she would get better value from a semi-retired mason named Pedley, 'an inoffensive old man' who had seen a good deal of the world, 'perhaps too much'. Pedley's reputation had suffered because he had built Birmingham's St Philip's church (now the cathedral) – of which there was local low opinion – built, as Shenstone explained, 'to the groom-porter's design'.[32] This was the architect Thomas Archer, once Groom of the Stole to Queen Anne and the first two Georges, and who retired to Umberslade, where his son Lord Archer was Henrietta's neighbour.† The reliable old Pedley did not have a workshop, nor did Henrietta have anywhere for him to work, so the precious urn and its pedestal and laurel wreath ornament were cut from

---

* Thomas Hands is in Gomme's list of Smith's craftsmen.
† Thomas Archer (1668–1743) designed the celebrated pavilion at Wrest Park, Bedfordshire, 1709–11.

Warwick stone at Smith's Marble Yard by Mr Collins, 'the best stone-carver' in Warwick. It was ready for collection at the end of February 1750. 'All this is good. Now for the bad,' she told Shenstone, at the start of her saga. The pedestal was in two pieces, one above the other, as they had tried every quarry but could not find a piece large enough, and on the urn the horn hung on a loop, rather than a riband:

> The next misfortune is owing to a mercenary, ill-natured rascal, who is a weekly carrier from Henley to Warwick; by whom I sent a letter last Saturday to Mr Hands to say that I would send my team for the vase and pedestal on Monday ... Mr Hands was not at home but his people sent the [carrier] to Mr Collins, who told him by word of mouth that the team must not come till Wednesday, for the things could not be sent safely before; which message the rascal never brought, nor even mentioned to my servants, though he saw four of them on Sunday in Henley, and spoke to two of them. If it had been wrote down, he would have brought it, and demanded Three-pence at least; but it was verbal and he did not think it worth delivery. So when the team got to Warwick on Monday, Mr Hands swore, Mr Collins fretted, both said the urn would be damaged; for they had bespoke cases of deal for every distinct part, and but one case was made; yet to send the wagon back empty they did not dare; so, in short, they packed it all up as carefully as they could. But the roads being very rough and bad, they with difficulty got home by One in the morning; the mouth of the French horn struck off, and two stones broke off the lower plinth, and a small notch off the urn, and one off the cap of it, but trifling. The foreman and another man came in the morning and mended the two stones very well as I had some of the same stone in the rough; and [they] have put the mouth of the French horn on again (for luckily it was not lost); and they say it is as strong as ever, and the paint will hide entirely the piecing.[33]

The urn was assembled and placed in the garden on the morning of 14 March 'and now makes a good figure under its canopy of oak. If the weather continues dry, it will be fit to be painted in a fortnight;

and the man who set it up will come at the same time to inscribe it. The letters are to be carved in [the] stone, and then blackened.'[34] The inscription, settled at last after a long debate, was from Horace: 'Debita sparges lacryma favillum vatis amici' ('You will sprinkle the glowing ashes of your poetic friend with due tears.')[35]

Just after the triumphal completion of Somerville's Urn another 'painter' came to visit, meeting her in Henley after church and riding to Barrells by her 'coach-side'. He was the landscape painter, Thomas Smith, a native of Derby, a man of about thirty who was making himself a reputation amongst the country house cogno-scenti of Middle England for his views of the more rugged parts of Derbyshire and the Lake District. Henrietta promptly bought eight Derbyshire views, and the artist was so pleased that he gave her one of Chatsworth.* He painted country houses and gardens to supplement his living, his *Views of Hagley, Newstead Abbey, Exton, Belton [the grotto, cascades and ruins] and Chatsworth*, engraved by Vivares and Mason, and published in 1749, were very popular. He was also to paint Abraham Darby's Works at Ironbridge well before Joseph Wright of Derby and Philippe-Jacques de Louthenbourg.[36] Smith had come from painting views at The Leasowes and on this visit, or later, he painted Somerville's Urn – the only surviving visual record of it. Smith impressed Henrietta, she saw him again several times and bought more of his prints, and on that first visit he was fascinated by her garden. He saw it first on the gloomy Sunday evening, with the moon 'just seen through the trees', the gloominess suiting the Long Walk, and he was delighted that the trees seemed to form a Gothic arch. Next morning, she told Shenstone:

> He got up at Seven and walked all over this place, and again with me, when I arose. He commends it more than I think it deserves. He agrees with you entirely in admiring the amphi-theatre of wooded hills [the view south to Oldberrow] that we see from the windows, and the situation of the Hermitage; which

---

* Smith's *Eight of the Most Extraordinary Natural Prospects of the Mountainous Part of Derbyshire*, engraved by Vivares, was not published until 1760.

> he thinks preferable to any in England. He laments my want of water; but thinks I might find springs (as indeed most people do). He liked the shell-urns [made by old Pedley on an earlier occasion], and the situation for the new one; as also the aspect of the kitchen-garden, and the pond and oak-tree; and agrees to moving the pales, so as to guide one to the Shrubbery . . . he is also against my painting the niche where the [Statue of] Venus is, for he says she is supposed to have been bathing, and to crouch herself in that manner . . . by way of hiding herself; and he would have the niche adorned with moss, &c. like some bathing place in a remote corner.

Pieces of looking-glass would give a watery look to her 'cave' and 'will have a good effect' from the front door.[37]

The entrance of Thomas Smith of Derby into her life brings Henrietta into focus as someone with ideas before her time, as someone who, had she but lived another ten years, might have become the patroness of the coming Midlands Enlightenment. She epitomises a truth, so persistently overlooked by history, that great inventions and cultural milestones do not suddenly spring fully formed, but are merely the larger bubbles in a cauldron of ordinary lives. Before the reputations of Matthew Boulton, of John Baskerville and of John Wall of the (Royal) Worcester Porcelain company have bubbled into greatness she will have left the scene, but they all enter her life, evidence of her 'nose' for interesting men, a talent that had not deserted her from her earlier days. Perhaps it is not unkind to liken her to a benign and lovely – for some are lovely – spideress, at Barrells, weaving her silken threads that somehow, in a country-side thick with dunderheads and fools, found out men of genius and (a few) women of wit and charm. Poor Thomas Smith was never to be much more than a provincial artist, though perhaps because he also died too early, in 1767, at only forty-seven or so. Henrietta's perceptive appreciation of his rugged views of Gordale Scar and other 'wonders of the Peak' encouraged him, for soon after their meeting he went to the Lakes. His *View of Darwentwater &c from Crow Park* – which perhaps she purchased when he returned

The Weekly Journal or British Gazetteer May 1721: 'Lucipher's new Row–barge for First–Rate Passengers' satirizing the fate of sleek South Sea Company profiteers and, in the top left corner, 'thy faithful cashier', Bob Knight, all consigned on the boat to Hell.

Paris, Les Promenades du Palais des Tuileries, *c.*1730: the fashionable scene which Henrietta rarely saw because of her 'imprisonment' in Le Roule on the Faubourg St. Honoré.

Extract from Chapman & Andre's 1777 map showing the location of Luxborough mansion and gardens beside the river Roding, the house Bob Knight cherished and from which Robert Knight took his title of Baron Luxborough.

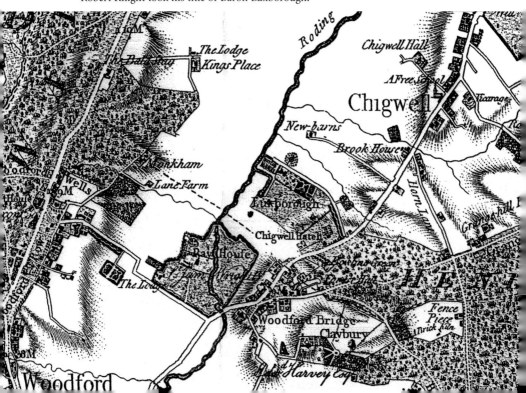

Robert Knight in his robes as Baron Luxborough, painted during his estrangement from Henrietta and in the last decade of her life.

Left Maddalena Henrietta, only daughter of Robert and Henrietta Knight.

Above Henry [Harry] Knight, only son of Robert and Henrietta Knight, painted just over ten years before his mother's death.

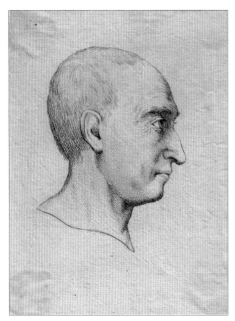

Above Henry Bolingbroke in middle age – as he called himself, the 'retired attainted Philosopher & Hermit'.

Above right Bolingbroke's beloved second wife and Henrietta's ally, Marie Claire.

Right Holles 'Holly' St John, Henrietta's youngest brother, a theatrical portrait that probably belonged to Henrietta, as Holly left her everything at his death. The portrait has had a chequered descent through the Knight family, at sometime folded into a small parcel, and subsequently extensively overpainted.

Opposite William Shenstone and his greyhound with The Leasowes as the backdrop.

And far be driven the fumptuous glare
 Of gold, from Britifh groves;
And far the meretricious air
 Of China's vain alcoves.

'Tis bafhful beauty ever twines
 The moft coercive chain;
'Tis fhe, that fov'reign rule declines,
 Who beft deferves to reign.

The Leasowes, vignette with the last two stanzas of
'The partially retir'd Venus' [see p.209] by William
Shenstone.

Right William Somerville of Edstone, author of *The
Chace* and Henrietta's first poet in the wilderness,
for whom she erected the memorial urn in her garden
at Barrells.

Top Thomas Robins the Elder's illustration of the garden at Woodside, Old Windsor; my text [pp.195–6] imagines the chinoiserie pavilion replaced by Henrietta's little classical shrine to Venus, and then some idea of the paths winding through her shrubbery and into her woods may be gained.

Below Thomas Robins the Elder's illustration of the Orangery at Woodside; my text [p.195] imagines the Orangery replaced by Henrietta's summerhouse and the south front of Barrells' house to give the flowery atmosphere of her terrace, bowling green and upper garden.

Right Somerville's Urn beneath the oak tree in Henrietta's garden.

Below Barrells House, designed by Joseph Bonomi the Elder and exhibited at the Royal Academy in 1796, showing the remains of Henrietta's entrance avenue to the right, but her Upper garden and shrubbery all 'cleared' to the hill of Skiltz on the left, western side.

to Barrells – has all the 'beauty, horror and immensity' of the composite legacy of Claude Lorrain, Salvator Rosa and Poussin, with the pastoral foreground of contented cows, the tree-fringed lake and dark encircling crags that rise to meet mountainous clouds, their undersides ablaze with light. Thomas Smith's was a truly Picturesque imagination, and his views were painted a full twenty years before William Gilpin's sketching tours of Cumberland and Westmorland, and his declarations that 'roughness' and 'ruggedness' were the essential ingredients of the Picturesque.[38]

And what did she do with Smith's Views? Why, she viewed them, and showed them to her friends, through her convex glass and her camera obscura. She must have brought the camera obscura with her from London, for none of the Birmingham 'toyshops' could yet command a specialist corner of the market as the London opticians such as John Cuff of Serjeant's Inn Gate in Fleet Street or Edward Scarlett in Soho Square. Scarlett advertised his optic glasses, camera obscura and microscopes in English, French and Dutch.[39] Henrietta's camera obscura (bought after the enthusiastic conversations in Pope's grotto?) was one of the smaller box travelling kind, or possibly one which collapsed into the faux binding of a book. At one time it developed a 'leak' of light and Shenstone took it to a friend for repair. She had asked if she could use it in her coach for looking at the countryside, but he thought 'not conveniently'. They both had convex glasses for looking at landscapes and their garden views. Henrietta's was three and a half inches in diameter, convex on one side and flat on the other, slightly smoked, and in a frame, rather like a large magnifying glass. Shenstone's was being 'fitted up by a Joiner' into a folding wooden case, to be used as by young men on the Grand Tour or Picturesque travellers in the Lakes 'suspended by the upper part of the case, holding it a little to the right or left [as the view dictated] and the face screened from the sun'.[40] He felt 'Smith's designs well colour'd will appear to great Advantage' through their glasses. At Henrietta's the lively and artistic Meredith girls, Patty and Harriet and their little sisters, who were already allowed to play with her miniature puppet theatre, now enjoyed her camera obscura as a 'show box' for both viewing and their own sketching. Later Shenstone thought of a 'small Improvement' of his own 'which consists in pasting all the Pictures on a long scroll of Canvas ... & so having a Roller behind & before, turning on an Axis, by which means one may by turning round the latter shew the Pictures with all the Ease imaginable ... '.[41] So, here in the mid-eighteenth century in rural Warwickshire is (almost) the silent movie!

The setting up of Somerville's Urn on that definite day, 14 March 1750, in Henrietta's fifty-first year, settled his ghost both in her memories and in her garden. At last her letters to Shenstone are freed from 'the irresistible subject of urns' and filled with the more varied activities of her days. She habitually celebrated her birthday on 15 July with a house party of friends, and though she saw no particular significance in being fifty, as she was in 1749, that birthday had provided her with a very special treat. She had seen her daughter, now calling herself Maddalena Henrietta, for the first time in several years in the previous summer, just after Maddalena, aged nineteen, had married Charles Wymondesold. Then, in 1749, the Wymondesolds announced their arrival at Barrells with a party of friends with whom they were travelling. Henrietta was so excited, she wrote putting off the Merediths saying that she and her daughter 'had not lain under the same roof' since Maddalena was six. She had heard that Charles Wymondesold was 'an exceedingly good-natured man' and to be sure he did seem to write sensible letters. She was afraid that he was 'used to his father's fine seats but here he will meet a cottage',[42] but all seemed to go off well, mother and daughter were truly reunited, Henrietta had her daughter back in her life by way of regular letters, and to the Wymondesolds' credit, they continued to call into Barrells on their summer journeys. Of her son Harry Knight she saw nothing, but knew he was well and was travelling in Europe. Letters from Battersea brought only sad news. She was surprisingly upset to hear of her brother Jack's death at

Naples, leaving only her and Harry now, and their nephew Frederick in charge at Lydiard. Harry Bolingbroke, who had sat by Pope's bedside and wept at his illness and death in 1744, was now feeling bitterly betrayed by the discovery that Pope had published clandestine copies of *The Idea of a Patriot King*. In Harry's eyes this was not quite the last betrayal. As he struggled to look after his beloved and sick wife Marie-Claire at Battersea, he was at first the eminence grise of the 'Boy Patriots' who saw Frederick, Prince of Wales, as their coming Patriot King – and then dismissed by them as a 'frustrated and embittered old man'.[43] When Marie-Claire died, after fearful suffering, on 18 March 1750 and Henrietta knew Harry's 'vast affliction' she wanted to go to him. Harry's grief was aggravated by the unseemly haste with which Marie-Claire's family sued for the inheritance due to them under French law.

Soon after she was given a glimpse of her own mortality, as she described to Shenstone on 13 May:

> Imagine you receive this from the Elysian shades, where it is next to a miracle but I had been, instead of writing to you from my parlour; which act is contrary to the rules of chirugery, and is full as much as I can execute in this scrawling fashion. But I was resolved to attempt for the first time what most people would have been unable to perform in six months; whereas it will not be a fortnight till tomorrow since I had a fall in my chamber in getting out of bed [which must have proved fatal] had I not been reserved by Fate for some other end, which I am as yet a stranger to . . .

Her surgeon 'young Mr Holyoake', the eldest of the three sons of Parson and Mrs Holyoake at Oldberrow, had been so skilled that 'eight or nine plasters are reduced to two', one over an eye, one on a knee; 'he has treated me in the French way and used no lenitives [i.e. drugs] nor kept my eye bound up longer than till it could open. I have been tractable and in spirits . . . and am now allowed to go once in the middle of the day to the Hermitage . . .'[44]

She convalesced reading Swift's *Works* (George Faulkner's Dublin edition published in 1735; Swift had died in 1745), *The Conquest of Mexico* in French, and Voltaire's tragedy of *Alzire*, of which William Somerville had given her his English translation. Shenstone was amongst her many visitors in June, and she was soon gardening again, optimistically opening views from her refuge in her wood. She used her 'Claude Glass' to choose interesting prospects, then 'framed' her views. 'I have put the white bench into the corner,' she reported to Shenstone, 'from whence one has a view of Skiltz [a hill to the west] and the Urn looks also well from it. I have made another opening in the Long Walk and am thinning the branches of the trees that lead to the Old Orchard so that now I discover three little edifices beside Oldborough [*sic* Oldberrow] church through the trees [to the south].' The remainder of this letter, thanking Shenstone for his visit, is typical of the thoughts that tumble from her mind at the end of a happy day. 'You could not, Sir, have said anything more flattering to me, than that there is a resemblance between my imagination and yours. It would be too vain in me to own that I think so; but I may say with truth that there is a great similitude in our way of life and our solitary amusements; and that may also cause a resemblance in our turn of thought.' She was pleased to have visitors appreciating her 'improvements', as pleased as he was to have The Leasowes praised, but she would not like Barrells 'a shew for the Public in general as Lord Cobham's [Stowe] which every body tires'. She realised that Hagley attracted visitors who spilled over to The Leasowes, but that was no shame 'nor do the beauties of Hagley in the least obscure those of your place . . .' but 'I would not have you (nor would I myself) execute our schemes all at once; for I think there is more joy in forming the plan and seeing it grow by degrees towards perfection, than there is in seeing it perfect.' She ended: 'I send you a goose, a gander, a mallard, two ducks and a rumpled egg shell, rural tribute Barrells' humbly pays to its Lord the Leasowes! Mrs Arnold's skills will tend the baby fowl'.[45]

In July Henrietta took the Wymondesolds and a widowed friend

Mrs Davies from Stratford to The Leasowes, and she spent her birthday with a party of friends. August was harvest-time for her wheat, and she fretted nervously whilst Captain Outing was gone to London to meet Robert on business concerning the Grosvenor Street house, which she had made over to the Wymondesolds, and, briefly, her wish to convert some of her invested capital (from Holly's and her father's legacies) into income, because her expenses on Barrells were so high. She felt 'perplexed by affairs and accounts, which I would willingly set to rights' and was feeling sorry for herself: 'I am alone, and must be a farmeress too, unknowing as I am; and am entertained (by letter only) with the reproaches of some, who ought to commend me for the money I have laid out here.'[46] Far from receiving guidance or practical support from Robert on the running of Barrells' estate out of her own pocket, all she got was a sharp letter from him about not living beyond her means.

On 15 August her 'trusty servant' James died. He had been brought up at Battersea, had come from London with her without a second's thought, and, as she said, he 'had lived with me for twenty-two years and was incorruptible where my interests were concerned'. She was distraught and more overcome as she realised 'the millions of affairs' and 'some not quite agreeable' that James had protected her from. On the day of his funeral she was stung by a wasp on her elbow, her whole arm swelled up ('no less hard, though much less beautiful, than that of Venus in her Shrine in my Walks') and she became so feverish that she had to be bled.[47] Once again the Holyoakes came to her aid, this time William the second son, apprenticed to his grandfather Mr Stephens the apothecary in Worcester, who knew Dr John Wall. Dr Wall was an amateur artist as well as a physician.[48] He was her ideal doctor, and became her friend, soon realising that it was worth calling at Barrells at dinner-time.

Another hot August afternoon brought a surprise visitor when a coach was forced to take a detour through Barrells' grounds. Permission was sought and granted and the lady in the coach found herself being invited in, Henrietta being 'most profoundly civil', and perhaps having a rather boring day. The lady was none other than Mary Delany's sister Ann, Mrs Dewes. The Dewes had a house at Wellesbourne, in the Avon valley east of Stratford, and another at Mappleborough Green on the higher ground just west of Barrells, to where Mrs Dewes had taken her three ailing children thinking they would benefit from the good air. Henrietta was sensible to the 'politeness, delicacy, softness and grace' which distinguished Ann Dewes, and she accepted an invitation to Mappleborough Green for the following week.[49] Mrs Dewes confided to her brother that Henrietta was 'entertaining' and that 'she had made her house and garden very pretty'. But to her sister she clearly expressed doubts, for Mary Delany replied to her from Dublin:

> Now for Lady Luxborough. I am vastly entertained at your being acquainted with her in spite of your prudence; but I really see no reason why her acquaintance is to be declined. If she leads a discreet life, and does generous and charitable things, she ought to be taken notice of, as an encouragement to go on in a right path, and your conversation and example may be of infinite service to her. She has lively parts, and is very well bred, and knows the polite world, and you may, I think, divert yourself with her as much as you can, and [Dr Delany] says you will only do a meritorious thing in so doing.[50]

One would think that the stainless Mrs Dewes had encountered the witch of Endor or some probationary gaolbird – what a pity that she should only remember fifteen-year-old stale gossip and not let appearances speak for themselves. Fortunately the Delanys were more worldly wise, though patronising in the extreme. Henrietta did go to Mappleborough Green, but she soon realised that Ann Dewes did not have the literary, artistic and gardening talents of her sister, and perhaps sensed the chill in her politenesses, for she decided that it was not worth the journey to Wellesbourne to keep their acquaintance. It was another of those near misses of history: if she had persevered with Ann Dewes, would she have met Mary

Delany? They were the same age; Mary was at court with Frances
Hertford; and had had her share of misery before she married Swift's
friend Patrick Delany and had gone to live and garden happily at
Delville, outside Dublin. The two of them would have indulged in
garden-talk all evening long – a fine match for each other.[51]

That autumn Henrietta was determined to 'keep garrison' at
Barrells: she had heard that Robert with Harry Knight and his new
wife Frances Heath (a South Sea Company heiress) were in the area
'and I believe they have all three a longing eye towards it'.[52] It seems
that Robert (or Lord Luxborough as perhaps we should now address
him) was looking for a country home for Harry and Frances Knight
in the territory that should one day be theirs. He was hovering, that
is for certain, and therefore all the more reason for Henrietta to fill
Barrells with her friends and relatives for protection. There were
her dearest Merediths*, who often stopped off between London
and Cheshire, and her neighbours the Holyoakes, Reynoldses and
Captain Outing.† These were her friends who sipped syllabub
beneath the trees and played bowls by moonlight on her birthdays.
She had her widowed intimates, Mrs Davies and Mrs Kendall, the
second a rich widow with a coach and six, who lived in Stratford.
In addition she cannily presided over good dinners and better conversation for a motley collection of distinguished gentlemen (who
might be called her protectors should the need arise, though perhaps
they never knew it): Lord Archer from Umberslade (very proud of
the obelisk in his park), her cousin Sir Peter Soame, another relative
a Colonel Hildersly, a Judge Chambers, and to these she added Dr
Wall from Worcester and the dashing Captain Robinson, who has
yet to be introduced.

Even for a hermitess there was 'nothing so terrible as parting
from friends', that moment when she stopped waving and turned

---

* Patty the eldest girl married a Mr Banks of Winstanley in Lancashire in 1750, and her
brother Sir William was a Member of Parliament.
† Reynolds and Outing were respectively vicar and curate at Wootton Wawen and
'Somerville's Aston' (now Aston Somerville), the home of William Somerville's heir, Lord
Somerville, just west of Broadway.

back into an empty house, when all her insecurities gathered to meet her. On one such autumn afternoon when 'to have taken leave and then have gone to bed, had been such an image of death, that I avoided it as much as possible, and endeavoured to banish [such thoughts] from my mind', she doubted she would win the battle. But then

> luckily a man [it was Shenstone's gardener, his 'trusty' Tom whom he often sent to help her] came to fell some trees and immediately looking upon him as upon a tutelar angel sent to my assistance, I never returned to the house, but walked, under his protection, all over my grounds, and particularly to the farther end of the Long Avenue; where I ordered a crooked row of scrub trees to be fallen, and a strait row of elms to be planted, and other views to be opened, by felling and transplanting about the Old Summer-house.

The day, if not saved already, was turned to the happy contemplation of 'root-seats' upon discovering a pile of roots she had set by, and then choosing a place where one might be built 'from which one shall just discover a bit of a Gloucestershire hill'.[53] This was most likely Willersey hill on the edge of the Cotswold scarp, about seventeen miles on a crow's flight south, on the Warwickshire and Gloucestershire border. In root-seats, along with root-houses the darlingest features of the Picturesque, art masqueraded as usefulness; for are not tree roots the gardener's bane, impossible to leave in the ground, difficult to dig out, and then impervious to burning? William Shenstone, ever an opportunistic gardener, had utilised roots and found stones into casual seats in many places on The Leasowes' circuit walks. The root-seats were good for damp and shady places (where they still refused to rot) and mosses and lichens enhanced their appeal. Once again, Shenstone and Henrietta were in front of the fashion. William Wright's *Grotesque Architecture or Rural Amusement*, which gave plans and ideas for using 'Rude Branches and Roots of Trees', was not published until 1767. In *The Ladies' Companion to the Flower Garden* of 1844, Jane Loudon suggested roots piled up and pegged together with moss or heath pushed into the crevices to make a comfortable seat.

Like so many gardeners Henrietta felt newly alive on 1 October; she loved the autumn. Shenstone was the opposite; when the leaves left his trees he sank into a gloomy hibernation, he would not reply to letters and he certainly could not be dislodged. Henrietta thought his natural tendency was aggravated by hearing of the poet Thomson's death in autumn; they had started discussing this foible then, and it became a perennial theme to which here she applies all her lyrical persuasion. She told him:

> I am partial to the autumn season, perhaps you will become so when grown somewhat older; and not exclaim against that pensive season (as you call it) which, if it does not afford all the gaieties of spring and summer, is however attended with fewer disappointments. Would you in spring enjoy the beauty of your parterre, a sudden shower drives you home; in summer you are obliged to shut out the delicious prospect of the ripened grain and the various labours of the peasant, lest, like him, you should be scorched by the sunbeams, which your spreading waters reflect the more strongly, or be catched, though under the shelter of an oak, by the merciless lightning: whereas in autumn, although more languid, the sun has still power to chear, and its gentle heat causes no pain; it still serves to ripen fruits, which are to be your consolation in winter; and though the days are short, every hour of them may be enjoyed in meads and groves, where indeed the trees lose their verdure; but it is no more than changing their dress (as some lowly nymphs have done of late) from a plain green gown to a rich brocade, mixed with ten thousand shades: and as it is wove by the hand of Nature, should still please in its variety.[54]

Later, her frustration got the better of her.

> How charitable it would be Sir, if you would take a trip to this little Retreat at this melancholy season! The English hang themselves, it is said, in the month of November – what then, if to indulge the splenetic humour which the density of the air and the shortness of the days incline you to, you should come

and spend them in my chimney-corner? Nothing will put you enough in mind of spring to make you regret it, unless it is the singing of my two Canary-birds, and they shall, if you please, be sent out of the parlour, after which the most profound silence will reign, and dulness be triumphant.[55]

She, on the other hand, was wary of winters: 'I begin to envy the ants, who are hid from the world, and the world from them' until the sun returns. Not having that facility, she philosophises: 'true, however, it is that winter in the country is too solemn to give pleasure, though it may give awe; and I love it as much as a child loves a rigid parent'.[56] In reality her winter days were busy, seldom without a traveller in distress as refugee from the frozen ruts of the lanes, as her clerical friends and others, such as Dr Wall, still had their journeys to make. Barrells' little farm community was forced into self-sufficiency, with enough to spare for visitors. The short days were packed with the business of surviving, unsheathing the summer-scented hay for the cows, unearthing root vegetables for the kitchen, collecting apples from the store, and feeding every living thing. Winter – and the winters seemed especially cold, and Barrells was snow- and ice-bound for weeks on end – was the bargaining of cold for warmth, in a kind of ritual dance. Henrietta prided herself on her home-made cheeses, now retrieved from the near-freezing dairy store. The milk came warm from the cows, gifts of hams and game were brought from the cold larders. Coals stored on delivery by the friendly colliers from Halesowen (who also carried her letters) and their own wood kept them warm, they baked their own bread, and wanted for little, except perhaps fresh air and exercise: 'I eat heartily, grow too fat, and have not tasted wine, beer nor cyder these two months or more' she wrote after one freezing spell, and she was 'in perfect health'.[57]

Once his dreaded autumn was over, Shenstone was only too happy to travel in the coldest weather, and more than once he came to Barrells at Christmas, or soon after. Henrietta wrote a poem to celebrate one of her winter house parties: 'Asteria in the Country to

Calydore in Town' was the title she gave it when Robert Dodsley wanted to publish it. Calydore has been identified as Captain Outing.* Did she intend it to remind him what was at stake when he was in town negotiating with Lord Luxborough? The scene is her book room, with a roaring log fire; Captain Outing reads from Pope's Homer or perhaps William Somerville's *The Chace*, and Mrs Meredith, her 'lov'd Johanna' (sometimes spelt Joana), and her daughters Patty and Harriet are present:

> Two Nymphs adorn'd with every pleasing art
> To charm the fancy or engage the heart
> Would with their pencil some fair Landskip trace
> Or stag, or hound – as just as in the chace . . .

Then, 'thro' trackless roads, o'er mountains pil'd with snow' comes Shenstone, 'our own Salopian bard', descending

> To lowly chat, & to as lowly fare
> At whilst to play, or loll in elbow chair.

She muses on memories, metaphors arise, and she is left alone:

> Silence & solitude her hapless Lot!
> Unjoyous days, & evenings full of thought
> Yet happy still; & still with pleasure fraught
> Were present bliss reflection on the past
> Her hoarded treasure then might ages last
> But much I fear Regret were too reviv'd –
> For sublunary joys are all short-liv'd.

> Why then, you cry, on me bestow your trash?
> A rhimeing Princess cuts a tinsel Flash.†
> Hold courteous Heroe! Tho' unskill'd in Art
> Alike my tongue, my pen, & friendly heart
> And rude my Lays, receive at least my pray'r,
> May happiness unchecquer'd be your share.

---

* Sir Calidore, the Knight of Courtesy, from Spencer's *The Faerie Queen*, Book VI.
† The Merediths had brought the latest London fad, for cutting decorations from thin sheets of lead.

CHAPTER EIGHT

'A Lady of Quality'

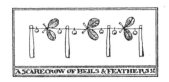

'I AM NO POETESS, which reproachful name I would avoid,' Henrietta had written to Captain Outing when she sent him 'Asteria in the Country to Calydore in Town'. She had a low opinion of her verses and hoped 'you will throw them in the fire when you have read them'.[1] Later, when William Shenstone and Robert Dodsley were conspiring to publish 'Asteria in the Country' and her lines 'Written at a ferme ornée near B[irmingham], 1749', she refused to be named, and so they were credited with the customary pseudonym, though rather unfortunately remembering Fanny Vane, to 'A Lady of Quality'. It is understandable, for what would the credit have been, to 'Lady Luxborough'? A name that was hardly *hers*, and Lord Luxborough's temper would surely not have improved had she used it so! Her title was all a flummery, a word she had had some fun with when she unintentionally strayed into the forbidden arena of politics in a letter to Shenstone:

> I do not conceive what could make it [that the Royal Mercy was not given to (Bosavern) Penlez?*] enter into my head, but when it did do so, I can easily conceive it would fly away with my pen; for so negligently I write, the first ideas that present themselves

---

* As a result of the Penlez riots in the Strand in July 1749 Bosavern Penlez and John Wilson were found guilty of rioting and sentenced to death. Wilson was reprieved. However, Penlez was denied the royal pardon. The case caused public outrage.

go off to my friends, unpolished and unconnected: but to others I give only a very little *flummery*, and so conclude. This word *flummery*, you must know, Sir, means at London, *flattery* and *compliment*; and is the present reigning word among the Beaux and Belles. Pardon my telling you what your Dictionary would *not* have told you and pardon me also for boasting of knowing something about the fashions my neighbours do not know, and which, thanks to Chance, I do know! – I hope this self-exaltation will not draw upon me the guilt of the arrogant Pharisee. My knowledge does not extend very far, as learned as I am . . . !²

This indeed was no poetess, to ponder for hours over two lines or less, for Henrietta, as she said herself, loved to write as the ideas and commentaries came tumbling from her brain. Letters were her lifeblood and in many ways the torpid Shenstone was her perfect foil, for though he (who *loved* to sit for hours on end introspectively writing reams of poetry) could often only manage one letter for her every four or five, at least she knew he understood most of her outpourings, as long as there were no politics.* But in her London life letter-writing was so easy; the quills lay ready, the ink in a silver stand, a sheet of fine paper had only to be taken from the drawer. For the farmeress at Barrells it was very different – 'my want of a pen and ink is really want of common necessaries, bread or water; yet the fact is so that I can come at neither that will make what I write intelligible'. She scoured her garden and fields for crows' feathers, but forever cursed them as the worst, apologising for 'the late rough notes of my croaking crow'.³ To which Shenstone replied: 'In the first place however I must premise that Crows shall never be esteem'd inauspicious Birds by Me, since they convey me Intelligence of Your Ladyship's Health & Welfare: & I think I may extend my Indulgence also to Ravens, with whose Quills, I presume, you wou'd be able to write more sprightly Things, than any other Person with the Quill of a [mockingbird].'⁴ Of the goose – after she had chased one of her own for a tail feather – she had more hopes,

---

* Whether she wrote political letters to Harry Bolingbroke can only be imagined, for none have survived.

imagining the quill of that bird would favour me as it did you; but I am disappointed, she is still stupid; and her sister, who served you so well, must have been bred at Paris, if one judges by her politeness: and if you have ever employed her in the Poetical Pieces you have sent me, I shall think she has studied at Parnassus. Why must the silly look of the goose entitle her to be the emblem of nothing but stupidity, when the more silly gravity of the owl allows him to be the emblem of wisdom? Henceforward I shall prefer geese to all other of the feathered kind; at least the geese of the Leasowes!⁵

But then came the wondrous Christmas turkey-quill letter from Shenstone. 'I never once thought or imagined,' she exclaimed, 'that turkies could produce a quill capable of writing so good a hand . . . surely the bird you killed for Lord Dudley and with whose quill you wrote to me, must have been a phoenix in disguise! How could we have been both so elegantly feasted on any common bird?'⁶ Shenstone had now warmed to the subject, one which now seems to us slightly bizarre:

> As to the Quills of Turkeys, (tho' Indeed, I, who am no Hero made use of one) I think they are singularly proper for your Military Men; & that whether you regard the Nature of the *Bird*, or the Temper of His Feathers, the Bird you know is remarkable for empty Noise and Ostentation, & then as to the Quill it may suit a person very well who has been accustom'd to write his meaning with the Point of a Sword. I believe he will not find much *difference*, were he to try them both alternately upon Paper. To your Ladyship I wou'd recommend the Quill of a *Black-bird*; a bird that has both *spirit* & *Elegance* in his Notes; but as he seems to want *variety* I must own I know no English Bird except the Throstle that unites those three Qualities of all you write & say.

He regretted for her sake that neither the song-thrush (throstle) nor lark nor nightingale would have 'writeable' feathers, and

> I must therefore leave you to make use of whatever Quill you please; well knowing that you cou'd not write disagreeably even

with the Quill of a *Bittern* – For me the Goose ... will still
retain a Feather; And, against the Time I write in verse, I nourish
a very fine Peacock whose harmonious Voice agrees to a tittle
with my Versification; as I fear your Ladyship has too plainly
experienc'd.[7]

Her disgust with the 'soot and water' ink provided in that bleak
house at Quarley in the wilds of Hampshire meant that she was
used to better – a concoction of powdered black or amber rosin,
boiled linseed oil and water at its most sophisticated – though soot
and water was commonly 'ink', especially in the countryside. That
so many of the letters she kept from the miserable time of her
separation have survived with torn sheets is perhaps evidence of
how often she was in dire need of writing paper. Occasionally ink
and paper could be ordered in Henley-in-Arden, but these were
usually on her shopping list in Birmingham, where Shenstone introduced her to Thomas Aris, the publisher of *Aris' Birmingham
Gazette*, who sold drawing and writing materials. A more intriguing
situation arose with Shenstone's friendship with John Baskerville
and Robert Dodsley, which began because the trio of poetic friends,
Jago, Graves and Shenstone, liked to have their poems printed in
the *Gazette*, and some of these were amongst the earliest pieces set
by Baskerville in his new typeface. Shenstone knew the Baskervilles
well enough to be dropped by Henrietta's chaise at their door on
Easy Hill 'to beg a Draught of Perry' on a hot September afternoon,
and be admitted to find them sitting in their parlour with 'a Busto-
maker'.[8] John Baskerville was in his forties, an independent, showy
little man with a taste for gold lace, and though built 'with the light
timbers of a frigate, his movement was solemn as a ship of the line'.[9]
For over fifteen years he had been running his profitable japan-
ning workshop, selling cabinets, clocks, mirrors, trays and the like,
veneered and varnished in imitation tortoiseshell or painted with
fruit. Henrietta had as likely bought a tray or two (at 6 guineas a
pair), for they were much admired. Baskerville had developed his
passion for printing, built his own press, and in October 1752 he

was fast progressing with testing the typeface of his Great Primer, as the new letter-punches were cut on steel, prior to being stamped into a copper matrix to form the printing type.[10] This was the making of printing history, a recipe for a thriller of industrial espionage, for Baskerville was determined that William Caslon, whose type was the most popular at the time, should not learn of his innovation. Caslon had several connections to Shenstone, and was a local man, so it was all a taut game.[11] Along with his printing Baskerville was making advances with papers and inks. His paper was made from silk rags and moulded on a fine wire mesh that left no wire-marks, and called 'wove' (though there is some controversy as to whether Baskerville or Whatman invented 'wove' paper). He sold this as writing paper: 'Superfine post gilt or plain, glazed or unglazed ... little inferior in smoothness to the finest abortive Vellum ... also quarto post gilt and beautifully decorated in the borders at two Shillings and six-pence the quire, octavo ditto at one Shilling and six-pence; and Messages at eight-pence the dozen.'[12] Shenstone and Henrietta were the first customers for some of this paper, buying it directly from Baskerville, though most went to London to be sold through Robert Dodsley.

Robert Dodsley, in his late forties when she met him, became an important figure in her life. He was a sometime footman, author of 'a little satiric play', *The Toy Shop* (not in the Birmingham sense but a children's toyshop), put on at Pope's suggestion for a successful run at Covent Garden in 1735. It was a dramatic satire of conversations between the proprietor of the toyshop and his customers, and it made Dodsley enough money to buy and open his bookshop at the sign of Tully's Head in Pall Mall.[13] He pursued his contacts well and published, and sold, works by Pope, Lord Bolingbroke, Elizabeth Rowe, Stephen Duck, Richard Graves, Richard Jago (who wrote an 'Essay upon Electricity'), John Dalton and Shenstone, of the characters in Henrietta's story, as well as others. Dodsley's lists delighted her and supplied her winter reading.[14]

So, there she is, supplied with writing and reading materials (and she also mentions a fire-grate bought from Matthew Boulton's toyshop) by courtesy of the early dawning of the Midlands Enlightenment!

Of course her ink could always freeze, as it did in February 1751, when her lack of response from Shenstone prompted her 'I hope your ink has thawed, which I am persuaded has been froze; for I am sure your genius cannot freeze'.[15] She tried whimsy:

> my bees join with me in inviting you to my little Library, where they rejoice in their labour and work abundantly. It is a situation that Virgil has not marked out for them; but I dare say, were he to inhabit this earth again, he would not fail to call in an army of these useful creatures to form a colony in his Study where he would view their works and fancy himself one of their fellow citizens.

Surely such fancies were 'all very entertaining to us hermits'.[16] Henrietta was having a troubled time. She had been unwell and Dr Wall was her most frequent visitor, and she was forever being reminded of the tiresome and unpleasant chores that James had protected her from (perhaps James had kept the bees in order), and how much she missed him. Worst of all, she had so hoped that her brother Harry would come to stay at Barrells, and now she knew he was ill at Battersea with a cancer of his face. She felt very alone, and kept lobbing letters into the silence from The Leasowes. True to her own 'autumn' temperament she found spring intimidating, full of false promises, nonetheless she tried temptation. 'Now to talk of your favourite season Spring,' she wrote to Shenstone in March, 'my Shrubbery is in its prime, I am laying sand on all the walks, the kitchen garden is much improved by being lengthened . . . and my brother Bolingbroke has sent some exquisite melon seeds and lettuce.'[17] The walks and the kitchen garden were the achievement of her new Scots gardener, who is never named, but he is her first professionally-trained gardener and he probably came to her via the travelling 'mafia' of workmen who frequented the big establishments, possibly even from Lord Dudley's, where she admired the greenhouses.

News finally came from Shenstone on 24 April that his brother Joseph had been seriously ill, and though he had thought of writing often, he had never actually got down to it, because his spirits were so low, 'so much injur'd by watching, and so much varyed by sudden hopes and fears'.[18] Joseph was not pronounced better till the end of May. She made endless enquiries about their welfare, but again no replies came. June was cold: 'I languish out this everlasting winter . . . confined to my chimney corner, without a flower to adorn my chimney-piece or a gooseberry my board.' Probably for the only time in her life, Henrietta became maudlin: 'I see nobody near to bestow my affections upon. Those few who deserve them are, for the most part, snatched from me by one awkward event or other, and I seldom find use for that member the tongue, which is supposed to be so essential to women. My ears are as useless to me, for the whistle of the wind is their only entertainment.' Her Stratford friend, Mrs Kendall, was doubly bereaved by the deaths of her son and her sister. The nation, or the part that had great hopes of the 'Patriot King', was devastated by the sudden death of Frederick, Prince of Wales. Henrietta noted that the Hanoverian hatred between father and son seemed mollified in the King's kindness to Princess Augusta and 'wee George'.[19]

For her, a garden project was the cure: 'I have made, or rather am making a court before my house' which was 'entirely gravel and perhaps the handsome sundial that is in the upper garden in the middle'. She had widened the entrance from Barrells Green, removing the stone gate piers and resetting them as the entrance to her court, with a gate, in line with the Aviary at the north end of the house. 'There will be low white posts and rails round the court, to prevent drunken coachmen going down the Terrace. – This is my own plan, and I am all over embroidered with dust and mortar daily; but should prefer it to embroidery of another kind.' She added that she longed for Shenstone 'as you are the only touch-stone of true taste that I can have recourse to here' to approve. He was not to see it for over a year, but at least Mrs Kendall's coach and six came, and she was relieved they had room to manouevre.[20]

The weather for Henrietta's birthday on 15 July, her fifty-second, was suffocatingly hot, and the company, which included Lord Archer and Judge Chambers and his wife and daughter amongst others, spent the evening in her garden. An additional entertainment was provided by Captain Robinson's Dragoons and their forty-three troop horses scampering 'at grass' in her Great Meadow, 'which with the tent of the Grass-guards really does make the scenery pretty from my windows'. She had heard one of the dragoons playing his German flute 'very well', and he offered to play for her birthday party. At the party they bowled and 'had our syllabub out of doors' with the sound of flute and bagpipes wafting across the ha-ha. She hoped that letting the meadow to the militia would prove profitable.[21]

Shenstone really was infuriating, she thought. Not only had she pleaded and watched for him to come to her birthday party, and neither word nor body came, but when he did write it was all of the company of Lady Duchesses, a Lady Di, a Lady Caroline, Lord Goodness-knows-what, Admirals and Colonels that demanded all of his attentions on their visits to his walks. Henrietta archly observed, 'I find The Leasowes is becoming the resort of the *beau monde*.' He had sent her a present (unspecified) to which she replied that she would have rather had his company.[22] In August she became conspiratorial: 'I cannot write much; yet I must tell you one secret which nobody in the neighbourhood knows, viz that my brother Bolingbroke is to send a set of horses from Bath on Saturday next, to fetch me to him.'[23]

Shenstone was forgotten, Barrells had to fend for itself, she was gone to Battersea to be with Harry. They had not been together for any length of time for more than twenty years, since the happy days at Dawley, and the birth of Harry Knight, and they had not been alone together since her childhood. And yet they knew the details of each other's lives, and there were all their ghosts to talk of – Frances Bolingbroke, grandmother Johanna, old Sir Walter,

Angelique, George, Jack, Holly, even 'Old Frumps' their father –
and Marie-Claire – undoubtedly they walked into the old church to
meet them all, and for Harry to shed a tear over Marie-Claire's
epitaph, which he had composed:

> Mary Clara des Champs de Marcilly, marchioness of Villette and
> Viscountess Bolingbroke born of a noble family bred in the
> Court of Lewis 14th; She reflected a lustre on the former by the
> superior accomplishments of her mind; She was an ornament
> to the latter by the amiable dignity and grace of her behaviour:
> She lived the honour of her own sex, the delight and admiration
> of ours. She dyed an object of imitation to both with all the
> firmness that religion can inspire.[24]

And then did they roam the old rooms and the still lovely gardens
that Harry tended, and laugh over their childhood memories? It
seems so, for Frances wrote to Henrietta: 'I am not in the least
surprised that you were pleased to return to the venerable seats of
your ancestors, and the abode of your first and happiest days; and
find nothing trivial or childish in the satisfaction you felt in seeing
old faces full of gratitude for obligations long since past and by you,
perhaps forgot; or in recalling some little lively incidents in the
earliest and innocent hours of youth.'[25] It is easier to dwell on distant
memories. Is it possible that Harry ever explained to her just how
he had needed Bob Knight's money and had allowed her to be
married to Robert; how he was sorry for all that had happened;
how he was delighted with the success she had made of Barrells?
Harry Bolingbroke was a man who bore his grudges to the end. Did
he realise that this was the one person in the world that he could
have no grudge against, and did he tell her so? Perhaps she sat by
him as he composed his own epitaph, rather on the lines of the
inscription at La Source:

> Here lies Henry St John, in the reign of Queen Anne, secretary
> of war, secretary of state, and viscount Bolingbroke: in the days
> of King George I and King George II something more and better.
> His attachment to Queen Anne exposed him to a long and severe

persecution: he bore it with firmness of mind. He passed the latter part of his time at home, the enemy of no national party; the friend of no faction; distinguished under the cloud of a proscription which had not been entirely taken off, by zeal to maintain the liberty, and to restore the antient prosperity of GREAT BRITAIN.[26]

It was not long before this was placed beside Marie-Claire's on Roubiliac's elegant double memorial in Battersea church. His darling Heriott and 'the old faces full of gratitude' cared for him to his end, and he died on 12 December, at the age of seventy-three. Immediately after his funeral, Henrietta quickly moved to the Wymondesolds in Grosvenor Street for three weeks. She was undoubtedly upset, and did not want to face the triumphant heir, her nephew Frederick, the 3rd Viscount St John from Lydiard. Her farewell to Harry was her farewell to Battersea, and she never saw her childhood home again.*

The pain of Harry's death aggravated all her ills, her swollen joints and painful hands, her headaches and sleeplessness: 'as our losses are irrecoverable,' she wrote to Shenstone, 'we ought I believe, endeavour to shake off the melancholy ideas they suggest, but I preach what I do not well practice'.[27] She returned to Barrells to the dispiriting news that Shenstone's brother Joseph had died, no doubt leading to an inescapable atmosphere of gloom and despondency

---

* The year after Henrietta's death, 1757, Frederick, whom his friends called 'Bully', married Lady Diana Spencer, the eldest daughter of the Duke of Marlborough; the marriage was made as a joke, by way of a *faux* proposal at a party at Vauxhall Gardens. There was no love, nor compatability. Frederick, despite Harry Bolingbroke's best efforts to cultivate his heir – or perhaps because of them – was a rake, though a talented rake who had an eye for horseflesh and owned the fabulous Gimcrack, which he commissioned George Stubbs to paint on Newmarket Heath. Lady Diana was a beauty but also an artist, and portrayed as such by Sir Joshua Reynolds. She gave birth to an heir, George, a daughter Charlotte, and a spare Frederick, in the early 1760s. In 1765 she left her husband, citing his cruelty and adultery, and taking refuge with her brother, now the Duke of Marlborough, who protected her. Their subsequent divorce 'rocked society'. Frederick, who had no happy memories nor affection for Battersea sold Henrietta's old home to Lady Diana's cousin John, who became Earl Spencer in 1765. Lady Diana, now free and in love with Topham Beauclerk, married him, and lived happily; their daughter Mary had a passionate affair, and four sons, with her half-brother George St John.

at The Leasowes. Dr Wall said that she must get away again –
'bathing and pumping' was his prescription – and so she arranged
to go to Bath, with two companions Mrs Lane and her maid Ann
Harrop, and stay at least until spring appeared. They travelled
through the lanes to Worcester and then on to Gloucester, spending
the night at the New Inn. They arrived at Mrs Hodgkinson's in the
Orange Grove the next day, 20 January 1752, and 'Lady Luxborough's
Arrival' was listed in the *Bath Journal* the following week.[28]

Bath was much changed from the quiet little spa town Henrietta
had first visited with her mother thirty years before. It was now at
the height of its fame, the triumphant work-in-progress of the
architect John Wood the Elder, and ruled over by Beau Nash. The
Orange Grove was the smartest corner of all, a pretty square between
the east end of the abbey and the river and Pulteney Bridge. It
sported Wood's new Dame Lindsey's Assembly House, and Nassau
House, designed by Lord Burlington for Prince William of Orange
(whose wedding celebration she had failed to attend all those years
ago) who was restored to good health by the Bath waters, an achievement advertised on the obelisk in the centre of the Grove, set up by
Beau Nash in 1734.[29] From her window Henrietta could watch the
fashionable company strolling in the Grove, or sitting in the shade,
for there were many seats beneath the trees, and the whole effect
was garden-like.

The Orange Grove was also a place of curiosity, supposedly the
site of King Bladud's oracle that told of the hot springs, and so
brought the Romans. This was the story in John Wood's *Description
of Bath*, freshly reissued in 1749, and required reading for every
visitor. Wood had convinced himself of the Roman glories that
Agricola had conferred on Bath, calling it 'Troy Novant', and these
mystical associations had inspired his rebuilding.[30] Blyden Doith,
Blyden the Soothsayer, or Bladud,* was the *Description*'s impressive
frontispiece drawn by William Hoare (one of the children at Quarley

---

* Who met his end *c.* 843 BC while trying to fly with leather wings.

House eighteen years earlier) as a tall, curly-haired and bearded figure in a loose cloak, with an ornate buckled belt, leaning on his bow. He was pictured in a landscape with what appeared to be the (Hoare family's) Stourhead temples as a backdrop, a figure not unlike William Shenstone wandering in his groves.

Henrietta had always looked upon buying new things as a tonic and in the Orange Grove she had many purveyors to hand, or close by: Frederick's the Bookseller's, a coffee shop or two, with jewellers, silk weavers, perfumiers and a glove-makers. Knowing that Shenstone loved 'baubles' she sent him some, which he ridiculed as 'elegant presents', and so in revenge she sent, in the care of her young servant Joe, 'a bit of dirty rock and a snail petrified by the water hereabouts'.[31] Having cheered him, she tempted him further:

> Bath is *your* place ... for Duchesses trudge the streets here unattended, we have also friendly Othellos, Falstaffs, Richards the Third and Harlequins, who entertain one daily for half the price of your Garricks, Barrys and Rich's. And what you will scarcely believe, we can also offer you friendly solitude, for one may be an Anchoret here without being disturbed by the question 'Why?' Would you see the fortunate and benevolent Mr Allen, his fine house and his stone quarries? Would you see our lawgiver Mr Nash whose white hat commands more respect and non-resistance than the Crowns of some Kings, though now worn on a head that is in the eightieth year of its age? To promote society, good manners and a coalition of parties and ranks; to suppress scandal and late hours are his views; and he succeeds rather better than his brother monarchs generally do – hasten then your steps, for he may soon be carried off the stage of life, as the greatest must fall to the worms' repast.[32]

She did see Mr Allen's 'fine house', Ralph Allen's Prior Park, where she met the luminaries Dr Oliver (of Bath Oliver fame) of the Bath Mineral Water Hospital (who had prescribed her cure), John Wood, William Hoare and Henry Fielding's sister, the writer Sarah Fielding.[33] At other times she benefited from 'the bathing and pumping', and enjoyed the resort-atmosphere of 'friendly conversation, friendly springs, friendly rides and walks, friendly pastimes to dissipate gloomy thoughts; friendly booksellers, who for five shillings for the season will furnish you with all the new books, friendly chair-men who will carry you through storm and tempest for sixpence'.[34] One person was less friendly though, for who should be staying in the Orange Grove but the exacting Mrs Dewes, at 'Mr Jones great house', who again was sent into a flurry of alarm at being seen with Henrietta. Once again she appealed to her sister and Mary Delany poured balm: 'I am really diverted at your difficulties about Lady Luxborough – your character is too well established to be hurt by an acquaintance with her, and Bath acquaintances are said to pass with the waters, and as people of fashion and reputation do not shun her I see no reason why you should do so in any remarkable way, but your own prudence and judgment can better direct you than I can.'[35]

Henrietta does not mention Ann Dewes' 'prudence and judgment' or anything else of her, and their meeting was towards the end of her stay in Bath. The zealous Selina, Countess of Huntingdon, may have crossed with her, too; the countess had been a friend of Marie-Claire Bolingbroke but did not hesitate to censure Henrietta as 'so odd, so engrossed with her poets and literary acquaintances that she gave neither time nor attention to her never-dying soul'.[36] How did the countess know? She may have wished Henrietta was an ardent Nonconformist like herself, but Henrietta's church was the one she was born into and her clerical friends gave her regular enough reminders of her soul. Besides, this was a commonplace charge to lovers of beauty in any form, and in his kindly and bucolic satire on Methodism, *The Spiritual Quixote*, Richard Graves made his hero Mr Geoffry Wildgoose admonish a gardening gentleman, saying

> that doubtless the pleasures we receive from gardens, woods and lawns and other rural embellishments, were the most innocent of any amusements; but that we should consider them as amusements only, and not let them engross too much of our attention;

that we ought to spiritualize our ideas as much as possible; and that it was worth while to enquire how far too violent a fondness for these merely inanimate beauties might interfere with our love of God, and attach us too strongly to the things of this world.*[37]

Henrietta's expedition to Claverton to see Richard and Lucy Graves was her most eagerly anticipated outing from Bath. She found the rectory down a 'rough, unfrequented road' behind a high wall, as Graves had written. It was an ancient house, modernised in Queen Elizabeth's time, with an enclosed entrance court where visitors were 'regaled with the sight and fragrance of all the flowers of the season'; this season being early spring. The gloomy hall, the walls covered with maps and chronological tables and cheap prints of foreign countries, gave on to the large, wainscotted parlour 'adorned with some fine prints, a few good paintings, and a bust or two over the chimney'.[38] Here Graves, 'who does not leave his wife an inch', presented his precious Lucy, young, tall and beautiful with a smile 'which, like the sun-shine so much admired in the landscapes of Claude Lorraine, diffused an additional chearfulness over every other object'.[39] Lucy Graves was twenty-two; her husband, born in 1715 and at Oxford with Shenstone, was thirty-seven. Graves, a Fellow of All Souls and unable to marry, had been a curate at Aldworth on the Berkshire Downs not far from Marlborough when he had fallen in love with the youngest daughter of Edward Bartholomew of Dunworth Farm. Lucy was fifteen. There were strong objections to any betrothal from both families, but Graves, enthralled by Lucy's 'good nature and good sense in her disposition

---

* There was an outcome: the gentle gardener, having given Wildgoose and his companion a bed for the night, rose early to find his guests already departed. Wildgoose, having spent the night wrestling with his fears that his good host had already set up idols in his heart, had gone out into the garden, opened the sluices of the cascade reservoirs and knocked a lead statue of a Piping Faun off its pedestal. On discovering this wilful damage, the gentleman was 'a little provok'd' at first, then laughed out loud, and set about repairing the Faun for his visitors, confident that they would find the amusing story more than made up for the shortage of water in the cascade. The gentle gardener was, of course, William Shenstone.

with sprightliness and artless freedom' as well as her 'eyes of such brilliant lustre' that he never knew their real colour, whisked his now-pregnant love off to London, where he married her secretly in August 1747. In London they lived quietly, Lucy gave birth to a son and then a daughter, and he sent her to school to finish her education. Having lost his fellowship Graves had been lucky enough to get the Claverton living. He had been ordained to the charge of 100 souls living in sixteen houses in the one-street village at the foot of Claverton Down on Sunday, 11 June 1749, given the church keys, and 'he tolled the bell of a church of his own for the first time'.[40]

At Claverton Richard and Lucy were living happily ever after. Henrietta found them devoted and very agreeable, and she made a point of her admiration of Lucy. They in their turn were enchanted with their visitor. It was early for the garden, but it was not to be missed, for the lessons of The Leasowes had not been lost on Graves, who practised 'allegro and penseroso, the chearful and the gloomy' in miniature, with roses, jasmines, lilacs and philadelphus, a serpentine walk of cypress and laurels, 'here and there an urn, with suitable inscriptions' and a rough rock-work arch over a fountain, green and mossy.[41] Henrietta was promised roots of a particularly good polyanthus and a Cornelian cherry, Cornus mas for Barrells. These new friends and their promise to come to see her made a happy ending to her stay. The Bath cure seemed to have worked and she journeyed home in May in the best of spirits. She had been greatly taken with some designs she had seen, by Prince Hoare, for moulded papier-mâché decorations that could be used instead of plaster for ceilings, and she had plans to redecorate her bedroom and dressing room.

That late spring and summer of 1752 saw her garden at its prettiest – even the reluctant Ann Dewes had allowed it was 'very pretty' and she had seen it with the August seediness setting in – and so in June and for Henrietta's St Swithun's Day birthday it must have been so. If that visionary artist of enchantment Mr Thomas Robins, who has given us the gift of seeing Honington, Painswick and Bath in the

1740s and 1750s, had painted Barrells – which unfortunately he did not – what pictures could he have made? Take his view of the orangery pavilion at Woodside near Old Windsor of 1750, framed in morning glory and jasmine, with ladies with lapdogs and a gentleman in blue with a black greyhound and her puppy – lapdogs were not Henrietta's style but Shenstone had a faithful greyhound and gave Henrietta one of her puppies, so there's a starting point! All the character of Henrietta's garden is here, it just has to be rearranged: all it needs is her house, or 'cottage', the south facing, lime-washed gable end with sash windows and a garden door added to the left of the pavilion. For pavilion read her summerhouse, built out from the back of an outbuilding, with a stuccoed front with columns, and a pediment, and the small stone vases that old Pedley had made her at the corners of the roof. There were no glass panes as in Robins' orangery, nor oranges, but inside she had a semicircle of busts, her brother Bolingbroke, Pope, Dryden, Milton, Newton, Locke and Shakespeare, her miniature pavilion of 'British Worthies', as at Stowe. Her summerhouse, bathed in late afternoon summer sunlight as the sun slipped round to the south-west, was for sitting with a book or taking tea with friends on a fine evening. Rather than lawn, as in Robins' painting, she had a paved terrace all along the front, with beds of her Austrian briar roses, and the artist would be taking his view from her bowling green. If he tipped his chair back he might fall over the ha-ha.[42]

A second Robins view of Woodside shows a Chinese pavilion with half a dozen gardeners at work. Henrietta had neither chinoiserie nor as many gardeners, but take these away and the view might be from her front door, across her carriage sweep to her Shrine to Venus. This had begun life as her 'grotto', a small brick cave, mortared and stuck with shells and spars, any she could find, with a backdrop of evergreens as Robins shows here. When she acquired the crouching Venus she found a home in the 'grotto' amongst moss-covered rocks, with ferns and ivies. Over all this Henrietta had built a new stuccoed pavilion, of simple classical shape with a pediment. 'O Venus Regina Guidi' was the motto placed over the shrine. She came back from Bath with a 'debris' of rock-work from Mr Allen's quarries and she also had some 'Bristol jewels' – these most likely amethyst, quartz or agate acquired from work-in-progress on Thomas Goldney's grotto at Bristol, begun in 1737.[43] Frances Hertford had visited this and described it to her and she saw it for herself on a visit to the Merediths at Henbury in the early 1740s. All these treasures were added to Venus' setting, along with some mirror shards for extra glitter, as the painter Thomas Smith had suggested.

So, to return to Robins' chinoiserie painting, take out the Chinese pavilion and insert Venus' classically-fronted shrine. The most fascinating thing about the painting is the detail of sanded or gravelled paths winding through shrubs, a Shrubbery, and the only contemporary image that I know that allows this glimpse of 'her' garden.

So let us begin at the beginning of the Barrells tour. This was elm country, those majestic, fluttering trees beloved of landscape painters, and the elms parted at Barrells Green to allow the sweep into Henrietta's drive. It was a straight drive, lined with elms and oaks, hollies and laurels which screened the views on either side. Its straightness was a relict of the direct ways of old England, before the serpentine had been invented. Had she been given more time Henrietta might have changed it, for she devoured Hogarth's hymn to the shallow, elegant, undulating double curve, his 'line of beauty' in *The Analysis of Beauty*, as soon as it was published (December 1753). She 'found a book which I did not imagine Hogarth capable of writing [and] never imagined his pen would have afforded me so much pleasure'.[44] But the drive remained straight, entering her gravelled court through a five-barred white gate, with a footgate at the side, set between stone gate piers. The court allowed a coach to pull up at her front door, then sweep around the sundial in the centre, and leave for the stable yard that was to the east of the drive. As she had said, the court was delineated with a white post-and-rail fence to prevent the overly excited horses or the drunken coachman from driving down her terrace.

From the house there was a choice of circuits, the longer to the east could be taken in the light chaise, otherwise with strolling and talking it could probably fill two hours or so. From the south terrace and the bowling green steps led down beside the ha-ha to the lower garden, which was simply a fenced semicircle of meadow flowers and grasses that projected into the rectangular Great Meadow, giving uninterrupted views to the north-west and south-east. It is imposs-ible to know if Henrietta made this 'bastion' viewpoint, for she does not mention it, but as she was an admirer of Stephen Switzer and his *Ichnographia Rustica* in which he showed his design for the Duchess' bastion at Grimsthorpe Castle (and she had met the anti-quary William Stukeley who had made a comical drawing of the ladies escaping from the woods to their viewing bastion) it does seem likely. It shows her usual economy without loss of style. The Barrells 'bastion' gave a view down the meadow (a field of 37½ acres) – where the militia troop horses had gambolled – to the old fish ponds along the valley stream, and moated Oldberrow Court (which unfortunately Lord Luxborough bought at about this time).

Regaining the higher level, the perambulators, or the chaise, set off down the Long Walk which was to the east along the naturally raised field boundary. This was a grass walk which she had cut from the boundary wood of chestnuts and Scots pines on the inner, north side, and from the grown-out hedgerow ash and elm on the field boundary. In one section she had planted an avenue of some healthy young limes which were already arching overhead in the desirable 'cathedral' effect. It was probably near the scented limes that she placed the seat, with a view across the meadow to the valleys of the Alne and Avon and her hopefully spied 'little bit of a Gloucestershire hill'. Mostly the canopy and spacing of the Walk were light enough for the grasses to grow along the 'lane', which was fringed with elder bushes and briar roses, honeysuckles, poppies, ox-eye daisies and perhaps corncockles and campions. Hers was a sustainable, country version of Frances Hertford's flower walk of stocks, daisies, campions, sweet williams and lupins along beside the cornfield at Percy Lodge.

At the field corner the Walk turned north, to wind through the remotest part of her wood, a bluebell wood in springtime. In the deepest corner of this remote wood was a clearing, where a pit had been dug for gravel for some long-forgotten purposes, which was now a grassy dell with wood anemones, ferns and primroses on the banks. On the rim of the dell was her Hermitage, built of rough-hewn chestnut palings with a thatched roof, and covered with flowering clematis, the sweetly scented white-flowered *Clematis flammula*. Thomas Smith had thought her Hermitage more prettily sited than any other that he had seen in the great gardens. Henrietta was only too pleased that it was now weatherproof, even in winter, and the tiled floor and sturdy wooden seats, well cushioned, made it possible for her to retreat there on the first and last warm days of the years. Being there on her own with a book was almost a holiday, freed from the cares of a farmeress. With visitors it was the favourite spot for the picnic tea.

Some visitors were more energetic than others, for Shenstone had written, 'I am to thank Miss Harriet for demolishing the Precipice by the Pitt side, & converting it into a Slope, which is the very thing I've been labouring at ever since I knew Barrells'; labouring *in thought* that is, whereas Harriet Meredith was all action. As was her sister all art, for Shenstone added, 'I am to thank Miss Patty for the little boy from Watteau; who, this minute, peeps at me over my Chimney-Glass, and looks exceedingly archly.'[45] Is it possible that Henrietta had a little Watteau, bought in Paris and there for Patty Meredith to copy?

The Hermitage was the farthest from the house, and the return along the north side of her woods was via a public right of way that ran from east to west, from Mount Pleasant at Ullenhall towards Mappleborough Green, across Barrells' land. It was a customary right of way, ages old and well used, and whilst Henrietta did not begrudge the travellers their right of passage, she was greatly vexed at the damage done by idle miscreants who scrumped her apples and cavorted in her Coppice. She had tried everything, fencing (broken down), a bank (climbed over) and a close avenue of abele, the fast growing white poplar, which, after endless uprootings and replacings, grew into a screen. Poor Shenstone at The Leasowes was equally 'open' to all who wandered the lanes and despairing of the perversity of human kind. He had been planting primroses beside one of his streams but feared they would not last, 'I would gladly enough compound the matter with the Mob if they wou'd leave me about *Half*, particularly those you were so kind to give me. But I fear they wont, for tho' there are Primroses to be gather'd in the Fields in Plenty yet if they can discover one that is apparently planted, they are sure to crop it. But 'tis chiefly done by Children & such as can't read, were I to publish my *Placard* as they have done at Hagley Park'.[46]

The poplar avenue led to her stables, and the drive, but her visitors could turn south, through her Coppice to the Kitchen Garden on the east side of the house, or to the Aviary on the north. This home coppice, the part of the wood nearest the house, which had been cut for everyday uses for years was fenced, and it was light and sunny, with patches of shade beneath full-grown oaks, where she was cultivating one or two moss seats. It was carpeted with the flowers she remembered from her childhood – snowdrops, primroses, violets, star of Bethlehem and wild hyacinths in spring, and the russet of the fallen chestnut leaves in autumn. She was forever exploring her Coppice, creating 'pictures'. She planted an avenue of rowan which she called her Service-Walk, perhaps because it led from the kitchen garden to the stables, but more likely because they were the native wild service tree (*Sorbus torminalis*) or the service tree of Fountainbleau (*Sorbus latifolia*). Equally she was overjoyed to find 'a kind of natural arbour in the Coppice with an oak in it, under which I have a mind to raise a bank of turf'[47] as a new home for the statue of the Piping Faun she had now acquired as a present from The Leasowes. Coppice melted into orchard, and her orchard surrounded the kitchen garden, made out of the old farmyard, and likely to have been low-walled in a utilitarian way. She had melon pits, but she does not mention peaches or apricots, those famous fruits of her old home at Battersea. Her very first visit to Shenstone in 1747 had been marked by his gift of 'the finest pine-apple I ever tasted' and she would surely have told him if she successfully grew them.

From the house's South Terrace the shorter 'circuit' to the west must have been especially pretty in the early evenings when the setting sun sparkled through the trees. Venus' Shrine could be approached by a footgate from the carriage sweep, and around and beyond it, rather as Thomas Robins had painted, the soft-edged gravelled paths led through the main area of Shrubbery, a sprinkled planting of lilacs, philadelphus, bay, myrtle, holly, sweetbriar roses and her Whitsun 'roses', *Viburnum opulus*, the snowball tree. Shenstone had mused 'what if you were to plant here & there a Yew-tree in your Shrubbery to look wild & to continue about ye size of your other Shrubs'.[48] She also had bushes of 'the *kind* laurestinus (*Viburnum tinus*) who is indeed a *friend in distress*, and most welcome in winter'.[49] Evergreens were really rather precious, the bay laurel, myrtle and laurustinus, Mediterranean plants though grown in England for at least 200 years, were used to walled and sheltered gardens, and so planting them out in an open, windy, Midlands shrubbery was quite an adventure: the native yew would add stability and shelter.

In his *The Flowering of the Landscape Garden* Mark Laird allows her into the pioneering company of Philip Southcote of Woburn Farm, Dickie Bateman's Grove House at Old Windsor (painted by Thomas Robins), Shenstone and Joseph Spence[50] amongst makers of medium-sized gardens, a very honourable place to be. These four, along with Sanderson Miller who will appear in a moment, all had subtle taste and the perception to make their gardens with far less resources than the great houses with their armies of gardeners and whole management structures to seek out and obtain the newest plants. These large and *much* smaller gardens have been lumped together in history in a very confusing way, and for Henrietta and for Shenstone at least, they were working in unsympathetic 'wilder-nesses' in the horticultural sense, which made their achievement all the more worthy.* Through all her time at Barrells Henrietta – who, after all, was familiar with the greatest houses in the land – remained dismissive of her grandest neighbours. She tolerated Lord Archer from Umberslade who set up the pompous obelisk in his park to celebrate his father's – the groom-porter's – peerage, and she noted with undisguised glee how the crowning golden ball arrived on the carrier's cart. She was polite, but nothing more to Ferdinando Dudley Lea, Lord Dudley, who clearly admired her – she preferred his greenhouses, of which she was openly envious. As to Hagley, fashionable Hagley, whose owner George Lyttelton was a political ally of Harry Bolingbroke's in the 1740s but who never seemed to acknowledge her as more than a 'garden visitor', she had sorted her priorities: 'I am not ashamed to own,' she wrote to Shenstone, 'that I like even a root-seat at the Leasowes better than I do the [sham castle] at Hagley . . . how many are there, besides myself, whose eyes oblige them (without knowing why) to be more delighted with the Banqueting House in Whitehall than with Blenheim [Palace], and with the front of [St Paul's] Covent Garden church than with St Paul's Cathedral.'[52] Was it a matter of degree, or a more social thing? Was she, for all her cheerful confidence, wary of being snubbed, or was it – and more likely – that this fashionable 'modern gardening' was so new that its lordly advocates had not yet realised it was too much an art to be left only to their professional gardeners. A love of one's landscape, perceptive ideas and 'hands-on' gardening – the controlling mind and eye – were necessary: those who 'gardened' merely for show were not for her.

---

* She did, in the spring of 1751, acquire seeds of 'the greatest curiosity of a flower – if I can but raise it!' The pod 'which is as big as a pine-apple and perfumes a room even now it is not in flower' was possibly *Magnolia virginiana*.[51]

At Barrells, the serpentine paths led slightly uphill to an open lawn known as the Upper Garden, and apparently the *only* garden before Henrietta's time, with a sundial (which she moved to the entrance court) and some beds of flowers. Flower beds were not her style, but Shenstone recommended her to plant peonies in her 'grove'. It is not impossible that, with the peonies in the grass, she had a colony of tall larkspurs, yellow daisy-flowered dorinicums and green hellebores, as William Robinson was to have at his wood's edge. The preferred habitats of flowers do not change. To the north of the Upper Garden was a second grove, the clearing she had made as the home of Somerville's Urn, which had settled comfortably underneath its canopy of oak branches. Just beyond it, and in view of the Urn, she had set a white bench 'from whence one has a view of Skiltz [a hill to the west] and the Urn also looks well from it'.[53] This spot in high summer had an 'edge of the cornfield' quality such as Stubbs and Gainsborough painted: there was no fence, her softly-scythed green grove lipped over a ditch and met the standing golden corn, which rippled away to the west. It was the perfect spot for remembrance of William Somerville the countryman. It also said something about the place of the 'modern' landscape garden, at that delicate moment of harmonious balance in the middle of the eighteenth century. Henrietta believed that her whole *ferme ornée* was her garden, and that she had endless prospects – 'Why don't your Ladyship throw all your Haystacks into ye Form of Pyramids, and chuse out places where they may look agreeably,' suggested Shenstone.[54]

Henrietta spent her fifty-third birthday in Oxford followed by visitors in August, Mrs Davies, Sir Peter Soame and his son, also Peter, and Captain Outing. At home in September a Mr Pixell decorated her bedroom and dressing room as she had planned, with papier-mâché festoons over the windows: Henrietta had not lost her touch for when Pixell (the son of Shenstone's friend Revd John Pixell?) went home she heard from Shenstone that his visit to Barrells had rendered him 'so vain ... it will take five or six weeks

Mortification to bring him down to the standard of other Vain-glorious Men'.[55] In October her manservant Price had a stroke, and as he could no longer manage the upper stairs he was nursed in her second-best bedroom, with Dr Wall in frequent attendance and often staying overnight, until Price died in early November. Shenstone brought Lord Dudley to see Barrells, and they all went over to Umberslade to see Lord Archer's obelisk on its windy hill, from which Henrietta took a chill which turned feverish. She was miserably ill all through Christmas, though it appears 'good Mrs Holyoake' was kind enough to sit with her.

Henrietta's low spirits lasted through January, and they were little helped by the news that her daughter had left Charles Wymondesold and eloped with Josiah Child. Henrietta, perhaps more than most, was aware of the perils of her daughter's position. '[T]his melancholy scene to her friends is, I suppose, an amusement to the public, who will divert themselves at her and her favourite's expense, whilst her Husband laments her folly.'[56] Wymondesold, never the most alluring of husbands, was awarded damages in the divorce suit against Josiah Child so the couple were exiled in Paris, from where Josiah wrote to Lord Luxborough that 'my dear Harriot' gave birth to a son, also called Josiah, on 28 January 1754. They were married in Paris on 3 May. From now on her daughter signed herself Henrietta Child, undoubtedly to be as distant from 'Maddalena Wymondesold' as possible. She clearly had her mother's brains and spirit, for she was clever enough to involve herself in Parisian circles and find gossip that intrigued Lord Luxborough, so much so that he never criticised her nor, more importantly, stopped sending her money for the support of little Josiah. Lord Luxborough was now, unfortunately, their lifeline: Mr Child was only a younger brother of Lord Tylney of Wanstead, and had little employment or money in Paris. Henrietta Child, who had been so close to her mother since they were reunited in 1748, with every sign of affection and mutual care – especially for the distraught Henrietta after Harry Bolingbroke's death – now had to make a choice between her parents. Her mother was clearly of little 'use' to her and it seems that she never wrote to her again. Henrietta was never to see her little grandson.[57]

So Henrietta was left with just one true correspondent – Frances Hertford. The Hertfords had become Duke and Duchess of Somerset at the end of 1748 and Frances had become engrossed in her new houses, Petworth in Sussex and Northumberland House in Westminster. But sadly the time to enjoy their new position was all too short, for the duke died in early 1750, leaving his widow her beloved Percy Lodge as her home for the rest of her lifetime. The two old friends exchanged letters once or twice a year now, understanding each other: 'when you write to me you give me pleasure,' wrote Frances in December 1752, 'when you do not, I love my own peace too well to fancy you are angry with me'. There was no anger left, only consolations and even unspoken farewells. Duchess Frances had a 'regular and religious family', her servants and her routine at Percy Lodge. She had always been inclined to piety and was now more so, with a daily ritual of prayers and breakfast, a little company, a walk in the garden, dinner at the old-fashioned early hour of three, then reading, more prayers and to bed. Henrietta thought privately that this was 'too much retired'.[58] They write of their books, but do not seem to read the same ones any more; they share their frailties – 'I pity your Grace as I do myself when I think of our being lately carried up and down stairs; we! who measured long tracts of land with our steps, and seldom sat down to rest!'[59] To which Frances replied: 'times are changed with us since no walk was long enough nor exercise was painful enough to hurt us, as we childishly imagined; yet after a ball or masquerade have we not come home very well contented to rest?'[60] This was to be Frances' last surviving letter, of 25 February 1754. She added:

> I will ingenuously own to you, dear Madam that I experience more true happiness in the retired manner of life that I have embraced, than I ever knew from all the flatteries and splendour

of the world. There was always a void; they could not satisfy
a rational mind; and at the most heedless time of my youth, I
well remember that I always looked forward with a kind of joy
to a decent retreat, when the evening of life should make it
practicable . . .'[61]

Henrietta's own 'dear Duchess' remained in character to the last;
she died quietly six months later at Percy Lodge.

Characteristically, Henrietta wanted one more turn around the
ballroom. She bought herself a new chaise, a light landaulet which
would take her around her own garden, as well as other people's.
She learned that the road from Crabbs Cross, six miles west of
Barrells, to Bromsgrove and Stourbridge was being turnpiked and
she rejoiced that this would make her journey to The Leasowes
easier. She was determined to go to see Lord and Lady Plymouth's
Hewell Grange, and also Enville, Lord Stamford's garden.

Enville's owner had been to Barrells, and Shenstone was giving
him a great deal of advice on his estate, another pioneering
garden of the Picturesque, set in a spectacular and dramatic landscape between the Stour and the Severn just west of Stourbridge.
Enville possessed ravines, rocks, trees and water and was given
all the trimmings: cascades, a hermitage, a Gothic boathouse and
'Shenstone's Chapel', this last in his honour. Shenstone is sometimes
given the credit for Enville, but Capability Brown, who came after
him, takes much of it – and of course, Nature's own role in such a
dramatic garden cannot be discounted.

Shenstone was also much involved with Sanderson Miller and
his gardens, and reported faithfully to Henrietta. It would be nice
to think that she saw Miller's own Radway Grange*, for he was a
character she would have found interesting, a talented amateur
architect with a taste for the 'rocaille' – rococo– and a talent for
friendship. At the age of thirty-four, in 1750, he explained his
priorities:

* About ten miles south-east of Stratford.

> At last I find that I have clear
> In Land six hundred pounds a year
> Besides a Piece for Wife & Daughters
> And something more for Woods & Waters
> And Laurel Walk & Strawberry Bank
> For which the Paymaster I thank.*[62]

Miller's Radway 'farm' was between his house (with the two new Gothic bay windows) and Edgehill, the Civil War battlefield (23 October 1642) and celebrated as the title of Richard Jago's long poem in praise of this middle England landscape. Radway was almost a *ferme ornée* in idea, at least the farm existed in the ornamental context, for Miller had used double hedges to shelter the pathway from house to hill, gradually introducing features along the way. Shenstone was scathing on his 'detestable' trees, stunted and sprouting ash, and hardly less happy with 'a little frothy water' and some new works which struck a false note:

> [the water] falls over 3 rustick arches, runs down, thro' broken stone-work, to a Bason in the midst of which is a Jetteau; and on each side tumuli or little mounds of Earth artificially cast up ... a juvenile Performance, & only retain'd because it is there & has cost him money. After this we viewed an artificial Terrass which gives a view of the Plain where the Battle was fought.

The side of the hill was clothed in woodland, of 'wild & *Forest-like* appearance', and the path terminated in 'an *Eye-trap*' – the end of a stable plastered and painted to look like a pedimented doorcase – a piece of counterpointed design that any twenty-first century gardener would be proud to own. Miller's *pièce de résistance* was his octagonal brick tower on the hill, with its Gothic upper room, shields on the ceiling, painted glass windows 'Gothick Niches & Gothick Cornice', though Shenstone felt that the way the stair broke through the floor was 'horrible'. Nearby was a 'ruin', partly the old gateway removed from Radway Grange with a turret added 'which

---

* The 'Paymaster' was William Pitt, whose reforms on subsidies had improved army pensions. Pitt was also a keen gardener.

is in reality some Poor body's chimney,' scoffed Shenstone, who was on the whole not impressed with the evident expense of all these constructions which vied with the serenity of such a remote place.[63] It is refreshing, then, that garden visiting did not *have* to be constant admiration.

Maybe Sanderson Miller took note of Shenstone's criticisms, for at Farnborough Hall, just four miles from Radway, he made improvements that, as at The Leasowes, took their cue from their setting, which showed an appreciation of the landscape for its own sake and 'which fitted well with the agricultural scene, contributing to it materially as well as aesthetically'.[64] Farnborough was owned by the 'good and wise' William Holbech II. How Henrietta would have loved it. Richard Pocock saw it at the time: 'Mr Holbech's . . . very grand terrace, winding round the hill for half a mile [with] an obelisk at the end which may be 80 feet high, and in another part an oval open summer house, with a room over the colonade. This terrace commands a fine view of the rich country, which is called the Vale of Red Horse, from a red horse near Tysoe, cut in the hill.'[65] Besides the obelisk and the oval summerhouse on legs, there was the 'elegant and costly' Pentagon Temple (now vanished), an Ionic temple, and a sturdy little octagonal game larder. In *Edge-Hill* Richard Jago celebrated the building of the terrace by Holbech and his estate workers:

> Hear they her Master's Call? In sturdy Troops,
> The Jocund Labourers hie, and, at his Nod,
> A thousand Hands o'er smooth the slanting Hill,
> Or scoop new Channels for the gath'ring Flood,
> And, in his Pleasures, find a solid Joy.[66]

Even Jago, a lifelong Warwickshire devotee, exaggerates here. Undoubtedly all the village men and lads were drafted in to dig and level the terrace, but 500 of the jocund souls was a little excessive – as was the term 'Flood' – the stuff of poetry but not landscape gardening in these quiet days *before* the advent of Lancelot

'Capability' Brown. Henrietta would have gasped at a labour force of five, or fifty, let alone 500, and the trouble with poetry is that it has exaggerated what was a gentle revolution, a refinement of the working landscape, and all the more wondrous for that. The 'Jocund Labourers' given regular work in the lulls of the farming year would have been glad, but they were not the armies yet to be drafted in for the canals and railways.

As a 'Lady of Quality' does not die, but merely fades away, I will leave her there; in her landaulet with a high-stepping pony, the painted wheels flashing as she drives along the terrace at Farnborough Hall, the terrace a little less manicured than it is today, but the buildings much as you find them now.[67] Perhaps she would walk into the honeysuckle-wreathed frame of Thomas Robins' painting of Honington, and take the progress around the lake to the fragile Chinese Tent and its Chippendale railings, to the little classical temples and the cascades.[68] For these gardens amidst the fields of middle England were the catalyst for the great landscape gardening revolution of the second half of the eighteenth century yet to come.

CHAPTER NINE

A Captivating Ghost

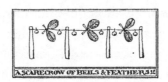

FIVE YEARS after Henrietta's death William Shenstone rewrote his 'motto' for his statue of Venus at The Leasowes, calling it 'Semi-reducta Venus' or the 'partially retir'd Venus'. Perhaps he was thinking of Henrietta, for even in part it offers an allegory for her life-story:

> To Venus, Venus here retir'd,
> My sober vows I pay:
> Not her on Paphian plains admir'd,
> The bold, the pert, the gay.
> Not her whose amorous leer prevail'd
> To bribe the Phrygian boy;
> Not her who, clad in armour, fail'd
> To save disast'rous Troy.
>
> Fresh rising from the foamy Tide,
> She every bosom warms,
> While half withdrawn she seems to hide,
> And half reveals her charms.
> Learn hence, ye boastful sons of taste,
> Who plan the rural shade:
> Learn hence to shun the vicious waste
> Of Pomp, at large display'd.
> Let sweet concealment's magic art
> Your mazy bounds invest,
> And while the sight unveils a part,
> Let fancy paint the rest.[1]

However pert and impetuous she had been in youth, however many young men she charmed, however she had failed, perhaps, to instil a Trojan fortitude into her adored Harry, she had lived much of her life on the rim of history. Now, she had come to the end of her twenty years of semi-retirement at Barrells, and of her demonstration of the 'magic art' of creating beauty from modest means.

Thankfully Henrietta did not lose her mind, and books were her great comfort. She read Francis Coventry's *Pompey the Little: The Life and Adventures of a Bologna Lapdog* with great amusement, and Madame de Maintenon's *Letters* and Edward Moore's *The Gamester*, 'the most modern English tragedy' exposing the vice of gambling. Besides Hogarth's *Analysis of Beauty* and Fielding's *Tom Jones* – of which she remarked 'Yet I might live at least five hundred years in this place before one quarter of the incidents happened, which are related in any one [of these six volumes]'[2] – she spent a good deal of time annotating the margins of *The Letters on the Study and Use of History etc by the Late Lord Bolingbroke* which had been published in 1752. She also had Voltaire's *Defence of the Letters*. Interestingly Mrs Delany happened to be reading the *Letters*, too; she was a woman of perception who knew how the world spoke, and she commented that 'there seems to be an ill design in them; but his style and manner of writing is charming. How grievous that such a genius should not have had a better heart?'[3]

For Henrietta, in her last summer of 1755, her good moments sparkle like her May anemones in the gathering gloom. Her friends urged her to 'fresh air and exercise' but she almost always ended up with a chill after an outing. Her legs were swollen and painful and she could walk no distance, relying on her landaulet to see her garden. The last (surviving) letter from Shenstone is dated 14 May, full of gossip about visits and visitors; she had been to visit Guy's Cliff in Warwick, where the shell room was 'the prettiest thing I ever saw of the kind'.[4] Richard and Lucy Graves from Claverton visited The Leasowes, and came over to Barrells with her polyanthus root and Cornelian cherry seedling. The Leasowes remained her grail, its delicate leafy enchantment shining before her like the fields of paradise: was it merely Shenstone she saw there, or her dream of the youthful, golden Harry? Her fingers became so swollen that she could not write, and her last letter to Shenstone was written for her, at midsummer, announcing that she would bring her guests, Sir Peter Soame and his son, on the following Saturday morning.[5] Whether she made that last visit we do not know.

The damp and freezing cold of February 1756 finally laid her low, and Henrietta died quietly, early in what she had always called 'the boisterous, baneful month of March'. Mrs Holyoake and her daughter nursed her, and Mrs Davies and Captain Outing were never far away. Though she had not been to church for some time Parson Holyoake gently offered her the Sacrament, which she received 'with great devotion', and he read prayers with her the night before she died. He assured Shenstone that 'nothing hath been wanting either to prolong her life or to prepare her for the other world'; 'though she had so great troubles and afflictions in this life' she was 'perfectly happy' at her end. Shenstone, who had characteristically been so sunk in his own winter's depression that Henrietta's death did not register with him until long after her funeral, endorsed the value of her neighbours and friends: he told Parson Holyoake of 'how much preferable your friendship was to that of the more gay and more capricious world', and ended 'whatever may be now expended upon embellishments at Barrells, it can hardly ever be the agreeable object from your house [Oldberrow Rectory] that it has been'.[6] It was a nice tribute, and perhaps the 'Partially-retir'd Venus' was his true epitaph for her.

Death in her fifty-seventh year was not unreasonable in the mid-eighteenth century; after all Duchess Frances had predeceased her by eighteen months and she had outlived all her siblings. Poor Shenstone only lasted another seven years, dying from a 'putrid fever' on 11 February 1763, aged forty-nine. But, having come this far with her, it would be unnatural not to lament the absence of another decade in Henrietta's life, or that she had a closer proximity to the thoroughfare of progress. A few more years, a few less miles, might have brought her closer to the beaten track. Her excitement at the prospect of a turnpike to within six miles of her only confirmed the sheer impassability of those Warwickshire lanes, axle-deep in the mud of a fecund countryside that both nurtured and constrained. Henrietta knew only too well that hers was a rich arable and pasture country, that the milk, butter and cream from her cows sustained her good health but equally that the muddy cascades that flowed from all the surrounding meadows every time it rained kept her a prisoner. It was no accident that she habitually visited The Leasowes in August, between haymaking and harvest, when the ruts had been flattened into dust; outings had to be taken when the roads permitted.

If only she had been allowed a little longer, for just at that moment as she left the whole fantasia of the English landscape garden tumbled into her nearer countryside. Mr Thomas Robins painted Honington in 1759; Coplestone Warre Bampfylde, that rather more staid miniaturist, a sometime pupil of George Lambert, who painted Stourhead and his own Arcadian valley at Hestercombe in Somerset, visited The Leasowes in November 1762.[7] Bampfylde would surely have had a meeting of minds with Henrietta. He may even have been related by marriage, for his wife, Mary, was the daughter of Edward Knight, a wealthy iron-master of Wolverley near Kidderminster. Either Robins or Bampfylde could have painted Henrietta's garden into posterity and fame.

Unjust though it seems, a landscape revolution could not be made by a lady in a chaise (even a coroneted one), but only by a hard-riding man. During the last years of Henrietta's life a Northumbrian in his mid-thirties, one Lancelot Brown, had come riding into Warwickshire, looking for landscape business. Brown's patron at Stowe, Lord Cobham, died in 1749, and though the head gardener had stayed in post he had taken time off to look around him. It was Henrietta's acquaintance Sanderson Miller who introduced Brown to his Warwickshire future clients, and Brown's jobs at Packington,

Charlecote and Warwick followed.*[8] At Warwick Castle Brown had 'set up on a few ideas of Kent and Mr Southcote', over which Henrietta would have enthused, making lawns planted with trees and shrubs (a shrubbery?) beside the River Avon, to which he introduced a cascade. Horace Walpole remarked 'One sees what the prevalence of taste does; little Brooke who would have chuckled to have been born in an age of clipt hedges and cockle-shell avenues, has submitted to let his garden and park be natural.'†[9] With the energetic and capable Brown, who rode endless miles to be at his clients' beck and call, the new wave of network-landscaping was beginning; unfortunately it was soon more the acquisition of acreages, than 'sweet concealment's magic art'.

Lord Luxborough presented himself at Barrells the very day after Henrietta died, to take charge, and take over his property. Her coffin, modestly adorned with the earliest spring flowers from her garden, was carried to St Peter's at Wootton Wawen where the Revd Reynolds led the prayers and she was buried. Back at the house, his Lordship took everything of apparent value and anything that immediately appealed to him, sorting through her papers and returning letters from people that mattered, so that some of her letters from Frances Hertford went back to her family, and those from William Shenstone were returned to him. Lord Luxborough was nothing if not capable and efficient; he must have taken a cursory look at the bundle of papers she kept from the time of their separation, pushed them into a strongbox and left them to be stored in the attic. Next to his other properties at Edstone and Oldberrow,

---

* Beyond the Midlands, it might be added, Brown's fame was being polished by working for the Hertfords' son-in-law, now Lord Northumberland, at Syon House and Alnwick Castle and for their Egremont cousins at Petworth.

† This 'little Brooke' was the same Lord Brooke that had been married to Frances Hertford's sister Molly, who had died in 1721. Henrietta had then known him perfectly well, she apparently owned a painting by him, but in all her twenty years at Barrells she was but twelve miles from his door, and yet she never mentions him. But then, Frances Hertford once told her that Lady Betty Smithson, to whom Henrietta was an 'honorary aunt', had journeyed into Warwickshire, perhaps to Warwick Castle, and yet had no idea of where Barrells was. Was Henrietta more conscious of being both isolated, and more *beyond the pale* than she allowed everyone to think?

Barrells and its garden and fields must have seemed fairly insignificant – it was merely subsumed into his local steward's responsibilities. He pensioned off her older servants, and kept a 'skeleton' staff to maintain the house. Perhaps Henrietta would have seen her clever Scots gardener to his next job with a good reference, or, if not, his discovery that his Lordship had no interest in gardens whatsoever would surely have prompted his hasty departure. Henrietta's garden was to be completely neglected for over thirty years.

In the house, one imagines, all Henrietta's pretty things were spirited away by Robert's succession of disgruntled mistresses; fortunately some of her pictures were left on the walls and Thomas Smith of Derby's painting of *Somerville's Urn* remained. What happened to the real urn, the Shrine to Venus, the Piping Faun and her 'bustoes' of Pope, Bolingbroke, Milton, Dryden and Shakespeare and their company can only be imagined; were they smashed, stolen, or spirited away? Is it possible that the urn, cut so carefully by Smith of Warwick's craftsmen, adorned with the French horn and wreath, or the smaller urns that the old master-mason Pedley had made for her summerhouse roof, still sit somewhere in a quiet Warwickshire garden unawares?

Two months after her death Lord Luxborough married his mistress, Mary, Lady de Quesne, but in the family history she is counted as 'a virago' and said not to have lived with him. Instead, at least as far as his time at Barrells was concerned, he imported a string of mistresses – at least three, one hilariously named 'Moll Clever Legs' – whom, rather tellingly, he tried to keep in the house by force of imprisonment.[10] Lord Luxborough's taste for imprisoning his women was not his only unpleasant habit, for apparently there were 'distinct touches of blackmail' in the way he extracted a large sum of money out of the Treasury, and in gaining his Irish titles. It seems that in occupying Sir Robert Walpole's Castle Rising seat in Parliament for seven years he had found out things the Walpole family would rather have kept secret, and so that was how 'Baron Luxborough of Shannon' became successively Viscount Barrells and finally Earl of Catherlough.[11] Lord Catherlough returned to his old Great Grimsby seat from 1762 to 1768, and finally sat in Parliament for Milbourne Port in Dorset (1770–2), a seat connected to Henrietta's old adversary Lord Lovel. For all his wealth and influence history was to remember Knight junior as 'less talented and far more odious' than the old Chief Cashier his father;[12] just a smattering of imagination would seem to suggest that his devious tricks had blighted Henrietta's, and perhaps even Harry Bolingbroke's lives, in more ways than we can ever know.

Harry Knight, Henrietta's son whom Lord Catherlough had taken away from her and protected so carefully, died in August 1762, aged thirty-three; he and his wife Frances Heath had no living children. Her daughter, Henrietta Child, had found married happiness with Josiah, but they were constrained from returning to England because of the large sum being legally exacted from Child by Charles Wymondesold in return for Henrietta's divorce. The Childs and their son Josiah roamed the Continent. For some time they were in Brussels, where Henrietta's considerable social skills that she had inherited from her mother, were used to gain them acceptance in the highest circles, with added 'information gathering' of the most discreet kind which could hardly be called spying, but which she relayed to her father, keeping Lord Catherlough sweet and financially supportive. Her beloved husband Josiah died in the winter of 1759–60 in Lyons. She came home to England briefly, but returned again to France when she married Louis Alexandre de Grimouard, Comte Duroure. Henrietta died in Marseilles on 1 March 1763 after giving birth to their son Ivor; she was thirty-three. Ivor eventually inherited his father's titles but left no heir. Henrietta's bloodline – all those generations of St Johns and consanguinity with kings – came to an end in Josiah Child. The 9-year-old boy came to England as his grandfather's ward after his mother's death but Josiah, preferring the gregarious continental life of his childhood, attached himself to an Italian family who took him to Paris. His grandfather Knight was furious and washed his hands of the boy's future (he was intended for the army) and so the young Josiah died in oblivion, somewhere on the Continent, of an unknown cause.

In 1764, his Lordship, in trying to collect the rent from his impoverished tenant at Moat Farm, Ullenhall, so the story goes, bargained for his comely daughter Jane Davies instead. The courageous Jane agreed to go to London and live with him, where he arranged for her to have lessons in French and music and dancing. Jane's first child, a son named Robert, was born on 3 March 1768, and Robert was followed by a brother, Henry Raleigh, and two sisters, Henrietta Matilda and Jane.[13] Jane Davies must have been just the amiable and submissive wife Robert Knight had always wanted, and they were happy together, so the story goes, for the last years of his life. He built a large extension, including a private chapel, on the north side of Barrells house, which would have ensured the destruction of the last vestiges of Henrietta's pretty home. His even greater building effort was for his Mausoleum, a brick pyramid – copied from the Tomb of Caius Cestus in Rome – which was sited beyond the end of Henrietta's Long Walk and the woods. Her hay and corn meadows had become his Park, and the Mausoleum was beside a new drive, leading to the East Lodge entrance. In his detailed local researches Andrew Craythorn found that Lord Catherlough planted walks of wild thyme, water-mint and salad burnet – so perhaps he found some gardening solace in his last, happier, days.[14]

Robert Knight KB, Earl of Catherlough, etc., an unkempt old man, died at Barrells on 30 March 1772, and he was buried in his Mausoleum. The coffin of Henrietta, Baroness Luxborough, was brought from Wootton Wawen to the Mausoleum, along with the coffins of their children, Harry and Henrietta. In that curious construction in Barrells Park they were together again as a family, as they had not been since the early 1730s in their house in Grosvenor Street.

Sadly Jane Davies died six months later giving birth to her fifth child, a daughter Caroline. The little girl lived for not quite a month and she, too, was buried in the Mausoleum, with the name Caroline

Knight. It is not known where Jane Davies was buried, but the considerable Knight estates and riches were put into a trust for Jane's four living children, who were allowed to take the name of Knight. When the eldest, Robert, became of age in 1789 he was a very rich young man, and Barrells was to be his for his lifetime. He commissioned the architect Joseph Bonomi to build his new house, a rectangular block of nine bays with a south-facing pillared double-height portico, not unlike Luxborough. It occupied the site of Henrietta's poor cottage, plus her terrace and bowling green. Bonomi's drawing of the new house, exhibited at the Royal Academy in 1796, shows a glimpse of the rear wing with an avenue, the old drive, leading off into the distance. Henrietta's entrance court on the west was completely redundant, and indeed the Bonomi drawing shows a completely open countryside westwards to the hill of Skiltz, meaning that artistic licence had disposed of her Upper Garden and Shrubbery, too! Robert Knight consulted Humphry Repton on a landscape scheme for his park, but this was apparently not carried out.[15] Henrietta's ha-ha was rebuilt, into the generous semi-circular curve of her Lower Garden. Her old Kitchen Garden and Aviary, completely lost in the rush of rebuilding, were replaced by a new, large walled Kitchen Garden, which demolished her precious, flowery Chestnut Coppice. Even in the farthest reaches of the wood, her Hermitage – crumbled into a heap of logs after thirty years of neglect – gave way to an Ice-House, which was excavated below her gravelly primrose dell. Of Henrietta's enchanting garden, *ferme ornée* or *negligée*, there was now nothing left to destroy.

Henrietta, though, had one more journey to make. Robert Knight had spent approximately £10,000 on his estate.* He and his wife Frances Dormer and their two daughters lived there and in London. He became High Sheriff of Warwickshire and, curiously, member of Parliament for the old St John seat of Wootton Bassett in Wiltshire. History repeated itself in other ways, too, for in 1808 Robert

---

* He sued Joseph Bonomi over something he did not like, but unsuccessfully so.

and Frances Knight separated; five years later she gave birth to a son, Henry Charles Knight, whom Robert refused to own, whereas Frances insisted the boy was his, and the heir to Barrells. Robert Knight lived on at Barrells, but neglected it, for fear of this false heir. Unable to contemplate the spurious Henry Charles having anything that was his, he began a scorched earth campaign, pulling down the stables and glasshouses, leaving the house and Kitchen Garden to rot, selling the park timbers (and the last of Henrietta's trees), destroying the north (Henrietta's) and east entrances – leaving it all to dereliction and decay, while he departed to live in London. Lord Catherlough's Mausoleum, hardly fifty years old, fell into disrepair and was vandalised, and, finally, in 1830 Knight arranged for a new vault to be built underneath St Mary's church at Ullenhall. And so, Henrietta, and Harry and Henrietta Child and her son Ivor, Comte Duroure, and Lord Catherlough and little Caroline Knight all made their last journey on farm carts, over Mount Pleasant – that 'rugged walk' that Henrietta used to take – to their final resting place.

All was not quite at peace just yet: when Robert Knight eventually died, aged eighty-six, in January 1855, he left properties to his two daughters, with the remainder, including the Barrells estate, entailed in a trust. The Knight claimants, Henry Charles and his cousin Charles Raleigh (the son of Jane Davies' second son) combined to break the trust, appointed new trustees and put everything – over 3,000 acres of land and all the buildings – up for sale in sixteen lots.[16] Barrells and its immediate surroundings were bought by a successful Birmingham linen draper who was expanding into church furnishings, William Newton, who restored the Bonomi house and his whole estate to prosperity. His son, Thomas Henry Goodwin Newton built a new church for Ullenhall,* but the parishioners were not willing to give up their ancient chapel. The nave of old St Mary's was demolished leaving the chancel as the mortuary chapel for the

---

* St Mary's church, designed by J. P. Seddon, 1874.

Knight family vault, where Henrietta and her children lay. Today the chapel remains a prettily isolated and peaceful sanctuary; the parishioners of Ullenhall still treasure the little thirteenth-century building and use it for services. The lanes around it, one called Gentleman's Lane, are still of a character that Henrietta would recognise from the days that she walked here. But everything else has gone, long ago. The Newtons' prosperous era lasted until 1924, when Barrells was put up for sale again, launched into the turbulence of the twentieth century, with nothing left to show that Henrietta and her *ferme negligée* were ever there at all. In the 1920s Barrells' wood was said to be haunted by the ghost of a beautiful but unhappy lady, and the local people did not like to pass at night.*

William Shenstone's The Leasowes fared little better than Henrietta's garden, except in one vital respect: Shenstone's friend and publisher, Robert Dodsley, kept a promise and published a plan and description of his garden in Shenstone's posthumously issued *Works*.[18] On receiving his 'valuable Present' of the first two volumes, Shenstone's friend the Revd John Pixell of Edgbaston wrote to Dodsley on 16 April 1764: 'I am pleas'd that You have given ye Publick the Ground-Plot of the Leasowes, that Posterity may, by having recourse, see what Rural Taste was in a state of Innocence before the Fall; for surely whatever Changes Time & Caprice may make, must be so many Deviations from Simplicity.'†[19] The kindly Shenstone was generous to his relatives and servants, but they did nothing but quarrel and issue writs against each other. Shenstone thought he had settled his beloved *ferme ornée* securely. He left it to his cousin John Hodgetts for his lifetime, and after that to another

---

* The unacknowledged Jane Davies looking for her baby daughter, the wayward Frances Knight seeking her son's inheritance, there are plenty of candidates for a Barrells' ghost besides Henrietta; though there was a time when she might have been overcome by curiosity, for during the Second World War Oldberrow Court farm was the headquarters for the Warwickshire Women's Land Army – the sight of the girls in their breeches and forage caps working in her Great Meadow would have assured her that the age of women 'gardeners' had arrived.[17]

† 'Time & Caprice' made many changes, all lovingly recorded by a careful local historian E. Monro Purkis.[20]

cousin, Edward Cooke; if either wished to sell it was to be offered to Lord Stamford's family at Enville.[21] No sooner was Shenstone gone than Hodgetts bought out Cooke's interest, and after two years he sold The Leasowes for £3,350 to a Mr Turnpenny or Tenpenny. Mr Tenpenny is credited as the owner of the published plan. However, he spent the four years of his residency chopping down groves and copses. The already pitiable *ferme ornée* tumbled down the nineteenth century, passing swiftly through a succession of owners, including a Mrs Apphia Peach, a widow from India who managed to marry Lord Lyttelton and so move into Hagley! At The Leasowes the price kept rising, the damage kept accruing. The house was rebuilt, becoming more important than the *ferme*; it was nothing more than a pleasant place, and nobody stayed long. After ten or a dozen changes of hands The Leasowes entered the twentieth century as a school for physical culture, then passed to Halesowen Golf Club. Such 'strange uses for the Arcadia of the inert, ease-loving Shenstone!' concluded local historian Mr Purkis.[22]

It is one of life's, and death's, little ironies that posterity has a better appreciation of wallflowers who write reams than, say, *paeonia* 'Duchesse de Nemours', a flower of glorious sparkling life, leaving not so much as a farewell note. History collects dullards but cannot grasp colourful lives. Henrietta was a peony; it may be stating the obvious to say that she was also a woman, and whoever sat down to write a life of a woman, except as a sovereign, a caring mother or indulgent lover? Shenstone was a wallflower, rooted at home, but relentlessly penning his poetry and aphorisms. Much of his poetry is breathless and indigestible, his *Men and Manners* is full of observations that only a sedentary person would consider worthy of writing down; for instance, 'A large, branching, aged oak, is perhaps the most venerable of all inanimate objects', which is perhaps allied to:

> All trees have a character analogous to that of men: oaks are in
> all respects the perfect image of the manly character: In former
> times I should have said, and in present times I think I am
> authorized to say, the British one. As a brave man is not suddenly

either elated by prosperity or depressed by adversity, so the oak displays not its verdure on the sun's first approach; nor drops it, on his first departure. Add to this its majestic appearance, the rough grandeur of its bark, and the wide protection of its branches.[23]

The retiring Shenstone would not, I think, have credited himself with the qualities of an oak, but he was – though stating the obvious again – a man, and a poet, with poetical friends. In short, it was Shenstone himself, and the interest in him, that enabled The Leasowes, despite all, to survive. Besides his own poems and the precious plan and description published by Dodsley, Joseph Heeley's *Letters on the Beauties of Hagley, Envil[le] and the Leasowes* was published in 1777 and Richard Graves set down his memories of Shenstone and his garden in his letters to William Seward, which were published in 1788.[24] Although Shenstone's reputation, like his garden, slumbered during the nineteenth century, in the 1930s Marjorie Williams applied her affectionate scholarship to her perceptive biography *William Shenstone: A Chapter in Eighteenth Century Taste* (1935) and to editing *The Letters of William Shenstone* (1939), for which she gathered important papers that had strayed to American archives. All this kept an awareness of The Leasowes alive, so that it survived into the later twentieth century as partly a private golf course and partly a public park, owned by Dudley Metropolitan Borough Council. It was *there* in physique if not in charms for garden historians to discover, and armed with the precious plan that Dodsley published, some fifty-nine hectares (147 acres) are now being subjected to a million pounds' worth of restoration under the Heritage Lottery Fund's Urban Parks Programme.[25] Whether the massive yellow machines and mechanical paraphernalia that are implicit in modern landscaping can recall the spirit of a place created with a finger-tip precision and love is open to question. Let Shenstone have the last word: 'Concerning scenes, the more uncommon they appear, the better, provided they form a picture, and include nothing that pretends to be of nature's production, and is not. The shape of the ground, the site of trees, & the fall of water are nature's province. Whatever thwarts her is treason.'[26]

As to her own literary heritage, Henrietta's ladylike persistence – 'I am no Poetess' – in her anonymity was only frustrating. In the summer of 1754 Shenstone had sent his publisher some poems, six of his own, five by Richard Graves and at least one by Henrietta. Robert Dodsley had barely contained his angst that she would not allow him to publish her name:

> But how can her Ladyship talk of being vain of the Post of Honour, as She calls it, which I have assign'd her in my Assembly of Wits? Does she not know that she is qualify'd by Genius as well as Birth, to keep the best Company and to shine the brightest? If she is ignorant of this, she is ignorant of what everybody else both knows and allows; and affords an eminent proof of how difficult it is to know one's self.[27]

Poor Henrietta, she knew herself well enough, and her husband Lord Luxborough too, who would not have regarded 'her' name as hers to use in a lowly literary connection! *The Letters of Lady Luxborough to William Shenstone Esquire* appeared only in 1775, published by Dodsley's son. This was nineteen years after Henrietta's death, and *perhaps more importantly* three years after Lord Luxborough's, for it would have been perfectly within his devious nature to suppress them.* The curious have always been delighted to discover that the author was none other than Lord Bolingbroke's sister, and beloved sister at that. In retrospect Harry was Henrietta's greatest joy, and curse. Perhaps the lesson of her life was that only at Barrells was she free enough to be herself, and beyond his power. After her death, as during her life, she attracted Harry Bolingbroke's Whig enemies. Horace Walpole, nowadays regarded as the patron saint of garden historians and whose garbled gossip has long been so attractive to those looking for an amusing footnote, wrote that 'she fell in love with Parson Dalton, and that they rhymed together'.

---

* The trouble was they were hardly *published* at all, but thrown into print, with little attention to dates or names and no annotations; *The Letters* are a confusing jumble.

Walpole 'never saw her more till she revived in Shenstone's letters, and was a great performer in his ballad of Arcadia, and that he [Walpole] thought these materials of her history promised well for entertainment in her correspondence, considering that she was sister both of Lord Bolingbroke and of Hollis [Holles] St John'. Henrietta would have loved her billing in the 'ballad of Arcadia'; but Walpole, aiming beyond her, could also be more snidely personal, calling her 'a high-coloured black woman' who wore her husband's miniature in her 'bush of hair' and, after her separation, she 'retired into the country, corresponded with the small poets of her time, but as there was no Theseus amongst them, it was said that like Ariadne she had consoled herself with Bacchus, although this might be a fable'.*[28] Henrietta's place in history is irrevocably tied to that of her closest relative Harry Bolingbroke, and invariably tainted by that association.

And what of Henrietta's childhood homes, Lydiard and Battersea? After Lydiard's long nineteenth-century decline the heavily-mortgaged estate was broken into lots and sold in the 1920s. When Swindon Corporation acquired the empty house and 147 acres of parkland in 1943 all they could do, in wartime conditions, was to throw a large tarpaulin over the house's ruinous roof to try to keep the rain out. Slowly, in the 1950s the great task of structural re-building began, soon overlaid with the restoration of the decorative plasterwork, the gilding and the rich wallpapers, which can now be seen. The house had neither electricity nor piped water so these were installed. It was first opened to the public in 1955.[29] Since then Lydiard has quietly prospered, some of the family's furniture and belongings have gradually found their ways back, as have many portraits of people Henrietta knew and loved; the lofty rooms now breathe scandalous whispers that would make her smile. There are

---

* Almost exactly 200 years later similar things were being said about Vita Sackville-West, a gardener of a certain age, who liked her wine and home-made cider, who had a bad fall, suffered from arthritis and experienced some disorientation; lead poisoning from the buckets and lead-bound barrels in which the cider was made was the trouble at Sissinghurst, as it was more than likely at Barrells.

the three portraits of her, the precious painting by Thomas Smith of Somerville's Urn, and other mementoes to make it familiar to a retired Venus. They are clearly very fond of her at Lydiard now, which makes a change from the mood in her later lifetime, when it was ruled by her sister-in-law, Jack's wife Anne Furnese – there was no one 'so avaricious, more selfish or more false' in Harry Bolingbroke's opinion.[30] Out in the gardens and the park lively restoration projects are under way, archaeologists of field and television are searching out the remains of park features and of Johanna St John's walled gardens, and these are exciting prospects. Lydiard today is a vibrant, lively and lovely place; it has the feeling that a lot of people love and value the house and park. On special occasions, such as the annual festival for the Friends of Lydiard Tregoze,[31] the doors of the St John Triptych in St Mary's are opened, and Henrietta's great-great-grandparents and their family, their faces framed in Elizabethan ruffs, gaze out into the world once more, just as she saw them 300 years ago.

At Battersea, which now brings to mind the Park, the power station and the dogs' home, the St Johns and the lavender fields are all but forgotten. Much of Henrietta's old home, the manor house, was demolished in the 1770s. A century later the last remnant, the family's wing, was replaced by a flour mill, which has in turn been replaced by a block of flats, though a block of flats designed by the architect Richard Rogers. The Jacobean oak staircase, the cedarwood panelling and plastered ceilings from Henrietta's home were scattered to new homes in Surrey and Philadelphia.*[32]

Battersea's St Mary's church was rebuilt in an elegant Georgian

---

* Sir Walter and the lady Johanna's 'owne house' is now called Old Battersea House. This was almost demolished by Battersea Council in the 1920s, to make way for more flats, but saved by a vigorous local outcry led by Colonel Charles Stirling, who then became the tenant. Colonel Stirling's wife filled the house with the De Morgan Collection, paintings by her sister Evelyn de Morgan, and works by Evelyn's husband, the ceramicist and friend of William Morris, William de Morgan. Mrs Stirling, who lived until a few days before her 100th birthday, wrote a history *The Merry Wives of Battersea* in 1956. After her death in 1965 the house was leased and restored by the American Forbes Foundation, as a home for the *Forbes Magazine* collection of Victorian paintings.

style in the 1770s, but the St John memorial window, with the golden falcon rising and the crusader's stars, was incorporated into the new building, and so Margaret Beauchamp, Henry VII and Elizabeth I gaze on present congregations as they did on Henrietta.*[33]

Of Henrietta's other places, the church where she was married, St George's in Hanover Square, still solemnises society weddings, many of the alleys and courts of St James's and Piccadilly would be familiar to her, and some of the houses in Grosvenor Street remain from her time. Leaving London for the west, she would find Lord Burlington's Chiswick, Mrs Howard's Marble Hill and Pope's Villa at Twickenham all protected by their fame, though the latter less than it deserves.[34] Not so Dawley of her happy memories where her son was born, where a short road of houses under the Heathrow flight paths named Dawley Ride is the only clue that it once existed. When Bolingbroke sold his 'poor farm' for a fortune of £26,000 in 1739 he included all the furniture and decorations – that he did not think to send some of these lovely things up to Henrietta at Barrells is to be regretted. The stone-coloured hall with its trophies of garden tools remained untouched for nearly thirty years, until Lord Paget sold Dawley and all was demolished in 1772.

To the north, beyond the M4 motorway, Frances Hertford's Percy Lodge, now restored to Lord Bathurst's name Richings, is still a place of lawns and trees and a bubbling stream, on the outskirts of Iver. The main house is gone, but the stables remain, used as part of Richings Country Club. The Hertfords' romantic hermitage on

* Some of the St John memorials were re-erected in the gallery, including the marble casket and urn by Peter Scheemakers for Holles St John, which Henrietta commissioned and paid for from her exile in 1738, and Roubiliac's elegantly draped urn with their portrait medallions for the Bolingbrokes. After Henrietta's and 'Bully' Bolingbroke's times, Battersea became very prosperous and fashionable. Four new stained-glass windows by John Hayward of Edenbridge were added between 1976 and 1982 to commemorate notable eighteenth- and nineteenth-century residents: William Curtis, who compiled a London flora and founded his *Botanical Magazine* (and who is buried in the churchyard); the painter J. W. M. Turner; the artist and poet William Blake and his wife Catherine Boucher, the daughter of a local market-gardener, who celebrated their marriage in the church in 1782; and General Benedict Arnold, who raised his flag with George Washington in the War of American Independence.

St Leonard's Hill at Windsor was rebuilt after they left in 1739. Its ensuing history has been fairly quiet.*

Travelling westwards down the A4, much of it the course of the old Bath road that Henrietta and the Hertfords travelled, there is little that survives from the eighteenth century. But turn north just short of Newbury and Frances Winchcombe's Bucklebury will be found fairly untouched by time, secure amidst thick hedgerow banks and narrow lanes. Farther west at Marlborough, where Henrietta first escaped her childhood, the Hertford's big red-brick house dominates the entrance court of Marlborough College and both house and garden have been respected. The immutable Mound still has the path winding to the summit, and at the foot there is a small grotto stuck with shells and pebbles, which I imagine is a souvenir of the Hertfords' more elaborate creation, this one perhaps made by some lovelorn Victorian schoolmaster. The course of the Kennet through the garden is as magical as it was in Henrietta's day and many of the walks can still be traced. The spirit of this place survives, despite new buildings to house the expanding school, and perhaps because of the youthful chatter and laughter that breaks out beneath the trees at intervals throughout the day.

In Warwickshire, at Barrells, the prosperous Newton era ended just after the 1914–18 War. The ensuing sale precipitated Barrells into an almost unbelievable catalogue of ruinous disasters, fires, neglect, the Newtons' marble staircase was blown up by the army during the Second World War, and then demolitions and more neglect and more sales.[36] Not a vestige remains of the place that Henrietta knew. Except, perhaps, that from an Ullenhall lane you may still peer southwards and hope for 'a little bit of a Gloucester-shire hill' through a gap in the trees, and look westwards for

---

* It was not this house, but the Royal Hunting Lodge farther up the hill which found fame as William Pitt's country retreat during the Seven Years' War (1756–63), then became the setting for Lord Harcourt's flower garden, so much admired by the poet and gardener William Mason. The Hertfords' house, rebuilt, was home in the 20th century to a motor racing driver, a rich American Theosophist and then the unpopular American ambassador Joseph P. Kennedy, the father of Jack, Bobby and Edward Kennedy.[35]

the nearer hills of Skilts (Skiltz in her day), two of her '*Eye-traps*'.

And why should anything remain? Henrietta was, after all, only a gardener and a farmeress, ephemeral stewardships at best. If the fireside conversations at Barrells ever veered to posterity (it was unlikely) she would have voted for The Leasowes to be saved, but never her own garden. It was, after all, insignificant; it was merely her personal salvation. She was only too aware of her slim resources in acreages and guineas, and she mourned above all her lack of a purling stream, and the consequent mossy cascades and fern-edged pools. Unlike so many of her contemporaries and successors, she was truly a gardener; she spent so long poring over Philip Miller's *Gardener's Dictionary* that Harry Bolingbroke once chaffed her of being in danger of becoming the most knowledgeable gardener in the country. She had cold frames and hot pits, her melons and cucumbers were abundant, though she could not afford a green-house: she and her good Scots gardener grew all the more usual vegetables and salads that her household required. Equally she was never happier than when out in her wood or coppice, prinking and pruning her walks, or trimming the vistas through the trees. Setting a seat or planning a hermitage was the joy of all joys. Transforming her wild wood into a garden, walking the pathways, planting the flowers, was – as it was for Gertrude Jekyll a century and a half later, and for Beth Chatto another century on – the most personal and most difficult of all forms of gardening, totally dependent upon the gardener's perennial presence.*

---

* Henrietta had the bounty of a floriferous countryside, snowdrops of many varieties (she once mentions a double-flowered, yellowish variety, almost like a small rose), aconites, violets, primroses, oxlips, cowslips, pink ragged robin (*Lychnis flos-cuculi*) and Roman hyacinths (*Hyacinthus orientalis*), both blue and white. She had Star of Bethlehem (*Ornithogalum umbellatum*) and its relatives Solomon's seal and butcher's broom, and almost certainly scillas, squills and grape hyacinths. Her favourites were her many-shaded and scented violets and their pansy cousins *Viola arvensis* and *Viola tricolor*. She does not mention tulips or lilies but at one time she had a fashionable display of auriculas on a stand, an 'auricula theatre'; these were nursery bred hybrids of alpine primulas in reds, purples and crimsons, and she may have had the 'frosted' varieties which appeared in about 1735, causing a sensation and craze for florists' societies. Her friends amongst Smith's craftsmen or the colliers from Halesowen may well have been early florists and

Spring was her flowering time, spangled carpets below, and apple, cherry, pear and thorn blossoms above, and all these gave way to her shrubbery of roses, philadelphus, lilacs and her Whitsun rose, *Viburnum opulus*. Her sand paths were fringed with foxgloves, scabious, spurges, cranesbills and grasses and mullein spires, and her woods wreathed in honeysuckles and clematis. Campions, willowherbs and meadowsweets all came to her aid, but their July flowerings turned her attention, as the attentions of all country gardeners, to her vegetables, herbs and fruits which would be her harvest for the cold months.*

In late summer her little farm turned to gold with the dry-cut hayfields and the ripened wheat. This golden countryside, laid out below a blue September sky tinged with the relief of harvest home, was the most glorious climax to the landscape's year. In the coppice they gathered chestnuts, riffling through the russet carpets of leaves; then it was time for the autumn's work to begin. Henrietta's *ferme negligée* was ever-changing and ephemeral. Hers was English gardening with few exotics, which melded into her surrounding agricultural countryside and the poppy-spattered meadows. Garden and countryside were all of a piece, delicately balanced, ruled by time and the seasons. Much of the escapade of her gardening was the fantasy of a fragile, hay-roofed hermitage of logs, the very insubstantiality of a stucco-fronted pavilion – mottoes were not carved in stone but written on cards – and the serendipity of a sanded pathway. All were a challenge to the elements; all would be washed away. That was the gardener's agreement with her God.

William Shenstone could not have been more perceptive than when he told Parson Holyoake 'whatever may be now expended upon embellishments at Barrells, it can hardly ever be the agreeable object from your house that it has been'.[37] It was not just that

the Midland & West Section of the National Auricula Society flourishes in Birmingham and in her countryside still.
* She acquired a 'machine' of *lignum vitae*, presumably a water pump, which she was pleased would allow her vegetables to be watered from the well or the rainwater tank; watering was only for essentials and definitely not her lawn or even her bowling green.

Henrietta was dead, but that her way of living was to be crushed out of existence. She had accomplished the art of living in the country, economically, charitably – dare I say it, sustainably – without abandoning her pursuit of the poetic and even frivolous in the way of beauty. Hers was a fine art; in landscape gardening terms it was swept aside by men with fortunes who amassed acreages and paid the highest price for privacy. The acme of English beauty for successive generations of the eighteenth and early nineteenth centuries was to be that expansive, rolling, tree-girt and *empty* park. Enclosures, agricultural and industrial revolutions, and most recently industrial and agricultural declines, these seemingly great juggernauts of history have rolled by, and Henrietta's essential ingredients of beauty and poetry have been lost. Gardening and farming, or farming and gardening, have lost their reciprocity and largely replaced it with a mutual disdain. Of course, beauty and interdependence do have a slim golden thread of history,[38] the great campaign that the visionaries of the Picturesque inspired. Is it too much to include Henrietta amongst those visionaries? Perhaps it is, for she left nothing tangible behind her to inspire anyone. Her garden is but a dream, and much of her *improving* gardening was dreaming. I think that endears her to us who struggle on; and, at the least, her story has been told.

ACKNOWLEDGEMENTS

Henrietta's husband, Robert Knight, Lord Catherlough, appears the villain of this piece, but her story could not have been written without him. Towards the end of his life, in 1770, he appears to have sorted out Henrietta's treasured letters from her brother, Lord Bolingbroke, and lent them to his political ally and friend, Sir Harry Burrard of Walhampton, then MP for Lymington, who was perhaps interested in writing about Bolingbroke. In 1892 these letters, found at Walhampton, were sold to the British Museum by the Burrard family [B.L. Add. Mss. 34196]. To a second cache of papers, those that Henrietta kept from 1735 to the 1740s concerning her separation from him, Lord Catherlough added the letters from their daughter Henrietta Child, and he saw that all these papers passed into the family, that is to his descendants from his union with Jane Davies. The value of this 'dusty bundle of old letters' was eventually appreciated by the Knight family historians, especially Mrs Catharine Octavia Higgon, M.B.E., J.P., who presented them to the British Museum via the Friends of the National Libraries in 1943.[B.L. Add. Mss. 45889]. For all these eventualities and the people that inspired them I am grateful, as I have been for the privilege of reading these letters in the Elysian light of the new British Library's Manuscripts' gallery where the atmosphere is such that a communion with long-dead subjects is far more likely than might be thought possible in the Euston road.

To that hardly less august institution and abode of fellow souls, the London Library, I am forever in debt for their treasure trove of books that one imagines are lost, particularly the solemn biographies of Harry Bolingbroke and a first edition of Henrietta's letters to William Shenstone. I cannot help wondering if a dusty bundle of these originals is still hidden away somewhere in an archive connected to Shenstone's executor John Hodgetts or the publisher Dodsley? And, if any light can be thrown on the mysterious *B. Faussett* who inscribed the London Library's copy of John Dalton's *Epistles* in 1745 and apparently cut out the capitals *H.L.* – Henrietta Luxborough? – I would be intrigued to know.

Unconventional though it may seem, I want to acknowledge my debt to the labours of three more and particular ghosts: to Helen Sard Hughes of Wellesley College in Massachusetts, who researched and published her ground-breaking biography *The Gentle Hertford* in 1940; to M. R. Hopkinson for her *Man of Mercury, A Sketch of Lord Bolingbroke and His Wives* of 1936; and to Marjorie

Williams, who resurrected William Shenstone's life and letters in 1935 and 1939. For the use of these and all my other published sources I am grateful, and I have made every attempt to acknowledge them accurately and adequately. Some of my more modern sources are included in the list of Selected Reading on page 233. I would like to acknowledge also the originals of Lady Hertford's letters and poems, and some of Henrietta's letters to her friend, which are in the Duke of Northumberland's collection at Alnwick Castle.

My thanks go to the present Knight family historian, Arthur E. Carden, for his enthusiasm and knowledge generously shared, especially for the text of *The Bull Finch in Town;* also to his brother, the architect Michael Carden, whom I knew through Hampshire Gardens Trust long before I realised he had any connection to Henrietta, and to other members of the family who own the portraits we have illustrated which are acknowledged separately. My thanks also go to Georgina Green for starting me off on Luxborough and the Knights, to Jonathan Lovie who first took me to Ullenhall, to Richard Hillier at Peterborough Central Library for his work on Thorpe Hall and Oliver St John, to Dr Christopher Taylor for his opinion on the relict gardens at Colleyweston, to Denise Todd for her researches on Battersea history, to Dr Terry Rogers for showing me Marlborough College, to Jennifer Meir for her expertise on Sanderson Miller, to Stephen Ch. de Crespigny of Kelmarsh and the French Hospital at Rochester, to Fraser Jansen and Hester Davenport of Windsor, and to the late George Moore of Elton, naval historian.

Daily panics, the need to know a very particular something, are the nature of a writer's life and I have many friends and neighbours who are used to my eccentricities and I thank them for their ever-ready responses. My additional appreciations go to Sarah Finch-Crisp and Caroline Allington at Lydiard House, along with my admiration and best wishes for the ongoing achievements of the Lydiard Restoration Project.

My literary agent Caradoc King and Michael Fishwick, then at HarperCollins, first recognised the enchantment of my '18th century gardening dame' and I thank them, and hope she still pleases them. The brilliant team at HarperPress of Arabella Pike, Kate Hyde, Vera Brice, Caroline Hotblack, Carol Anderson, Annabel Wright and Lizzie Dipple have managed to make *My Darling Heriott* the most pleasing of all my sixteen books (so far) to work on; my thanks to them, along with my hope that if they have felt the pull of Henrietta's spell, then my readers will also!

JANE BROWN,
March 2006.

SELECTED READING LIST
FROM MODERN SOURCES

[all published in London unless stated otherwise]*

Balen, M., *A Very English Deceit: The Secret History of the South Sea Bubble and the First Great Financial Scandal*, 2002.
Brown, J. and Sykes, C.S., *The Garden at Buckingham Palace: An Illustrated History*, 2004.
Carswell, J., *The South Sea Bubble*, rev. ed., 1993.
Colley, L., *Britons: Forging the Nation 1707–1837*, 1992.
—— *In Defiance of Oligarchy: The Tory Party 1714–60*, 1982.
Eves, C.K., *Matthew Prior: Poet & Diplomatist*, 1973.
Friedman, T., *James Gibbs*, 1984.
Gomme, E.A., *Smith of Warwick: Francis Smith, Architect and Master-builder*, Stamford 2000.
Graves, R., *The Spiritual[l] Quixote or the Summer Ramble of Mr Geoffry Wildgoose* [1773] ed. Clarence Tracy, 1967.
Harris, J., *Gardens of Delight: the Rococo English Landscape of Thomas Robins the Elder*, 1978 [rare, but a beautiful volume].
—— *The Palladian Revival: Lord Burlington, His Villa and Garden at Chiswick* [Montreal 1994], 1995.
Hicks, C., *Improper Pursuits: the Scandalous Life of Lady Di Beauclerk*, 2001.
Hunt, J.D. and Willis, P., eds., *The Genius of the Place: The English Landscape Garden 1620–1820*, 1975.
Hunt, J.D., *William Kent: Landscape Designer*, 1987.
Jacques, D., *Georgian Gardens: The Reign of Nature*, 1983.
Jones, M.K. and Underwood, M.G., *The King's Mother: Lady Margaret Beaufort Countess of Richmond and Derby*, 1992.
Kramnick, I., *Bolingbroke and His Circle: The Politics of Nostalgia in the Age of Walpole*, 1968.

Laird, M., *The Flowering of the English Landscape Garden: English Pleasure Grounds 1720–1800*, 1999.

Martin, P., *Pursuing Innocent Pleasures: The Gardening World of Alexander Pope*, 1984.

Symes, M., *The English Rococo Garden*, 1991.

Uglow, J., *Hogarth: A Life and a World*, 1997.

—— *The Lunar Men: The Friends Who Made the Future 1730–1910*, 2002.

Vickery, A., *The Gentleman's Daughter: Women's Lives in Georgian England*, 1998.

Willis, P., *Charles Bridgeman and the English Landscape Garden*, 1977 (reprinted and revised ed., Newcastle upon Tyne 2002).

NOTES

FOREWORD

1 Nathaniel Hawthorne, *The Scarlet Letter*, 1850, London: Everyman, 1992 edn, p. 55.
2 *Historical Manuscripts Commission Report*, Castle Howard Ms VI (1897), pp. 143–4, quoted by J. D. Hunt, *William Kent, Landscape Garden Designer*, London: A. Zwemmer, 1987, p. 46, and in Tom Williamson, *Polite Landscapes: Gardens and Society in Eighteenth-Century England*, Stroud: Alan Sutton, 1995, p. 59.
3 G. M. Trevelyan, *England under Queen Anne*, vol. 1 *Blenheim*, London: Longmans, Green and Co., 1936, the opening to Chapter 1.

CHAPTER ONE
On Being Henrietta St John

1 L. V. Grinsell, H. B. Wells, H. S. Tallamy and John Betjeman, *Studies in the History of Swindon*, Swindon: Swindon Borough Council, 1950, pp. 98–9.
2 Ibid, pp. 50–1.
3 Ibid., p. 98.
4 John Andrews and Andrew Dury, *Map of Wiltshire* (1773), a reduced facsimile, Devizes: Records Branch of the Wiltshire Archaeological Society, 1952.
5 Thomas D'Urfey (1653–1723), 'A Ballad of Andrew and Maudlin' (1700), in John Barrell and John Bull, eds., *The Penguin Book of English Pastoral Verse*, London: Allen Lane, 1974, pp. 246–7.

6 Alexander Pope (1688–1744), 'Summer, the Second Pastoral' (1709), in ibid., p. 253.
7 See *Country Life*, 105, n.d., pp. 606, 670, 734.
8 Michael K. Jones and Malcolm G. Underwood, *The King's Mother: Lady Margaret Beaufort, Countess of Richmond and Derby*, Cambridge: Cambridge University Press, 1992, pp. 27–8.
9 Ibid., pp. 39–40.
10 Ibid., pp. 2–3, quotation from Shakespeare, *Richard the Third*, Act 1, scene 3 and Act 4, scene 2.
11 Jones and Underwood, *The King's Mother*, p. 2.
12 Ibid., p. 65.
13 Ibid., p. 165.
14 See ibid., pp. 154–5 on Collyweston. The garden is described in *Royal Commission on Historical Monuments (England), Northamptonshire*, London: HMSO, vol. 1, 1975, p. 30, with additional notes in *Northamptonshire*, London: HMSO, vol. 4, 1982, p. 187, by Christopher Taylor, who has added in a note to the author (2004) that the remains of Collyweston indicate both a garden and a designed landscape of importance, but it is difficult to date them exactly to Lady Margaret's time. Jones and Underwood, *The King's Mother*, refer to documents in the archives of St John's College, Cambridge. The site is now privately owned pastureland but can be seen in part from the Collyweston to Ketton road.

15 M. R. Hopkinson, *Married to Mercury: A Sketch of Lord Bolingbroke and his Wives*, London: Constable & Co., 1936, p. 31.

16 H. Poynton, FRS, *Paper on the Notable Doings etc., of Oliver St John, the Builder of Thorpe Hall*, read before Peterborough Natural History, Scientific and Archaeological Society, 9 November 1909 (1910) p. 7, quoting Thomas Carlyle.

17 Ibid., p. 1.

18 Antonia Fraser, *The Weaker Vessel: Woman's Lot in Seventeenth-Century England*, London: Weidenfeld & Nicolson, 1984, p. 44.

19 Poynton, *Oliver St John*, p. 16.

20 Nikolaus Pevsner, *The Buildings of England, Cambridgeshire*, 1996, p. 502 on Wisbech. See also Pevsner, *The Buildings of England, Bedfordshire and the County of Huntingdon and Peterborough*, 1968, pp. 353–5 for Thorpe Hall.

21 Alec Clifton-Taylor and A. S. Ireson, *English Stone Building*, London: Gollancz in association with Peter Crawley, 1983, p. 149.

22 Poynton, *Oliver St John*, p. 16. The Chief Justice's son Francis St John retained Thorpe Hall, and at his death in 1705 his son, also Francis, inherited. This Francis, a baronet in 1716, died the same year as Henrietta, 1756, and Thorpe passed to his daughter Mary, who had married Sir John Bernard of Brampton, and their son Robert Bernard inherited in 1766. In 1789 all the contents were sold, and with the death of Mary Bernard (with a nice sense of fate) the Chief Justice's lease of Thorpe manor land reverted to the Dean and Chapter of Peterborough Cathedral, who sold the Hall etc. to Lord Fitzwilliam in 1809. For this and the later history see a paper by Richard Hillier (pub. *Cambridgeshire Life*, December 1976) and Peterborough Central Library Local Studies Collection.

23 Antonia Fraser, *Cromwell: Our Chief of Men*, London: Mandarin, 1995, p. 399.

24 See Elizabeth Crittall's entry on Lydiard Tregoze, in R. B. Pugh and Elizabeth Crittall, eds., *Victoria History of the Counties of England: Wiltshire*, London: Oxford University Press for the Institute of Historical Research, 1957, p. 88.

25 John George Taylor, *Our Lady of Batersey: The Story of Battersea Church and Parish Told from Original Sources*, London: George White, 1925, Appendix G, p. 404, quoting Symon Patrick (1626–1707). See also *The Works of Symon Patrick DD, Sometime Bishop of Ely, Including his Autobiography*, ed. Revd Alexander Taylor, 9 vols., Oxford: Oxford University Press, 1858.

26 Ibid., p. 403.

27 Ibid.

28 Poynton, *Oliver St John*, p. 16. See also Symon Gunton, *The History of the Church of Peterburgh*, ed. Symon Patrick, originally published by Richard Chiswell, London, 1686, which contains 'A Short and True Narrative of the Rifling and Defacing of the Cathedral Church in the Year 1643' written by Francis Standish, pp. 333–40 in facsimile edition published Peterborough and Stamford: Clay, Tyas, Watkins and Clay, 1990.

29 Taylor, *Our Lady of Batersey*, p. 87, n. 83, quoting the diary of Lady Mary Rich, aunt of Mary Rich married to Henry St John, BM Add. Ms 27351, 27357.

30 G. E. C. (Cockayne), *The Complete Peerage*, 8 vols. Saint John, London: G. Bell & Sons, 1887–98, p. 332, quoting Edward Harley, 2nd Earl of Oxford, *Memoranda on the Peerage*, and Bishop Burnet, *History of My Own Time*.

31 John Evelyn, *Diary*, 29 May 1660, ed. Philip Francis, Folio Society, London, 1963, pp. 119–20.

32 G. E. C., *The Complete Peerage*, p. 332.

33 George de Pellissari's family is detailed by P. H. Ditchfield in 'The Family of Riou', *Proceedings*, The Huguenot Society, 10, 1912–14. D. C. A. Agnew,

*Protestant Exiles from France in the
Reign of Louis XIV*, 3rd edn, 2 vols.,
Edinburgh: privately published, 1886,
vol. 1, p. 425, mentions Julie Pelissary
(*sic*), Angelique's half-sister, being
naturalised in England in 1685 with a
large number of fellow Huguenots,
likely to have included Angelique. Julie
was sponsor at the baptism in The
Hague, 1688, of the daughter of Isaac
Monceau de la Melonière, later a
colonel of one of William III's
Huguenot regiments. Most of
Angelique's relatives appear to have
stayed in France. When Harry
Bolingbroke was in Paris in 1712 he
met her 'grande amie' Mlle Aissé and
other connections but there is no
mention of him renewing these
acquaintances in his exile. For this
information I am indebted to S. Ch.
de Crespigny and Randolph Vigne of
the French Hospital at Rochester.

34 Hopkinson, *Man of Mercury*, p. 31.
35 H. T. Dickinson, *Bolingbroke*, London:
Constable, 1970, pp. 2 and 315, n. 6.
36 Sheila Biddle, *Bolingbroke and Harley*,
London: Allen & Unwin, 1975, p. 58.
37 Trevelyan, *England under Queen Anne*,
vol. 1, *Blenheim*, London: Longmans,
Green & Co., 1936, p. 118.
38 Biddle, *Bolingbroke and Harley*, p. 61,
quoting Lord Chesterfield's *Character
of Lord Bolingbroke* in Bolingbroke,
Works, ed. David Mallet, 5 vols.,
London, 1777, vol. 1, p. xv.
39 Biddle, *Bolingbroke and Harley*, p. 60.
40 Ibid., p. 61, quoting Lord Chesterfield
who heard him speak.
41 Graham Greene, *Lord Rochester's
Monkey*, London: Bodley Head, 1974,
p. 24.
42 Edward Bulwer-Lytton, 1st Baron
Lytton, *Devereux* in the Knebworth
edition, London: Routledge, n.d. (orig.
pub. 1829), p. 306. An editorial note
has been added saying that though
Devereux was published as a novel the
words Bolingbroke speaks are taken
from his 'similes, illustrations or
striking thoughts' in his writings. This
speech continues:

I have paid the forfeit of my errors
– when my motives have been pure,
men have seen a fault in the
conduct – when my conduct has
been blameless, men have
remembered its former errors, and
asserted that its present goodness
only arose from some sinister
intention: thus I have been termed
crafty, when I was in reality rash,
and that was called the
inconsistency of interest which in
reality was the inconstancy of
passion. [Pp. 306–7].

On p. 307 Lord Lytton has added:
'This I do believe the real (though
perhaps it is a new) light in which
Lord Bolingbroke's life and character
are to be viewed', i.e. 'that there are
certain incompatible qualities which
can never be united in one character –
that no man can have violent passions
to which he is in the habit of yielding,
and be systematically crafty and
designing. No man can be all heat,
and at the same time all coolness.'
Lord Lytton's close reading, his
political experience, extravagant
lifestyle and disastrous marriage gave
him an uncommon sympathy with his
fictional character that amounts to a
biographical portrait.
43 Hopkinson, *Married to Mercury*, p. 31.

CHAPTER TWO
My Darling Heriott

1 G. M. Trevelyan, *England under Queen
Anne*, vol. 1, *Blenheim*, London:
Longmans, Green & Co., 1936,
pp. 308–11 for this description of the
great storm of November 1703 with its
strikingly similar weather pattern to
that of October 1987.
2 Ibid., p. 309, but see also Bella
Bathurst, *The Lighthouse Stevensons*,
London: HarperCollins, 1999,
pp. 60–1.
3 Trevelyan, *England under Queen Anne*,
vol. 1, *Blenheim*, p. 309.
4 Ibid., but see also my *The Garden at*

Buckingham Palace: An Illustrated History, London: Royal Collection Publications, 2004, p. 122.

5 *The Journeys of Celia Fiennes*, 'From London to Oxford and thence into Sussex' (*c.* 1694), London: Macdonald, 1983 edn, p. 59.

6 Daniel Defoe, *A Tour through the Whole Island of Great Britain*, ed. Pat Rogers, Exeter: Webb & Bower, 1989, Letter 2, p. 176.

7 Ibid., pp. 172–9.

8 Richard Steele, *The Spectator*, ed. Donald F. Bond, 1965, no. 454. Monday 11 August 1712.

9 John George Taylor, *Our Lady of Batersey*, London: George White, 1925, p. 68.

10 Stella Pates, *A Piers Plowman Manuscript and the St John 'Rising Falcon' Crest*, Report No. 36, Swindon: The Friends of Lydiard Tregoze, 2002.

11 *The Grand Quarrel: From the Civil War Memoirs of Mrs Lucy Hutchinson; Mrs Alice Thornton; Ann, Lady Fanshawe; Margaret, Duchess of Newcastle; Anne, Lady Halkett, & the Letters of Brilliana, Lady Harley*, ed. Roger Hudson, London: Folio Society, 1993, p. 4.

12 Taylor, *Our Lady of Batersey*, p. 85 and n. 73 records that the church vaults were opened in 1875 and the inscription on her coffin plate was recorded 'Here rests the body of the Honble Lady Johanna St John late pious prudent consort of Sir Walter St John who exchanged this life for an immortal crown Jan. 15th 1704 in the 56th year of her marriage.' The date is Old Style, i.e. the year beginning on 25 March, so this becomes 1705 (which makes the date of Walter and Johanna's marriage 1649, the year of King Charles' execution).

13 Taylor, *Our Lady of Batersey*, pp. 86–7.

14 Walter Sichel, *Bolingbroke and his Times*, vol. 2, *The Sequel, March 1715 to December 1751*, London: J. Nisbet & Co., 1902, p. 463, 'Prefatory Memoir of Henrietta St John'.

15 Papers relating to Frances Winchcombe, including her music book, are in the British Library.

16 A. L. Humphreys, FSA, *Bucklebury: A Berkshire Parish*, published by the author at York Lodge, Reading, 1932 (printed by 'my old friends Messrs Strangeways, printers of skill and patience), Appendix A, p. 315, letter from W. Stratford to Thomas Coke, 11th September 1705 (Cowper Ms vol. 3, p. 62) tells of Betty Winchcombe's death. Bolingbroke was so devastated, in contrast to his coolness to his wife's ailments, that it is easy to suppose that the vivacious Betty was his favourite, and possibly his own fever was the outcome.

17 Humphreys, *Bucklebury*, Appendix A, p. 319, letter of 1st May 1708 (Bath Ms vol. 1, p. 190), Henry St John to Robert Harley.

18 H. T. Dickinson, *Bolingbroke*, London: Constable, 1970, p. 69, Henry St John to Lord Orrery, 9 July 1709.

19 Hopkinson, *Married to Mercury: A Sketch of Lord Bolingbroke and his Wives*, London: Constable & Co., 1936, p. 75.

20 In 1706 Thomas Coke was appointed Vice-Chamberlain to Queen Anne, and his portrait by Michael Dahl shows him to have been a fitting candidate for 'Sir Plume' in Pope's *The Rape of the Lock*; but there were other names, notably Sir George Brown, a relative of Arabella Fermor the victim of the 'rape' and the poem's dedicatee. *The Poems of Alexander Pope*, one vol. ed. of Twickenham text, ed. John Butt, London: Methuen, 1965.

21 *The Journeys of Celia Fiennes*, 'Into Derbyshire and Back', pp. 199–203, has her description of Bretby and its garden at the time of Lady Mary's wedding. This garden naturally influenced Melbourne Hall, which has never been substantially altered. Tom Coke also designed a garden at Cranford, next door to Dawley, for the Earl of Berkeley, and ornamental buildings for other friends. Tom Coke's coffin plate is in the library at Melbourne; he died on 16 May 1727 in

his fifty-third year. See also Howard Usher, *The Owners of Melbourne Hall*, Melbourne Hall Trust, 2003.

22 Ibid., p. 25.

23 Lucy Moore, *The Thieves' Opera: The Remarkable Lives of Jonathan Wild, Thief-taker, and Jack Sheppard, House-breaker*, London: Viking, 1997, pp. 46–7. Sally Salisbury, born Sarah Pridden, 1692–1714, was the model for Hogarth's *Harlot's Progress* and John Cleland's *Fanny Hill*; her *Authentic Memoirs* were published in 1723 by Captain C. Walker.

24 Graham Greene, *Lord Rochester's Monkey*, London: Bodley Head, 1974, p. 24.

25 Biddle, *Bolingbroke and Harley*, London: Allen & Unwin, 1975, p. 61.

26 William Shakespeare, *Richard the Second*, Act 2, scene 1.

27 Edward Bulwer-Lytton, 1st Baron Lytton, *Devereux*, in the Knebworth edition, London: Routledge, n.d., but first published 1829, p. 307, and see chapter 1, n. 42 above. The distant cousin was Paulet St John, Earl of Bolingbroke, Baron St John of Bletsoe, MP and Recorder for Bedford 1663–81. The name Bolingbroke is derived from the medieval market town at the crossing of the Boling Brook, four miles west of Spilsby, fourteen miles north of Boston in Lincolnshire. The castle was built by the Earl of Lincoln in Henry I's reign and through confiscations and awards it came to John of Gaunt with his marriage to Blanche of Lancaster, and so Henry IV was born there. He made it Crown property, Elizabeth I repaired it, and the Parliamentarians laid siege to it in the Civil War.

28 G. E. C. (Cockayne), *The Complete Peerage*, 8 vols., London: G. Bell & Sons, 1887–98, p. 332.

29 Linda Colley, *Britons: Forging the Nation 1707–1837*, New Haven, CT, and London: Yale University Press, 1992, p. 46.

30 Ibid.

31 Humphreys, *Bucklebury*, Appendix A,

p. 430, letter of 14 September 1714, Dean Swift to Viscount Bolingbroke.

32 Hopkinson, *Married to Mercury*, pp. 102–3.

33 Ibid., p. 123.

34 *Letters Written by the Late Right Honourable Lady Luxborough to William Shenstone Esq.*, published for J. Dodsley in Pall Mall, London, 1775, Letter X, 28th May 1748.

35 Humphreys, *Bucklebury*, Appendix A, pp. 430–1, letter of 5 May 1716, Viscountess Bolingbroke to Dean Swift.

36 Ibid.

37 Ibid., letter of 4 August 1716, Viscountess Bolingbroke to Dean Swift.

38 BL Add. Ms 34196 (note: some of the letters from Harry Bolingbroke are incomplete, possibly from censorship, but equally possibly torn by Henrietta in her need for writing paper in her imprisonment in Grosvenor Street or in early days at Barrells).

39 Ibid. f. 1.

40 Ibid. f. 7.

41 Ibid.

42 Humphreys, *Bucklebury*, records that The Rt Hon. Frances Viscountess Bolingbroke was buried at St Mary's church 'in linnen' on 28 October 1718. The estate was inherited by Winchcombe Howard Packer MP, the son of her third sister Mary and Robert Packer of Shillingford. Mr Humphreys adds the bitter note (p. 35) that in 1728 Harry Bolingbroke, then living at Dawley, went down to Bucklebury and marked 1,100 trees, presumably those he had planted some twenty years earlier, for felling without telling the Packers.

43 BL Add. Ms 34196. f. 9.

44 Ibid. f. 9.

45 Ibid.

46 Ibid. f. 5.

47 Hopkinson, *Married to Mercury*, pp. 137–40, and see also Nancy Mitford, *The Sun King*, Harmondsworth: Penguin, 1994, pp. 157–60 for descriptions of St Cyr.

48 Peter Martin, *Pursuing Innocent Pleasures: The Gardening World of Alexander Pope*, Hamden, CT: Archon Books, 1984, p. 121 quoting *Correspondence of Jonathan Swift*, ed. Harold Williams, vol. 2, Oxford: Clarendon Press, 1963, p. 461.

49 BL Add. Ms 34196. f. 9.

50 Sichel, *Bolingbroke and his Times*, vol. 2, *The Sequel*, pp. 154–5, and Hopkinson, *Married to Mercury*, p. 149; letter dated 28 July 1721.

51 BL Add. Ms 34196 f. 19 and Sichel, *Bolingbroke and his Times*, vol. 2, *The Sequel*, pp. 500–1, letter 24 June 1722.

52 Hopkinson, *Married to Mercury*, p. 149.

53 Martin, *Pursuing Innocent Pleasures*, p. 122.

54 Ibid., p. 265, n. 51, refers to Pope's letter to Joseph Spence in Spence, *Observations, Anecdotes and Characters of Books and Men*, ed. James M. Osborn, 2 vols., Oxford: Clarendon Press, 1966, vol. 1, p. 271.

55 Martin, *Pursuing Innocent Pleasures*, p. 133, and n. 51, p. 265 quoting *The Works of Alexander Pope*, ed. W. Elwin and W. J. Courthope, 1871–9, vol. 8, pp. 478–9, 'Reflexions upon Exile', 1717.

56 Park Floral de La Source, 8 kilometres south-east of Orléans, is now a publicly owned pleasure park open from April to November, with the source of the Loiret at its heart.

57 Martin, *Pursuing Innocent Pleasures*, pp. 166–7.

58 Sichel, *Bolingbroke and his Times*, vol. 2, *The Sequel*, p. 155.

59 Hopkinson, *Married to Mercury*, p. 150. See also Brean S. Hammond, *Pope and Bolingbroke: A Study of Friendship and Influence*, Columbia, MO: University of Missouri Press, 1984, p. 44.

60 Sichel, *Bolingbroke and his Times*, vol. 2, *The Sequel*, p. 155.

61 Ibid., pp. 166–7.

CHAPTER THREE
'Bright Marian'

1 Joseph Addison (1672–1719), *The Spectator*, no. 37, 12 April 1711, in J. D. Hunt and P. Willis, eds., *The Genius of the Place: The English Landscape Garden 1620–1820*, London: Elek, 1975, pp. 140–1.

2 L. V. Grinsell, H. B. Wells, H. S. Tallamy and John Betjeman, *Studies in the History of Swindon*, Swindon: Swindon Borough Council, 1950, p. 74.

3 John Aubrey's *Natural History of Wiltshire* was published in 1847, ed. John Britton, but see also R. B. Pugh and Elizabeth Crittall, eds., *Victoria History of the Counties of England: Wiltshire*, London: Oxford University Press for the Institute of Historical Research, 1951, pp. 77 and 87.

4 Helen Sard Hughes, *The Gentle Hertford: Her Life and Letters*, New York: Macmillan, 1940, p. 15.

5 Ibid., p. 7, letter from Lord Weymouth to Frances Thynne.

6 Ibid., pp. 34–6, fragmentary letter.

7 Ibid., p. 26, Lord Hertford to Lady Hertford, 23 October 1715.

8 Ibid., pp. 34–6.

9 Elizabeth Singer (1674–1737), 'Love & Friendship', in *The Miscellaneous Works in Prose & Verse of Mrs Elizabeth Rowe*, 2 vols., printed for R. Hett at the Bible & Crown in the Poultry; and R. Dodsley at Tully's Head in Pall Mall, 1739, vol. 2, p. 26.

10 *The Journeys of Celia Fiennes*, 'The Later Journeys, c.1701–3, Another Journey from Wiltshire to London via Marlborough', London: Macdonald, 1983, pp. 371–2.

11 Alexander Pope's *Windsor Forest* was written in 1704–13 and first published in 1713 as a celebratory metaphor for Queen Anne's England. It was very popular. The catalogue of rivers, lines 337–46, invites declamation and conjures a bird's eye view of the Thames valley of that day:

First the fam'd Authors of his
 ancient Name,
The winding Isis, and the fruitful
 Tame:
The Kennet swift, for silver Eels
 renown'd;
The Loddon slow, with verdant
 Alders crown'd:
Cole, whose clear Streams his
 flow'ry Islands lave;
And chalky Wey, that rolls a milky
 Wave:
The blue, transparent Vandalis*
 appears;
The gulphy Lee his sedgy Tresses
 . rears:
And sullen Mole, that hides his
 diving Flood;
And silent Darent, stain'd with
 Danish blood.
 *Wandle

The Poems of Alexander Pope,
 Twickenham edn, gen. ed. John Butt,
 vol. 1, *Pastoral Poetry and an Essay on
 Criticism*, ed. E. Audra and Aubrey
 Williams, London: Methuen, 1961,
 pp. 182–4.
12 Frances Hertford, 'Verses Ocassion'd
 by Seeing the River Kennet Frozen
 Over', in Hughes, *The Gentle Hertford*,
 p. 51.
13 *The Journeys of Celia Fiennes*, 'The
 Later Journeys, c. 1701–3', pp. 371–2.
14 Hughes, *The Gentle Hertford*, p. 51,
 Frances Hertford to Mrs Thynne,
 9 July 1719.
15 Ibid.
16 John Gay (1685–1732), *The Shepherd's
 Week*, 'Prologue', in *The Poetical Works
 of John Gay*, ed. G. C. Faber, London:
 Oxford University Press, 1926.
17 Hughes, *The Gentle Hertford*,
 Henrietta St John at Lydiard to
 Frances Hertford, 30 October 1726,
 pp. 127–8.
18 Ibid., pp. 127–8, Frances Hertford to
 Henrietta St John, 1 November 1726.
19 Ibid., pp. 131–3, Frances Hertford to
 Henrietta St John, 7 September 1731.
20 Elizabeth Singer was born in Ilchester,
 Somerset, on 11 September 1674; her
 autobiography, published on her
 orders by her brother-in-law
 Theophilus Rowe, is included in *The
 Miscellaneous Works in Prose and
 Verse of Mrs Elizabeth Rowe*, 2 vols.,
 London, 1739, in vol. 1, p. xiv.
21 Charles Kenneth Eves, *Matthew Prior:
 Poet and Diplomatist*, New York:
 Octagon Books, 1973, p. 89.
22 Ibid.
23 Ibid., and 'To the Author of the
 Foregoing Pastoral by Mr Prior', in
 *The Miscellaneous Works of Mrs
 Elizabeth Rowe*, vol. 2, pp. 14–15.
24 Elizabeth Rowe, 'On the Death of Mr
 Thomas Rowe', in *The Miscellaneous
 Works of Mrs Elizabeth Rowe*, vol. 2,
 pp. 112–15.
25 Verses translated from *Il Pastor Fido* in
 ibid., p. 145.
26 *Letters Written by the Late Right
 Honourable Lady Luxborough to
 William Shenstone Esq.*, Dublin: Caleb
 Jenkin, 2nd edn, 1776, letter of
 16 October 1748, which has led to
 speculation that Henrietta was a pupil
 of Handel, though there is no evidence
 for this – or her musical talent. She
 would have met him frequently in the
 1720s as he was popular amongst her
 circle.
27 John Sheffield, Duke of Buckingham's
 garden, designed with the help of
 Royal Master Gardener Henry Wise,
 was one of the sights of London at this
 time. See my *The Garden at
 Buckingham Palace: An Illustrated
 History*, London: Royal Collection
 Publications, 2004, pp. 37–46.
28 Peter Bicknell, comp., *Beauty, Horror
 and Immensity: Picturesque Landscape
 in Britain 1750–1850*, catalogue of an
 exhibition at the Fitzwilliam Museum,
 Cambridge, 1981, Cambridge:
 Cambridge University Press, 1981,
 pp. 26–7.
29 Peter Martin, *Pursuing Innocent
 Pleasures: The Gardening World of
 Alexander Pope*, Hamden, CT: Archon
 Books, 1984, p. 2.
30 Bicknell, *Beauty, Horror and
 Immensity*, p. 26.

31 Richard Hewlings, *Chiswick House and Gardens*, London: English Heritage, 1989, describes the garden at various stages, and in this instance before 1727. The 1728–9 paintings by Pieter Andreas Rysbrack (1690–1748) of the Orange Tree Garden, the Bollo Brook, northern Pond and Tuscan pavilion, of the alleys with their eye-catchers and the view of the Bagnio and the Upper River are now in the house.

32 Linda Colley, *In Defiance of Oligarchy: The Tory Party 1714–60*, Cambridge: Cambridge University Press, 1982, p. 192.

33 Ibid., pp. 207–8.

34 Hughes, *The Gentle Hertford*, pp. 127–8, Frances Hertford to Henrietta St John, 1st November 1726.

35 Pope, *Windsor Forest*, line 341.

36 *The Gentleman's Magazine*, 72 (2), 1802, p. 725 (quoted in *The Victoria History of the Counties of England, Middlesex, Elthorne Hundred*, London: Oxford University Press for Institute of Historical Research, n.d., vol. 3, p. 265, but see also Peter Martin, *Pursuing Innocent Pleasures*, chapter 5, pp. 119–44 for a comprehensive study of Bolingbroke at Dawley.

37 Terry Friedman, *James Gibbs*, New Haven, CT: Yale University Press, 1984, for analysis of Gibbs' contemporary buildings. However, Friedman admits there is little evidence on Dawley.

38 As note 36 above.

39 *Letters [of] Lady Luxborough to William Shenstone*, pp. 22–3, 28 April 1748.

40 Friedman, *James Gibbs*, p. 141.

41 David Jacques, *Georgian Gardens: The Reign of Nature*, London: Batsford, 1983, p. 22.

42 Martin, *Pursuing Innocent Pleasures*, p. 132, confirms the poem was written by Pope.

43 Both Friedman and Martin have 'Dawley Farm'. Friedman includes an attribution to A. Ballantyne, *Voltaire's Visit to England 1726–1729*, [London]: Smith, Elder & Co., 1893, p. 39. Martin discusses the authorship in *Pursuing Innocent Pleasures*, pp. 132–3 and 265, note 48, suggesting Pope in possible collaboration with Swift.

44 Martin, *Pursuing Innocent Pleasures*, p. 133.

45 David Jacques, 'The Art and Sense of the Scriblerus Club in England 1715–35', *Garden History*, 4 (1), p. 48.

46 *Letters [of] Lady Luxborough to William Shenstone*, pp. 22–3, 28 April 1748.

47 Peter Willis, *Charles Bridgeman and the English Landscape Garden*, London: Zwemmer, 1977, p. 79.

48 See Hewlings, *Chiswick House and Gardens*, p. 89, for this famous remark in context.

49 Jonathan Swift to Alexander Pope, 29 September 1725, in *Jonathan Swift: Major Works*, ed. Angus Ross and David Woolley, Oxford: Oxford University Press, 2003, p. 472.

50 Alexander Pope, 'Essay' from *The Guardian*, 1713, in Hunt and Willis, eds., *The Genius of the Place*, pp. 204–8.

51 Ibid., p. 205.

52 Pope, 'The Gardens of Alcinous from Homer's *Odyssey*', in *The Genius of the Place*, p. 206.

53 Voltaire to Pope from 'My Lord Bolingbroke's House, Friday at Noon, November 16th 1726', in Alexander Dyce, *Memoir of Pope*, in *Poetical Works of Alexander Pope*, Covent Garden, London: Bell & Daldry, 1831, 3 vols., vol. 1, pp. lxxiv–lxxv.

54 Anthony Beckles Wilson, 'Alexander Pope's Grotto at Twickenham', *Garden History*, 26 (1), Summer 1998, p. 39.

55 Ibid., p. 37, quoting a letter to Edward Blount from *The Correspondence of Alexander Pope*, ed. George W. Sherburn, 5 vols., Oxford: Clarendon Press, 1956, vol. 1, p. 296, 2 June 1725.

56 John H. Hammond, *The Camera Obscura: A Chronicle*, Bristol: Adam Hilger, 1981, pp. 71ff.; Addison's 'Pleasures of the Imagination' was in *The Spectator*, 25 June 1712.

57 Hammond, *The Camera Obscura*, p. 72.

58 Jonathan Swift, *Gulliver's Travels*, ed.
   R. DeMaria Jr, London: Penguin
   Books, 2003, 'A Voyage to Lilliput',
   p. 30.
59 Christopher Hussey, *English Gardens
   and Landscapes 1700–1750*, London:
   Country Life, 1967, pp. 41–3.
60 Mark Laird, *The Flowering of the
   Landscape Garden: English Pleasure
   Grounds 1720–1800*, Philadelphia:
   University of Pennsylvania Press,
   1999, pp. 83–8, gives a tantalising
   description of the garden at Whitton,
   which was begun in the 1720s, but
   little chronicled until 1735 when
   Bolingbroke left Dawley. The house
   was built about 1732 but the garden
   centred on Gibbs' earlier greenhouse,
   so Gibbs would seem to be the
   connection between Pope, Dawley and
   Whitton. Henrietta could only have
   seen Whitton in embryo, with hardly
   time to appreciate the American
   shrubs and trees which were being
   grown here for the first time.
61 *Marble Hill House, Twickenham: A
   Short Account of its History and
   Architecture* abridged from Marie P. G.
   Draper, *Marble Hill House and Its
   Owners*, 1970, London: Greater
   London Council, 1977, p. 7.
62 Moody is the gardener; 'Quartridge'
   was his wage paid quarterly as was
   usual. *The Poems of Jonathan Swift*, ed.
   Sir Harold Williams, 2nd edn, 3 vols.,
   Oxford: Clarendon Press, 1958, vol. 2,
   pp. 407–11.
63 See Lord Bathurst in James Lees-
   Milne, *Earls of Creation: Five Great
   Patrons of Eighteenth-Century Art*,
   London: Hamilton, 1962, p. 26. Pope's
   Epistles, though moral and political,
   were addressed to leaders of gardening
   fashion: Richard Boyle, 3rd earl of
   Burlington (1695–1753) at Chiswick
   and Londesborough in Yorkshire;
   Richard Temple, 1st Viscount Cobham
   (1669–1749) at Stowe; Allen Bathurst,
   Baron (later Earl) Bathurst (1684–1775)
   at Cirencester and Richings; and
   Viscount Bolingbroke at La Source
   and Dawley. *The Epistle to Burlington*,

1731, contains the immortal line
'Consult the Genius of the Place in
all', followed by the subtleties of
landscaping skills combined until:

> Nature shall join you, Time shall
>   make it grow
> A work to wonder at – perhaps a
>   Stow'.

64 *Correspondence between Frances,
   Countess of Hertford afterwards
   Duchess of Somerset and Henrietta
   Louisa Countess of Pomfret between
   the Years 1738 and 1741*, ed. and pub.
   Richard Phillips, 6 Bridge Street,
   Blackfriars, London, 1805, 2 vols.,
   vol. 2, pp. 259ff. with letter dated
   26 February 1741.
65 Ibid.
66 Jacques, *Georgian Gardens*, p. 22.
67 Ibid., p. 19, quoting Stephen Switzer,
   *The Nobleman, Gentleman and
   Gardener's Recreation*, 1715.
68 Peter Willis, *Charles Bridgeman and
   The English Landscape Garden*, 1977
   ed., p. 22.
69 Ibid.

CHAPTER FOUR
The Honourable Mrs Knight

1 Brook Taylor (1685–1731) was son and
  heir to John Taylor of Bifrons in Kent.
  Educated at St John's College,
  Cambridge, he was a mathematician
  who pioneered planetary motion,
  calculus and catenaries and became a
  fellow of the Royal Society in 1714. He
  published *Linear Perspective*, 1715, and
  further *Observations*, 1719. He married
  a Miss Brydges in 1721; she died in
  childbirth in 1723. He married Sabetta
  Sawbridge of Olantigh in 1724 or 1725,
  but she, too, died in giving birth to
  their daughter Elizabeth. He succeeded
  to Bifrons in 1729 but had little time
  to enjoy that lovely house and garden.
  Bolingbroke's mention to Henrietta of
  Taylor's marriage to Sabetta supposes
  that she was interested. This is just
  another pointer to the escalating
  evidence that Henrietta's marriage was

not based upon love and compatibility but upon infatuation and money.

2 M. R. Hopkinson, *Married to Mercury: A Sketch of Lord Bolingbroke and his Wives*, London: Constable & Co., 1936, p. 153.

3 Helen Sard Hughes, *The Gentle Hertford: Her Life and Letters*, New York: Macmillan, 1940, p. 122, quoting Elizabeth Rowe to Frances Hertford.

4 Ibid.

5 *Letters of Lord Bolingbroke*, BL Add. Ms 34196, f. 40.

6 Ibid.

7 Ibid., f. 43 and printed in Walter Sichel, *Bolingbroke and his Times*, 2 vols., London: James Nisbet & Co., 1901–2, vol. 2, p. 519.

8 John Carswell, *The South Sea Bubble*, 1960, rev. edn, Stroud, Glos.: Alan Sutton, 1993, p. 46.

9 E. J. Erith, A. R. J. Ramsey et al, *The True and Lamentable History of Robert Knight Esquire and the South Sea Bubble together with The Rise and Fall of the House called Luxborough*, [Woodford]: Woodford Historical Society, 1987, p. 10.

10 Carswell, *The South Sea Bubble*, 1993, p. 52.

11 Erith, Ramsey et al., *The True and Lamentable History*, pp. 25–6. Ben Jonson's 'To Sir Robert Wroth' (1616) opens:

> How blest art thou, canst love the
>   countrey, Wroth,
> Whether by choice, or fate, or both;
> And, though so neere the citie, and
>   the court
> Art tane with neithers vice, nor
>   sport.

J. Barrell and J. Bull, eds., *The Penguin Book of English Pastoral Verse*, 1974, pp. 153–6.

12 Erith, Ramsey et al., *The True and Lamentable History*, pp. 25–6.

13 That Bob Knight commissioned Sir James Thornhill (though no evidence of work carried out survived) led to speculation that Luxborough was similar to the Childs' great Wanstead

House, where Thornhill worked. Of course, it was nowhere like Colen Campbell's Wanstead, in either size, scale or quality.

14 Erith, Ramsey et al., *The True and Lamentable History*, p. 13.

15 Ibid., p. 14, notes the death of Martha Knight as 1718, with her burial in St Mildred's Bread Street vault.

16 The elaborate memorial put up by Lord Luxborough to his parents in St Mary's at Wootton Wawen states that she died on 27 July 1723, aged thirty-seven – making her birth year 1686, and her age at marriage fifteen.

17 Isaac Kramnick, *Bolingbroke and his Circle: The Politics of Nostalgia in the Age of Walpole*, Harvard Political Studies, Cambridge, MA: Harvard University Press, 1968, p. 66.

18 Carswell, *The South Sea Bubble*, 1993 edn, pp. 62–3, 194, 201, and Malcolm Balen, *A Very English Deceit: The Secret History of the South Sea Bubble and the First Great Financial Scandal*, London: Fourth Estate, 2002, pp. 182–3, are both much taken with the still unravelling mysteries of Bob Knight's bookkeeping.

19 Kramnick, *Bolingbroke and his Circle*, p. 66.

20 James I's mulberry enterprise on Crown Land opposite the west gate of (Lower) St James's Park is documented in my *The Garden at Buckingham Palace: An Illustrated History*, London: Royal Collection Publications, 2004, p. 21.

21 Jenny Uglow, *Hogarth: A Life and a World*, London: Faber & Faber, 1997, p. 85.

22 Kramnick, *Bolingbroke and his Circle*, pp. 67–9.

23 Carswell, *The South Sea Bubble*, London: Cresset Press, 1960 edn, p. 225.

24 Kramnick, *Bolingbroke and his Circle*, p. 68.

25 Carswell, *The South Sea Bubble*, 1960 edn, p. 225.

26 Balen, *A Very English Deceit*, pp. 191–2. Robert Surman was Bob Knight's

nephew, the son of his sister Sarah and a haberdasher Philip Surman, recruited to the Sword Blade Bank then as Deputy Cashier at the South Sea Company. Surman was sacked in 1721 but resumed his banking career, and bought Valentine's Mansion at Ilford, which survives in public ownership. Surman died in 1759.

27 Balen, *A Very English Deceit*, pp. 202–3.

28 Ibid., p. 207.

29 Ibid., p. 208, where Malcolm Balen recounts his discovery of this subterfuge.

30 Carswell, *The South Sea Bubble*, 1960 edn, p. 267. Despite Bob Knight's 'gifts' to Queen Caroline, presumably carried to England by Robert, he was not to be pardoned until after Walpole's resignation in 1742. His saviour was the then Secretary of State Lord Gower, who remembered that he owed his own fortune to Bob Knight's advice when he was manager of the Sword Blade Bank.

31 John Page was MP for Great Grimsby 1727–34 and then for Winchester 1741–68.

32 BL Add. Ms 34196. f. 45.

33 Ibid. f. 50.

34 Lord Bolingbroke to Henrietta Knight from Dawley Farm, 3 June 1728, BL Add. Ms 34196 (printed in Sichel, *Bolingbroke and his Times*, vol. 2, p. 523).

35 Ibid.

36 Ibid.

37 Ibid.

38 Hughes, *The Gentle Hertford*, p. 63, letter from Frances to her mother Mrs Thynne, 1721. The Grosvenor Street houses were new-built, i.e. 1720–5; the exteriors of nos. 45, 50, 51, 52, 58, 59 and 60 are conserved from this period.

39 James Thomson (1700–48) *The Seasons*, 1730. There are many versions; my quotation is taken from a late nineteenth-century miniature edition, undated, pub. Crosby Lockwood & Son; there is a Clarendon

Press, Oxford, edition of 1981 edited by James Sambrook.

40 Richard Savage (*c.* 1697–1743) died in poverty in a Bristol gaol.

41 Stephen Duck (1705–56) entered the Church but took his own life in a fit of depression.

42 Hughes, *The Gentle Hertford*, pp. 135–6. Christopher Hibbert, *The Grand Tour*, London: Thames Methuen, 1987, pp. 20 and 39, describes the 'swarms' of Englishmen and their 'bear leaders' in Paris in the late 1720s.

43 William Knight (1731–67) spent his life in France except for a short spell at Oxford *c.* 1745. He was well provided for by his father. He married but left no children when he died in Reims.

44 'The Memoirs of a Lady of Quality' by Fanny Vane was published as 'the notorious' chapter 81 in vol. 2 of Tobias Smollett's *The Adventures of Peregrine Pickle*, 1751.

45 BL Add Ms. 34196 f. 78, printed in Sichel, *Bolingbroke and his Times*, vol. 2, pp. 530–2.

46 Alexander Pope, *The Dunciad*, Book IV, lines 557–63 in *The Poems of Alexander Pope*, ed. John Butt, one-volume edition of the Twickenham text, London: Methuen & Co., 1963, p. 795.

47 Henrietta Knight to Frances Hertford in Hughes, *The Gentle Hertford*, pp. 135–6.

48 Smollett, *Peregrine Pickle*, vol. 2, p. 78.

49 Henrietta Knight to Frances Hertford, in Hughes, *The Gentle Hertford*, pp. 133–4.

50 The Queen's remark, made after the royal couple had been seen to bed, is in *Lord Hervey's Memoirs*, ed. Romney Sedgwick, Harmondsworth: Penguin Books, 1984, p. 41.

51 Henrietta Knight to Frances Hertford, in Hughes, *The Gentle Hertford*, pp. 133–4.

52 Jane Roberts, *Royal Landscape: The Gardens and Parks of Windsor*, 1997, p. 11. See also Sheila and Pat Rooney, *St Leonard's Hill, Windsor: House,*

Hermitage and Hill, Windsor: Windsor Publications, 1991.

53 Verses by John Dalton (1709–63) from Hughes, *The Gentle Hertford*, p. 170. Dalton was the son of the Revd John Dalton, rector of Dean in Cumberland from 1705–12, a living provided by the Lowther family. He went up to Queen's College, Oxford, aged sixteen, gained his BA in 1730, MA in 1734 and Fellowship (which precluded marriage) in 1741.

54 Dalton in Hughes, *The Gentle Hertford*, pp. 170–1.

55 Henrietta Knight in ibid., pp. 172–3.

56 John Milton, *Comus and Other Poems*, ed. F. T. Prince, London: Oxford University Press, 1968, lines 859–66.

57 Frances Hertford, John Dalton and Henrietta Knight in *The Gentle Hertford*, pp. 174–8.

58 John Dalton, 'To the Honourable Mrs Knight in answer to a copy of verses from her', in *The Gentle Hertford*, pp. 180–1.

CHAPTER FIVE
'Poor Fat Fanfan'

1 This letter dated 9 or 20 October 1734 is the first surviving in BL Add. Ms 45889; these letters were kept by the Knight family after Henrietta's death and eventually given to the British Museum in 1943 by Mrs Catharine Octavia Higgon MBE, JP, who was a descendant of Robert Knight's liaison with Jane Davies. Typed versions of these letters are in *The Knights of Barrells*, compiled by Arthur E. Carden, also a descendant, in 1993. This was a limited edition of sixty copies; Warwick Record Office, Lydiard Tregoze, the Society of Genealogists, the University of Warwick Social History Centre and the British Library all have deposited copies.

2 Henrietta Knight to Frances Hertford in Hughes, *The Gentle Hertford: Her Life and Letters*, New York: Macmillan, 1940, pp. 141–3.

3 Ibid.

4 Kenneth Woodbridge, *The Stourhead Landscape*, London: The National Trust, 1986, pp. 12–13.

5 Mary, Lady Chudleigh (1659–1710), 'To the Ladies', quoted by J. Paul Hunter, 'Couplets and Conversation', in *The Cambridge Companion to Eighteenth-Century Poetry*, ed. John Sitter, Cambridge: Cambridge University Press, 2001, p. 23.

6 Peter Martin, *Pursuing Innocent Pleasures: The Gardening World of Alexander Pope*, Hamden, CT: Archon Books, 1984, p. 142.

7 Joan Lane's entry for Henrietta (Luxborough) in the *New Dictionary of National Biography*, 2004, quotes Lord Egmont's *Diary* for 11 August 1736: 'I heard in town that Mr Knight had separated from his wife (daughter of My Lord St John) finding her in bed with Dr Peters her physician but allows her £500 a year out of respect to her family.'

8 John St John to Henrietta Knight, 6 July 1736, BL Add. Ms 45889. (Note: these letters of 1736 and into 1737 were kept by Henrietta as a record of the sequence of events of her separation and move to Barrells; they are (unless otherwise stated) in Add. Ms 45889 and in Carden's *The Knights of Barrells*.)

9 Henrietta Knight to Robert Knight undated but April 1736.

10 Henrietta Knight to Robert Knight undated but March or early April 1736.

11 Ibid.

12 Henrietta Knight to Robert Knight, 14 April 1736.

13 Lord Bolingbroke to Henrietta Knight, 22 April 1736.

14 Bob Knight in Paris to Lord Bolingbroke, undated but in sequence.

15 Lord Bolingbroke in Paris to Robert Knight in Grosvenor Street, London, 30 April 1736 in sequence.

16 Fragment of a letter, Lord Bolingbroke from Calais to Henrietta Knight in London, 10 May 1736. This and other torn letters in this sequence indicate

how desperately short of writing paper Henrietta was during her imprisonment in Grosvenor Street at this time.

17 Lord Bolingbroke in France to Robert Knight in London, 25 June 1736.

18 John St John at Lydiard to Robert Knight in London, 29 June 1736.

19 John St John at Chipping Warden to his sister Henrietta Knight, 6 July 1736.

20 Noted by Mrs Higgon as on the reverse of one of the Copy Book 'My dearest Life' letters of March/April 1736 but more likely the other way around, i.e. Henrietta in her imprisonment practised her Copy Book pleadings to Robert on the back of this old love letter, which was therefore inadvertently saved!

21 Ibid.

22 Mary, Lady Chudleigh, 'To the Ladies'.

23 Robert Knight at Kingsclere to Henrietta Knight at Barrells, 13 July 1736.

24 Lord Bolingbroke from Argeville to Robert Knight, 30 August 1736.

25 Ibid.

26 Ibid.

27 Ibid.

28 M. R. Hopkinson, *Married to Mercury: A Sketch of Lord Bolingbroke and his Wives*, London: Constable & Co., 1936, p. 239, Viscountess Bolingbroke to the Countess of Denbigh, 25 October 1736.

29 Lord Bolingbroke from Argeville to Robert Knight, 30 August 1736, but see also *Letters of Lord Bolingbroke*, BL Add. Ms 34196.

30 Lord Bolingbroke to Henrietta Knight at Barrells, 25 September 1736.

31 Hopkinson, *Married to Mercury: A Sketch of Lord Bolingbroke and his Wives*, London: Constable & Co., 1936, p. 239, Viscountess Bolingbroke to the Countess of Denbigh, 25 October 1736.

32 Amanda Vickery, *The Gentleman's Daughter: Women's Lives in Georgian England*, New Haven, CT, and London: Yale University Press, 1998, p. 80.

CHAPTER SIX
'Asteria'

NOTE: Where the date only is given as the reference this means *The Letters of the Right Honourable Lady Luxborough to William Shenstone Esq.*, 1775. All the BL Add. Ms 45889 letters are in the sequence saved by Henrietta and the Knight family as referred to above.

1 Helen Sard Hughes, *The Gentle Hertford: Her Life and Letters*, New York: Macmillan, 1940, p. 144 has this letter from Henrietta Knight at Barrells (1736) to her father Lord St John, indicating that the letter was given to Lady Hertford.

2 Lord Bolingbroke from Argeville to Henrietta Knight at Barrells, 7 December 1736, BL Add. Ms 45889.

3 Hughes, *The Gentle Hertford*, p. 144, Henrietta Knight (1736) to Lord St John.

4 William Shakespeare, *As You Like It*, Act 2, scene 1, set in the Forest of Arden.

5 Stephen Greenblatt, *Will in the World: How Shakespeare Became Shakespeare*, London: Jonathan Cape, 2004, has atmospheric early chapters on Stratford and Warwickshire.

6 Andrew Craythorn, *Barrells Hall from Riches to Ruins*, privately published, 2003, pp. 8–10.

7 Robert Knight from Kingsclere to Henrietta Knight, 13 July 1736, BL Add. Ms 45889.

8 Hughes, *The Gentle Hertford*, p. 145, 16 January 1739, letter to Lady Hertford signed S. Cholmondeley. Seymour Cholmondeley was Henrietta's cousin or the S may have been an A, for her Aunt (Ann) Cholmondeley.

9 Andor Gomme, *Smith of Warwick: Francis Smith, Architect and Master-builder*, Stamford: Shaun Tyas, 2000, p. 514, records payments to Francis Smith in 1736–7 for the work being done in Henrietta's first winter.

10 Hughes, *The Gentle Hertford*, pp. 152–3, Henrietta Knight to Lady Hertford, 26 June 1742.

11 Lord Bolingbroke to Henrietta Knight, 20 March 1737, BL Add. Ms 45889.

12 Easter Sunday 1748.

13 18 December 1748.

14 Robert Knight to Henrietta Knight, 13 July 1736, BL Add Ms. 45889.

15 Henrietta Knight to Robert Knight, 14 April 1736, BL Add. Ms 45889.

16 18 December 1748.

17 Hughes, *The Gentle Hertford*, p. 145, letter to Lady Hertford signed S. Cholmondeley, 16 January 1739.

18 Lord Bolingbroke to Henrietta Knight, 20 March 1737 (catalogued as 1736), BL Add. Ms 45889.

19 Peter Martin, *Pursuing Innocent Pleasures: The Gardening World of Alexander Pope*, Hamden, CT: Archon Books, 1984, p. 142.

20 William Somerville (1675–1742) published *Hobbinol* in 1740, and a poem on hawking, 'Field Sports', in 1742.

21 Richard Graves, *The Spiritual Quixote*, 1773, London: Oxford University Press, 1967 edn, has descriptions of the Cotswold Olympic games, p. 38 and note, p. 479.

22 William Somerville, 'Song to Asteria' is taken from the text in Arthur E. Carden's *The Knights of Barrells*, Falmouth, 1993 (copy in Warwick Record Office) but was also published in *Dodsley's Collection*, 1775, vol. 4, p. 295.

23 Somerville's second 'Song' is from *Shenstone's Miscellany 1759–1763*, edited from the Ms (p. 61), by Ian A. Gordon of the University of New Zealand, Wellington, Oxford: Clarendon Press, 1952, p. 35.

24 Hughes, *The Gentle Hertford*, p. 157, Henrietta Knight to Frances Hertford, 19 July 1742.

25 Hughes, *The Gentle Hertford*, pp. 156–7, Henrietta Knight to Frances Hertford, 19 July 1742.

26 Robert Knight in London to Henrietta Knight at Barrells, 22 April 1742, BL Add. Mss 45889 ff. 42–4.

27 Bolingbroke had reported to Henrietta on 15 October 1738 that her youngest brother Holly's death would bring her 'some advantage'. Holles St John was only twenty-eight, and little is known of his life except that it was apparently rather colourful and he had a passion for the theatre. Carden, *The Knights of Barrells*, p. 323, has a reproduction of a portrait of a young man, with a family likeness to Henrietta, wearing theatrical costume, and a blond wig with the moon symbol of Diana the huntress on his head! Expert analysis has shown that the canvas had been folded several times, and the portrait extensively restored. It had descended through the Knight family and so may have belonged to Henrietta at Barrells.

28 Robert Knight in London to Henrietta Knight at Barrells, 22 April 1742, BL Add. Ms 45889 ff. 42–4.

29 Hughes, *The Gentle Hertford*, p. 150, Frances Hertford at Percy Lodge to Henrietta Knight at Barrells, 6 June 1742.

30 Ibid., pp. 151–2, Henrietta Knight in reply to the above (1742).

31 Ibid., pp. 153–6, Frances Hertford to Henrietta Knight, undated but early July 1742.

32 Ibid.

33 Ibid.

34 James Waylen, *A History Military and Municipal of the Town (Otherwise Called the City) of Marlborough and More Generally the Entire Hundred of Selkley*, London: John Russell, 1854, quoting a letter from Lady Hertford to the Countess of Pomfret, 25 June 1741.

35 Ibid., note on Newbury ashes added.

36 Ibid., Lady Hertford to Countess of Pomfret, 25 June 1741.

37 Hughes, *The Gentle Hertford*, pp. 150–1, Frances Hertford to Henrietta Knight, 6 June 1742.

38 Ibid., pp. 156–7, Henrietta Knight to Frances Hertford, 19 July 1742.

39 Ibid., pp. 158–60, Frances Hertford to Henrietta Knight, 1 August 1742.

40 Ibid., pp. 160–1, Henrietta Knight to Frances Hertford, 20 August 1742.

41 Ibid.

42 Henry Bolingbroke to Henrietta Knight, 10 August 1745, BL Add. Ms 34196.

43 John Dalton's 'Epistle the Second' is dated 15 August 1744, and it was published in 1745.

44 Hughes, *The Gentle Hertford*, p. 213, Lady Hertford to her son Lord Beauchamp.

45 Ibid., pp. 276–7, Lady Hertford to Lord Beauchamp, 12 August 1743.

46 Ibid., pp. 383–5, Lady Hertford to Lady Luxborough, 4 May 1747. The following year the Hertfords became Duke and Duchess of Somerset and Frances' attentions were diverted to her new homes, Northumberland House in London and Petworth in Sussex. The Duke died on 7 February 1750, leaving Percy Lodge to her, so that once again it became her beloved home.

47 *Letters Written by Lady Luxborough to William Shenstone*, July 1748 with the 'Pastoral Elegy' from Revd Perks, pp. 41–2.

48 Jenny Uglow, *The Lunar Men: The Friends Who Made the Future 1730–1810*, London: Faber & Faber, 2002, p. 21, quotes Birmingham's historian William Hutton 'drawing breath' when he extolled the wealth of nations gathered for the local craftsmen – metals, jewels, fossils, shells, skins, coral, horn, bone and ivory – from which Henrietta, with Franky Holyoake working at Boulton's, would have acquired 'scraps' for her grotto.

49 Anthony Beckles Willson, 'Alexander Pope's Grotto in Twickenham', *Garden History*, 26 (1), Summer 1998, pp. 42–4.

50 Thomas Goldney's grotto in Bristol was started in the late 1730s but not completed until 1764. Frances Hertford visited it, and Henrietta may have done so while staying with the Merediths at Henbury. The 1740s saw the start of the real enthusiasm for grottoes with the professional builders, the Lane family, working at Oatlands and Painshill in Surrey, and Wardour in Wiltshire. Designs by William Kent and Thomas Wright were only for grottoes in the grandest parks. See Barbara Jones, *Follies & Grottoes*, 2nd edn, London: Constable, 1974, pp. 152ff.

51 John Harvey, *Early Nurserymen*, London: Phillimore, 1974, pp. 104–5.

52 4 June 1749.

CHAPTER SEVEN
Lady Luxborough

NOTE: Where the date only is given as the reference this means *The Letters of the Right Honourable Lady Luxborough to William Shenstone Esq.*, 1775.

1 John Carswell, *The South Sea Bubble*, 1960, Stroud, Glos.: Alan Sutton, 1993 edn, p. 238.

2 E. J. Erith, pp. 20–2 in E. J. Erith and A. R. J. Ramsey et al., *The True and Lamentable History of Robert Knight Esquire and the South Sea Bubble together with The Rise and Fall of the House called Luxborough*, [Woodford:] Woodford Historical Society, 1987.

3 *Select Letters between the Late Duchess of Somerset, Lady Luxborough, Miss Dolman, Mr Whistler, Mr R. Dodsley, William Shenstone & Others from Original Copies ('the gift of an elegant friend')*, 2 vols., London: Thomas Hull, 1778, vol. 1, William Shenstone to Richard Jago, 17 September 1747.

4 William Shenstone (1714–63), *Men & Manners*, was published by the Golden Cockerel Press, Waltham St Lawrence, 1927, edited with a biographical essay by Havelock Ellis from which these quotations have been taken. Much of Shenstone's work, e.g. *The School-mistress* (1742), was published in his lifetime.

5 Richard Graves, *The Spiritual Quixote or The Summer's Ramble of Mr Geoffry Wildgoose*, ed. Clarence Tracy, London: Oxford University Press, 1967, pp. 130–5, has the story of Utrecia Smith as Ophelia in 'Mr Graham's Story'. Graham meets Ophelia at a country ball; she 'who had the

character of a learned lady and a great wit' was suffering from the death of her former fiancé. After a patient courting of two years Graham was determined to marry her, but whilst he was in London he received an anonymous letter blackening her character, accusing her 'of drinking spirituous liquors for her private amusement', and instead of facing Ophelia he was distracted by the flirtatious Lavinia. Ophelia saw them together, which brought on a fit of distraction and, within a few months, her death. The mortified Graham left the country and rambled all over Europe for nearly five years, until his mother's legacy enabled him to settle far away from his native countryside, at Bath, change his name and live out his days.

6 E. Monro Purkis, *William Shenstone: Poet and Landscape Gardener*, Wolverhampton: Whitehead Brothers, 1931, pp. 39–40.

7 Ibid., p. 64.

8 Dr Samuel Johnson, *Prefaces Biographical and Critical to the Works of the English Poets*, 1779–81, on Shenstone, p. 206.

9 Ibid.

10 'A Short Account of Thomson's Visit', 30 August 1746, in *James Thomson 1700–48: Letters and Documents*, ed. Alan D. McKillop, Lawrence: University of Kansas Press, 1958.

11 11 August 1747.

12 Ibid.

13 Lady Luxborough to Lady Hertford, *Percy Family Letters & Papers*, vol. 30, ff. 199–200, quoted in McKillop, ed., *Thomson: Letters and Documents*, p. 210. Henrietta added, 'We have at present a great dispute about the Seasons of the Year, his dislike being particularly to Autumn' being aggravated by the memory of Thomson's death. In her letter to Shenstone of 16 October 1748, which was about the 'autumn' debate, she commented 'your flowers all withered when Thomson died'.

14 James Thomson, *The Castle of Indolence*, quoted by Shenstone in *The Letters of William Shenstone*, ed. Marjorie Williams, Oxford: Blackwell, 1939.

15 'Written at a *ferme ornée* near B[irmingham] 1749' was 'polished' in 1751 and eventually published by Robert Dodsley.

16 12 December 1749.

17 Robert Holden, entry for Woburn Farm, in *The Oxford Companion to Gardens*, eds. G. Jellicoe, S. Jellicoe, P. Goode and M. Lancaster, Oxford: Oxford University Press, 1986, p. 611.

18 [1] July 1748.

19 Ibid.

20 Sir Thomas Browne, 1605–82. His *Hydriotaphia* (*Urn Burial*) and *The Garden of Cyrus* (1658) and *Letter to a Friend* (1690) were part of her education, and probably in her library.

21 Letter to Shenstone, 25 April 1750.

22 *The Letters of William Shenstone*, ed. Williams, William Shenstone to Lady Luxborough, 26 November 1749.

23 Ibid., 28 January 1750.

24 14 February 1750.

25 28 December 1749.

26 *The Letters of William Shenstone*, William Shenstone to Lady Luxborough, 13 November 1749.

27 Andor Gomme, *Smith of Warwick: Francis Smith 1671–1738 Architect and Master-builder*, Stamford: Shaun Tyas, 2000, p. 39.

28 Andor Gomme's *Smith of Warwick* gives details of all these works and more, but I have extracted only the clients and craftsmen that Henrietta knew or mentioned.

29 28 April 1748.

30 2 August 1750.

31 4 January 1749.

32 *Letters of William Shenstone*, 7 December 1749.

33 14 March 1750.

34 Ibid.

35 Arthur E. Carden, compiler, *The Knights of Barrells*, Falmouth, 1993, p. 73 has this careful translation of the inscription by Gilbert Stapleton, p. 24.

36 Thomas Smith (*c.* 1720–67) (perhaps overshadowed by Joseph Wright of Derby) has paintings in Derby, Manchester and Bristol art galleries and also at Chatsworth. See also note 38 below.

37 14 March 1750.

38 For 'A View of Darwentwater etc' (which belongs to King's College, Cambridge) see Peter Bicknell, *Beauty, Horror and Immensity: Picturesque Landscape in Britain 1750–1850*, Catalogue of an exhibition at the Fitzwilliam Museum Cambridge 1981, Cambridge: Cambridge University Press, 1981, p. 75.

39 *Letters of William Shenstone*, ed. Williams, pp. 158–9, letter of August 1748 and John H. Hammond, *The Camera Obscura: A Chronicle*, Bristol: Adam Hilger Ltd, 1981, pp. 77–83.

40 Leslie Parris, *Landscape in Britain c.* 1750–1850, an exhibition at the Tate Gallery (now Tate Britain), London: Tate Gallery Publications, 1973, p. 124.

41 *Letters of William Shenstone*, ed. Williams, p. 171.

42 24 June 1749.

43 H. T. Dickinson, *Bolingbroke*, London: Constable, 1970, pp. 294–5.

44 13 May 1750.

45 30 June 1750.

46 31 August 1750.

47 Ibid.

48 Dr John Wall (1708–76), an original partner in the (Royal) Worcester Porcelain company and prime mover in its establishment in 1751.

49 31 August 1750.

50 Mrs Dewes to Bernard Granville Esq., of Calwich, Ashbourne, Derbyshire by way of London from Mapleburrough Green, 12 August 1750, and Mrs Delany to Mrs Dewes, 24 August 1750, in *The Autobiography and Correspondence of Mary Granville, Mrs Delany etc.*, ed. Lady Llanover, London: Richard Bentley, 1861, vol. 2, pp. 577–8 and 584.

51 Mary Delany, 1700–88, was Henrietta's contemporary and a keen gardener, but there the similarities ended; she was a favourite at Court, a friend of Horace Walpole and a patient constructor of exquisite cut-out flower pictures, all of which have ensured her fame. As Mary Granville she too was at Longleat and would have met Frances and Henrietta there but it was at Longleat that her first unhappy marriage to Alexander Pendarves was arranged. Mary was a favourite at Court. See Ruth Hayden, *Mrs Delany and her Flower Collages*, London: British Museum Press, 1980.

52 31 August 1750.

53 19 December 1749.

54 16 October 1748.

55 13 December 1749.

56 11 September 1748.

57 18 December 1748.

CHAPTER EIGHT
'A Lady of Quality'

NOTE: Where the date only is given as the reference this means *The Letters of the Right Honourable Lady Luxborough to William Shenstone Esq.*, 1775.

1 Henrietta's poem 'Asteria in the Country to Calydore in Town, 1747–8 opens:

> To you, my Friend,
> From chearless hearths, & lonely
>   grots I write,
> Which once were scenes of
>   Friendship & delight'

and describes the company and talk around the fireside at Barrells. This comes from f. 53 of the Ms of *Shenstone's Miscellany*, in Ian A. Gordon, ed., *Shenstone's Miscellany 1759–63*, 1952, pp. 30–4. 'I am no Poetess' etc. is from Henrietta's letter to Shenstone of 28 April 1748.

2 29 November 1749.

3 4 January 1750.

4 *Letters of William Shenstone*, ed. Marjorie Williams, Oxford: Blackwell, 1939, 30 December 1748.

5 4 January 1749.

6 18 December 1748.

7 *Letters of William Shenstone*, 30 December 1748.

8 Frank E. Pardoe, *John Baskerville [1706–75] of Birmingham: Letter-Founder & Printer*, London: Muller, 1975, p. 33.

9 Jenny Uglow, *The Lunar Men: The Friends who Made the Future, 1730–1810*, London: Faber & Faber, 2003, p. 23, quoting William Hutton, *The European Magazine*, November 1785.

10 Pardoe, *John Baskerville*, Ibid., 23–4.

11 *The Correspondence of Robert Dodsley 1733–1764*, ed. James E. Tierney, Cambridge Studies in Publishing and Printing History, Cambridge: Cambridge University Press, 1988, p. 145, n. 6.

12 Pardoe, *John Baskerville*, p. 42.

13 *The Correspondence of Robert Dodsley*, ed. Tierney, p. 5.

14 Richard Jago (1715–81) was at Oxford with Shenstone and Graves, was ordained and spent his life in three Warwickshire parishes. His long poem *Edge-Hill* (1767) celebrates his landscape. Tierney, *The Correspondence of Robert Dodsley*, p. 201, notes his 'Essay upon Electricity' (which is interesting in the context of Erasmus Darwin and the Midlands Enlightenment, see Jenny Uglow, *The Lunar Men*, chapter 1) and also Ilse Dusoir Lind, *Richard Jago: A Study in Eighteenth-Century Localism*, n.p., Philadelphia, 1945.

15 13 February 1751.

16 31 August 1750.

17 20 March 1751.

18 *Letters of William Shenstone*, ed. Williams, 24 April 1751.

19 Ascension Day (June) 1751.

20 16 April 1751.

21 Ascension Day (June) 1751 and Wednesday, 10 July 1751. It was army tradition to send the horses out to grass for a month, the 'grass month', usually July. Henrietta's Great Meadow was an ideal place for Captain Robinson's troop horses and their 'Grass-guards' from Worcester, a contact possibly made through Dr John Wall. Her poem 'Lines written at

a *ferme ornée* near B[irmingham]' was sent with this letter of 10 July 1751.

22 1 August 1751.

23 21 August 1751.

24 John George Taylor, *Our Lady of Batersey: The Story of Battersea Church and Parish Told from Original Sources*, London: George White, 1925, p. 178.

25 Helen Sard Hughes, *The Gentle Hertford: Her Life and Letters*, New York: Macmillan, 1940, p. 409, Duchess of Somerset to Lady Luxborough, 31 December 1752, p. 409.

26 Taylor, *Our Lady of Batersey*, p. 177.

27 20 January 1752.

28 Marjorie Williams, *Lady Luxborough Goes to Bath*, Oxford: Blackwell, 1946, p. 11.

29 See John Wood, *An Essay Towards a Description of Bath 1742–3*, Bath: W. Frederick, 1749; also Tim Mowl and Brian Earnshaw, *John Wood: Architect of Obsession*, Bath: Millstream, 1988.

30 Peter Borsay, *The Image of Georgian Bath, 1700–2000*, Oxford: Oxford University Press, 2000, pp. 51ff.

31 29 February 1752.

32 Ibid.

33 For a colourful portrayal of Bath society in the early 1750s see Williams, *Lady Luxborough Goes to Bath*.

34 29 February 1752.

35 *The Autobiography and Correspondence of Mary Granville, Mrs Delany*, ed. Lady Llanover, 3 vols., London: Richard Bentley, 1861, vol. 3, pp. 108–9.

36 Selina, Countess of Huntingdon, quoted in Williams, *Lady Luxborough Goes to Bath*, p. 26.

37 Richard Graves, *The Spiritual Quixote or The Summer's Ramble of Mr. Geoffry Wildgoose*, 1773, ed. Clarence Tracy, London: Oxford University Press, 1967, pp. 329–31.

38 Ibid., pp. 184–223, where Graves tells the story of Lucy and himself as the characters of Charlotte Woodville and Mr Rivers.

39 Clarence Tracy, *A Portrait of Richard Graves*, Toronto and Buffalo: University of Toronto Press, 1987, pp. 64–5.

40 Ibid., p. 78.

41 Williams, *Lady Luxborough Goes to Bath*, p. 49.

42 John Harris, *Gardens of Delight: The Rococo English Landscape of Thomas Robins the Elder* (1716–1760), London: Basilisk Press, 1978. Robins painted two views of the Woodside garden, the Orangery and the Chinese Pavilion and both are referred to here. See also Michael Symes, *The English Rococo Garden*, Princes Risborough, Bucks.: Shire Publications, 1991.

43 For Thomas Goldney's grotto see also Symes, *The English Rococo Garden*. Goldney Grotto is owned by the University of Bristol.

44 16 March 1754.

45 *The Letters of William Shenstone*, ed. Williams, 13 November 1749, p. 233.

46 Ibid., p. 187.

47 8 September 1749.

48 Mark Laird, *The Flowering of the Landscape Garden: English Pleasure Grounds 1720–1800*, Philadelphia: University of Pennsylvania Press, 1999, p. 113. Sadly, Henrietta was just too early for the influx of American shrubs, the magnolia, kalmia, hydrangea, cornus and rhododendrons, and the maple, birch and acacia trees that would have delighted her. These were being grown in great house gardens and parks and in London in the 1740s but none seemed to reach rural Warwickshire.

49 Ibid.

50 Ibid., chapter 3, 'The First Shrubberies: Circuits, Clumps and Axiality' and pp. 109–13.

51 20 March 1751.

52 28 December 1749.

53 30 June 1750.

54 *Letters of William Shenstone*, ed. Williams, 1939, p. 285.

55 Ibid., 30 September 1752, pp. 341–2.

56 2 February 1753.

57 This would seem the appropriate place to comment on a myth that gained credence in a memoir *The Family Business* by the printer W. B. Clowes, London, *c.* 1955, that the Clowes family had royal ancestry through an illegitimate son of Frederick, Prince of Wales and a Miss Knight. The son, Charles Knight, settled in Windsor in 1779, when he was twenty-nine (where he married and had a son, also Charles Knight, who became Windsor's 'No. 1 citizen', which has kept the interest alive). Charles Knight the elder was thus born in 1750. Sad to say Henrietta's reputation has inclined the identity of the 'Miss Knight' to Maddalena Henrietta, who was, of course, Mrs Wymondesold at that time. The *Letters [written by] Lady Luxborough* reveal that Henrietta and her daughter were reunited in the summer of 1748, shortly after Maddalena's marriage, at the age of nineteen, to Charles Wymondesold, a South Sea Company contact of her father, Robert Knight. We know Wymondesold was a rich but dull dog and there were no children of the marriage. They stayed at Barrells in June/July 1749, and in September 1750 Henrietta met them in Stratford-upon-Avon for dinner. Mother and daughter were affectionate, they corresponded and exchanged presents. In June 1751 Henrietta sent Maddalena some of Shenstone's home-distilled eau de jasmine. However, the spacing of their meetings (which would never have occurred between say November and May because of the difficulties of travelling) does not preclude Maddalena giving birth to a child that Henrietta knew nothing about, or would certainly not have mentioned to Shenstone. It was likely that Maddalena, a favourite of her sometime guardian Lord Bolingbroke, would have met his friend the Prince of Wales. If Wymondesold had accepted the child as his own, which was surely likely for a royal bastard, Henrietta would certainly have known and celebrated her grandson by telling Shenstone, probably several times over. The child, Charles Knight, knew nothing of his parentage, and was

brought up by a distinguished bachelor clergyman and Greek scholar, Revd James Hampton. In an unpublished ms *Charles Knight: A Forgotten Genius*, Judith Hunter and Derek Stow reveal the royal patronage extended to Revd Hampton, possibly on account of his ward. Charles Knight was apprenticed to a publisher and set up as a bookseller in Windsor (why Windsor we do not know) where his most eminent customer was the young George III (his half-brother?).

It is a nice story, but the connection with Maddalena Henrietta is still tenuous. Henrietta Luxborough was quick enough to hear of her daughter's elopement with Josiah Child in early 1753, and the correspondence between – as she now styled herself – Henrietta Child and her father Robert Knight was kept in the family. Typescripts are included in A. Carden, comp., *The Knights of Barrells*, Falmouth, 1993, and the originals are in BM Ad. Ms 45889. These letters show that Charles Wymondesold was prompt and vicious in his legal proceedings against Josiah Child (perhaps because of the previous shame), which forced the Childs to remain in Europe, dependent upon the support of Robert Knight, Lord Catherlough, until Josiah Child's death in early 1760. But did Henrietta Child's undoubted success in European courts stem from her royal liaison? (Note: I am indebted to Fraser Jansen, bookseller in Windsor, and Hester Davenport for much of this information.)

58 The Duchess of Somerset's 'regular and religious family' and routine are described in her letter to Henrietta of 31 December 1752, in Hughes, *The Gentle Hertford*, pp. 408–11. Henrietta's comment to Shenstone is dated 2 February 1753.

59 Hughes, *The Gentle Hertford*, pp. 411–13, Lady Luxborough to the Duchess of Somerset, 13 February 1754.

60 Ibid., p. 413, the Duchess of Somerset to Lady Luxborough, 25 February 1754.

61 Ibid.

62 Sanderson Miller (1716–80) has a chapter in Michael Symes, *The English Rococo Garden*, but for this rhyme, dated 13 December 1750, and further information see Barbara Jones, *Follies & Grottoes*, 2nd edn, London: Constable, 1974, pp. 398–9.

63 *The Letters of William Shenstone*, pp. 252–3 for his description of Radway; but see also Jennifer Meir, 'Sanderson Miller and the Land-scaping of Wroxton Abbey, Farnborough Hall and Honington Hall', *Garden History*, 25 (1), Summer 1997, pp. 81–106.

64 Meir, 'Sanderson Miller', pp. 93–9. Farnborough Hall is owned by the National Trust and open on certain days during the summer season. Check 01295 690002 for details.

65 Quoted in ibid., p. 95.

66 Ibid., p. 94, quoting Richard Jago.

67 See note 64 above.

68 Honington Hall is privately owned but open by appointment with Benjamin Wiggin Esq., Honington Hall, Shipston-on-Stour, CV36 5AA, tel. 01608 661434.

CHAPTER NINE
A Captivating Ghost

1 *The Works in Verse & Prose of William Shenstone, Esq.*, 2 vols., Edinburgh: Donaldson, 1768, vol. 2, pp. xxviii–xxix.

2 23 March 1749.

3 *The Autobiography and Correspondence of Mary Granville, Mrs Delany*, ed. Lady Llanover, 3 vols., London: Richard Bentley, 1861, vol. 3, p. 116, Mrs Delany to Mrs Dewes in Bath, postmarked 30 April 1752.

4 27 April 1755.

5 18 June 1755.

6 William Holyoake to William Shenstone, 29 March 1756, at the end of *Letters Written by the Late Honourable Lady Luxborough to William Shenstone Esq.*, 1775. *The Letters of William Shenstone*, ed.

Marjorie Williams, Oxford: Blackwell, 1939, William Shenstone to William Holyoake, 21 April 1756.

7 Philip White, *A Gentleman of Fine Taste: The Watercolours of Coplestone Warre Bampfylde (1720–91)*, Taunton: Hestercombe Gardens Project (now Trust), 1995.

8 Dorothy Stroud, *Capability Brown*, new edn, London: Faber & Faber, 1984, pp. 55ff.

9 Ibid., p. 61.

10 Andrew Craythorn, *Barrells Hall from Riches to Ruins: An Account of this Famous Warwickshire Mansion, Seat of the Knights and Newtons of Ullenhall and the Celebrated Lady Luxborough*, privately published, 2003 (proceeds to Ullenhall Parish Council for the upkeep of the Old Chapel, Ullenhall), p. 41.

11 John Carswell, *The South Sea Bubble*, 1960, Stroud, Glos.: Alan Sutton, 1993 rev. edn, pp. 238–9.

12 Ibid.

13 Craythorn, *Barrells Hall from Riches to Ruins*, p. 44, but see also Arthur E. Carden, comp., *The Knights of Barrells*, Falmouth, 1993, for the discovery of Jane Davies' story.

14 I find this hard to believe, but Andrew Craythorn, who did a great deal of local research on Lord Catherlough, states this positively in *Barrells Hall from Riches to Ruins*, p. 43.

15 Stephen Daniels, *Humphry Repton: Landscape Gardening and the Geography of Georgian England*, New Haven, CT, and London: Yale University Press, 1999, p. 268, in the Gazetteer compiled with John Phibbs, has the commission for Barrells from Robert Knight (before) 1796, i.e. mentioned in William Peacocke's *Polite Repository* for that year.

16 Craythorn, *Barrells Hall from Riches to Ruins*, pp. 53–4.

17 Ibid., pp. 68–71. Craythorn describes how he first went to Barrells for a Scout camp and was inspired by camping beneath the trees of the derelict garden and tales around the camp fire within sight of the ruined house.

18 The plan of 'the Loosroes', the seat of Mr Tenpenny, and accompanying description are taken from vol. 2 of *The Works in Verse & Prose of Wm. Shenstone Esqr.*, Edinburgh: Alexander Donaldson, 2 vols., 1768. The loyal Dodsley had prepared *The Works* with Robert Graves' assistance, and the two volumes were published in 1764 shortly before Dodsley's death. The Edinburgh edition is the 3rd.

19 *The Correspondence of Robert Dodsley 1733–64*, ed. James E. Tierney in the Cambridge Studies in Publishing and Printing History, Cambridge: Cambridge University Press, 1988, pp. 467–8, documenting the difficulties over Shenstone's will. The letter from John Pixell from Edgbaston, 16 April 1764, is printed in ibid., p. 487. Tierney also documents Shenstone's work as an editor.

20 E. Monro Purkis, *William Shenstone: Poet and Landscape Gardener*, Wolverhampton: Whitehead Brothers, 1931, has all the advantages of an historian knowing his locality well, with a thorough bibliography of major and minor sources.

21 Tierney, ed., *The Correspondence of Robert Dodsley*, pp. 476–87, acknowledges the work of Dr Francis Burns of Newman College, Birmingham, who has pursued this legal history for his thesis 'William Shenstone: A Biographical and Critical Study', University of Sheffield, 1970.

22 Purkis, *William Shenstone*, p. 136.

23 *Men & Manners by William Shenstone*, selected and introduced by Havelock Ellis, Waltham St Lawrence: Golden Cockerel Press, 1927, pp. 24–5.

24 Richard Graves, *Recollection of Some Particulars in the Life of the Late William Shenstone Esq., in a Series of Letters from an Intimate Friend of his to [William Seward] Esq., F.R.S.*, London: J. Dodsley, 1788.

25 'The Leasowes Restoration 1997–2001 or How to Spend Money', *Garden*

History Society News, no. 51, Winter
1997.

26 Shenstone, *Men & Manners*, selected
and introduced by Havelock Ellis,
p. 25.

27 *The Correspondence of Robert Dodsley*,
ed. Tierney, letter to William
Shenstone, 3 May 1755, p. 201.

28 *The Autobiography and Correspondence
of Mary Granville, Mrs Delany*, ed.
Lady Llanover, vol. 2, p. 579. For
'Henrietta's revenge' see Tim Mowl's
candid *Horace Walpole: The Great
Outsider*, London: John Murray,
1996.

29 A leaflet *Under the Council's Wing: An
Introduction to Restoration And
Conservation at Lydiard Park.*, *c.* 1995,
is available at Lydiard Park, Lydiard
Tregoze, Swindon, Wilts. SN5 9PA.

30 BL Add. Ms 34196, Henry
Bolingbroke, Battersea, to Henrietta
Knight, 10 August 1745.

31 The Friends of Lydiard Tregoze have
an annual gathering, an annual report
and are kept in touch with the
Heritage Lottery Funded Lydiard Park
Project: www.lydiardpark.org.

32 The De Morgan Collection has now
moved to 38 West Hill, Putney, tel. 020
8871 1144, www.demorgan.org.uk. Old
Battersea House is open to group visits
by arrangement in writing with Mary
Ann Danner, Director of
Administrative Resources, Forbes Inc.,
60 Fifth Avenue, New York, NY 10011,
USA, with a copy to The Administra-
tor, 30 Vicarage Crescent, London
SW11 3LD.

33 Reg Prescott, Len Bridge and Tom
Hartman, *A Guide Book to Battersea
Parish Church*, printed by Embassy
Press, 341 Battersea Park Road,
London SW11 4LS, 1997.

34 Chiswick House, Burlington Lane,
W4 2RP, is owned by English Heritage
and open Wednesdays–Sundays and
Bank Holiday Mondays, Easter to
31 October, but please check on
www.english-heritage.org.uk/visits.
Marble Hill is also owned by English
Heritage but has more restricted
openings, so please check the same
website. Pope's Grotto is owned by
St James's Independent School for
Boys and applications to visit should
be made to the Headmaster.

35 See Sheila and Pat Rooney,
*St Leonard's Hill, Windsor: House,
Hermitage and Hill*, Windsor: Windsor
Publications, 1991.

36 Craythorn, *Barrells Hall from Riches to
Ruins*, pp. 66ff.

37 *The Letters of William Shenstone*, 21
April 1756.

38 See Melanie Louise Simo, *Loudon and
the Landscape: From Country Seat to
Metropolis, 1783–1843*, New Haven, CT,
and London: Yale University Press,
1988, Chapter 5; see also Gillian
Darley, *Villages of Vision*, London:
Architectural Press, 1975.

INDEX

Page numbers in *italics* denotes an illustration
n stands for footnote